W.I.L.D.

What Is Life Definitively

by A. Radical

ISBN 978-1-9701-0912-2

Copyright © 2019 by by A. Radical

All rights reserved, including the right of reproduction in any form, or by any mechanical or electronic means including photocopying or recording, or by any information storage or retrieval system, in whole or in part in any form, and in any case not without the written permission of the author and publisher.

This is a work of fiction. Names, characters, places, and incidents either are the product of the author's imagination or are used fictitiously. Any resemblance to actual events or locales or persons, living or dead, is entirely coincidental.

Published August 2019

ANEWPRESS

Thought Map

Forewarn	1
Foreword	3
Onset	11
Method	17
Thesis	29
Debt of Proof	31
Rule Bound Action	37
Platform/Space	41
Time & Motion	47
Order	69
Random	77
Balance	89
Value	97
Information	125
Objects	161
Subjects	165
Interface	183
Concepts/Ideas	229
Will & Volition	271
Campaigns & Missions	297

Resources, Skills & Tools 311
Enemy 317
Plan/Strategy 325
Story 329
Mathematics 339
Systems/Technology 345
Program(A Way) 355
Objective & Victory Conditions 391
Compulsion 399
Gamemaker & Player 417
Extent 431

Forewarn

"The unexamined life isn't worth living."
Socrates

[WARNING]: This work is well ahead of its time; so much so, that it might as well be an epiphany from the distant future. There is no polite way to go about this, no appropriate time to be inappropriate. The following presentation is unapologetically candid. Going where no mind has dared before, it contains explicit adult content, elements and ideas that may not be suitable for small minded audiences. This text may also challenge many prevailing societal narratives and some of its core beliefs. W.I.L.D. is a constructive response to the status quo. It touches on topics that are viewed as already settled, though they in fact, remain unsettled and really just exist as controversial and taboo. For some minds, this will be disturbing. **Reader discretion is advised.**

What would you do if you had something to tell someone, something that they needed to know, but is likely to arouse their ire? What if you already knew that they will not only become angry with what you have to say, but may also despise you initially for sharing it with them? Would you tell them, regardless? Would it be wrong if you didn't?

You think you know, but you have no idea of how engrossed you are in what philosopher, Immanuel Kant, referred to as "nonage" – naivete/oblivion. We interrupt your regularly scheduled moment of going through the motions of your life experience, in which you give inadequate consideration to – for good reason – to bring you the reality of our reality. This text will be the most adult conversation you will ever engage in or be privy to. And by adult, we are not referring to mere biologically developed adults, but primarily the ripened in psyche. Sure to test the emotional fortitude of even the most self-proclaimed opened of minds, the following dares to traverse the highest strata of thought – by delving beneath all the white noise of superficial biases, disingenuous arguments, deliberate and inadvertent deception/propaganda, hypocrisy, rampant cynicism, small talk, redundant entertainment, callous indifference, false bravado/disguised insecurities, questionable pathology, inherited beliefs and sarcasm – in earnest pursuit of what is actually true in our existence.

Foreword

Dedication & Inspiration: This book is dedicated to all the people this author has come in contact with over my life experience, as well as all the ancestors of modern humanity who contributed to rendering it actual. W.I.L.D. is a culmination of their efforts. It is a tribute to those who have trouble reconciling what they have been told life is about, with their own life experiences. This effort is also for those who take notice that something is just not right about our existence, those who are as confused by life as this writer was prior to articulating this text. This literary offering is to the benefit of the sincerest of truth seekers and also in defense & recognition of the hopeless, the unjustly marginalized and suffering – and their future descendants.

What is its purpose: This effort is meant to edify, empower and stimulate thought, to enlighten and awaken the consciousness of the reader to a broad range of topics that are relevant to each other and more importantly, to readers themselves. It is to help the populous achieve a higher understanding of our life experience.

Why write on this particular topic: Out of a sense of civic duty/public service. The intention was to fulfill a need, the shortage of certainty. It would've been a work that this author would have appreciated reading or learning about in my formative years, instead of becoming more and more confused by the world. Despite our impressive technological advancements, most people are still confounded by what it is to be alive. These are matters that must be addressed openly in a public forum and not in secret by a privileged few or condescendingly in entitled language.

Limitations and scope of book? Written from a cerebral and common sense perspective, this is the extremes of imagination articulated within the bounds of rationality.

Advice on how to read the book: To enhance your reading experience, as difficult as it can be – withhold your final appraisal until absorbing the entire text in totality. Ingest it in sequential order or you may inadvertently take the content out of context. You are recommended to approach from an objective vantage point, while being hyper-aware of your reflexive emotional responses. As you read, be wary of yourself and what your mind is doing. The information will be misunderstood, if one does not view the aquarium(the content) from an outside view, rather than as a fish swimming in it.

Experiences had or incidents that occurred during writing: Even as the author, I found myself conflicted both in developing and completing this work. Intense astonishment and cognitive anguish had to be endured, similar to what you the reader are about to experience. There was a fear of even undertaking and completing this project. Not only daunting in itself, the author is aware that a substantial segment of those the text was written to enlighten, may misconstrue and forgo its substance and overreact reflexively to its surface. Also pondered, was the notion that this work may receive more backlash than financial reward or may not even be appreciated/accepted during this writer's lifetime. While drafting, there were also moments where this author even questioned if the border where insanity and sanity converge, is where this work sits.

Before we delve into the primary subject matter, there are some items worth addressing and other things to keep in mind. Their inclusion will become apparent or are explained in more depth as you read further along:

- This text is an informal inquiry into overall life experience. Though composed in plain terms, this facet should not discount it from being considered as a cerebral grade expression.

- W.I.L.D. is written by a member of the masses for our empowerment and overall well being. The author is without professional licensure, but compensates by maximizing the capability to contemplate. This composition also relies heavily on the best exertions from some of the most renowned thinkers in recorded history.

- Though initiated by a single author, it is the foundation of the world's first living document based on the topic of objective truth. W.I.L.D. welcomes sincere and well thought public collaboration for future publication. Due to mankind being inherently error prone, no intellect gets it all right. Multiple minds genuinely working in concert to solve a problem, usurp a singular one attempting to do so. Readers are encouraged to constructively challenge the ideas put forth, as well as make valid suggestions, in order to continuously improve upon this work until its full completion.

- Be mindful that history's most ingenious ideas and inventions were all unorthodox when initially discovered, realized or introduced. Everything that is presently considered conventional, was once viewed as unconventional before being accepted. In fact, the historical record shows that genius is rarely recognized in its own lifetime. This renders most people in any given present generation as unqualified to immediately recognize such quality of thought, initially.

- Human beings have a tendency to overcomplicate things. Often times we overlook the obvious.

- We justify our actions, with one justification or another, before we act them out. Our justifications for these actions, including what we choose to believe – are not always rational.

- Culture and technology has removed us far from the actuality of life experience, to the point that we are extremely alien to it. Sociologist, Jean Baudrillard, said that we view life as a "hyperreality". Despite the advent of the Enlightenment and science's many discoveries and inventions since, Plato's allegory of the Cave still very much applies to modern day human society, on a whole.

- Our perception can be different from reality. Reality's truth(s) isn't always as we desire it to be. Just because an assumption is popular, does not render that opinion true. Truth exists independently outside of our emotions and beliefs. In a human society of lies, the truth will appear absurd and/or offensive and its orator(s) combative. This is more of a characteristic of truth and the environmental conditions it is dispensed in, than being attributable to any intention of this scribe. The truth will set you free, but first truth antagonizes. Applying objective truth to all of life – risks insulting the beliefs of everyone, including this writer's. An attribute of the truth is that it hurts, varying in intensity, depending on our emotional attachment to some falsehood that it undermines. A false belief is the antithesis of truth, such information is a lie. If truth does not align with what we believe, we avoid or attack it in irrational and emotional displays. Some truths are uncomfortable for us emotionally, but all truths are ultimately neutral. Preferring not to think or talk about them does not render inconvenient truths vanquished.

- Do not be fooled by terms such as "civilization" or "first world" or even by our advanced technology. We have always existed in the wilderness. A worldwide, year long electrical power outage would quickly reveal, that we have only been pretending to be separate from the wild.

- The ways our life experience can be viewed:
    - the way you've been told experience is or how you believe it is.
    - the way experience appears.
    - and the way experience actually is.

We view things from a subjective perspective, as if another and better alternative isn't available. To ascertain objective truth, one has to reconcile their own subjective view with the actual objectivity of experience. One has to view the world as if one is an object that is a part of the aggregate.

- We are susceptible to delusion, due to the natural embellishing of our imaginations.

- Some portions within this text, you may find familiar and obvious.

- Though capable of intellect, people operate primarily on emotion, rather than cerebrally.

- If you are too close or immersed into something, it is hard to see it for what it really is.

- We are gullible, a necessary feature more than a defect – for purposes of adapting moment to moment.

- There is more than one way to accomplish a feat, including ascertaining the fundamental truth(s) of life experience.

- Some new words and phraseology/terms will be introduced in this work to replace antiquated, burdensome, confusing, gender biased or overly used ones. For instance:
    - "Axial" means neutral or objective or universal.
    - "The Wild" and "the Wilderness"(capitalized) substitute for the words – universe, cosmos, macrocosm and megacosm.

- "Perone" and its variants, substitutes for the word "person" and its alterations.
- "Exact" and its variations & "actual(s)" will substitute as another term for "truth"(be alert of the context some words are used in).
- "Relatively Neutral" means objective or centered.
- "Uni-being" is in reference to people collectively.
- "Yestory" substitutes for "history".
- "Himind(high-mind)" and "Cereve(seer-eve)" substitute for human. "Cere" translates to "man", "Reve" means "woman".
- "Fevale" replaces "female".
- "Wezence", "wezentic" – replaces "romance" and "romantic".
- "See-Level" or "See-World" or "Experiential Level" are terms that substitute for the "material" or "physical world".
- "Synergy" is another term for moral.

- Some people that we mostly disagree with, tend to make some statements at times that we agree with. Conversely, some people that we mostly agree with, can utter some words that we disagree with – from time to time.

- There are aspects to experience that exist that we don't even know that we don't know about yet, as there always has been.

- Some assertions conveyed in this effort are repeated, out of necessity, due to overlapping with multiple other points being expressed. Other repeated points are for effect.

- Even with all of this preparation, you may still be left befuddled at the end of the book. There's no shame in that, it is advised that you absorb this work in manageable portions, rather than importing it in full. Even then, you may find that you will likely have to reread it on multiple occasions to effectively mine its complete value.

We now advance humanity into the next phase of our evolution.

Onset

"Those who are able to see beyond the shadows and lies of their culture will never be understood, let alone believed by the masses."
Plato

Though theoretical physicist, Albert Einstein, is credited with putting forth a notion of a possible theory of everything, an explanation that effectively articulates our life experience – respectfully, this declaration is false. At least to the point of recorded history, if not all of the tenure of human beings(particularly homo sapiens), we have been seeking answers to our existence. Due to our inherent curiosity, it has been since our very emergence that we've been asking questions such as – why are we here, why are we alive? Why is life the way it is? Why is there something rather than nothing – why does everything happen? Is there something deeper going on, is there an ultimate meaning to life experience? Is there a G0d or is existence all the result of happenstance? How are we to conduct ourselves? Is it possible that our reality is not actually reality and what would that mean? What happens to us after we die, is there an afterlife? Can life's fundamental absolutes ever be realized?

Mythology and religion, for all of their faults, deserves the honor of the distinction as being the first entities in recorded history to seek a theory of everything. They both arose out of our need for explanation of what was going on in our life experience. Folklore and religion also share the similarity that both are not based in facts. In fact, religion is often referred to as "faith". Philosophy then took the reins, as far as the presocratics forward and science then followed.

What's interesting is, while we have been surviving, technologically advancing and establishing civilization – at least to the point of known history – philosophy, religion and science – have been prevalent institutions and all three have made attempts to explain our experience. Notwithstanding their often times shared contemptuous relationship, another commonality that they share is that despite their lasting tenure, the trio has proven to be inept in providing conclusive answers to our being alive.

Religions may start with noble intent, but eventually they become a state or some other assumed authority's, tool to pacify populations or groups. Military leader, Napoleon Bonaparte, alluded to this when he stated, "religion is here so the poor don't murder the rich". Religion reinforces a culture and even in Western so called "free" societies, culture tells the population how to be. Religion essentially provides a service of offering emotional solutions, such as reassurance for coping with hardships in life. These are appealing offerings that, for the most part, philosophy and science do not compensate for in their exchanges with the general public. Religion connects with people on an emotional level, not a rational one.

The issue with religion is that it tends to have heavy influence over substantial segments of the population. Its practitioners tend to assert that their particular religion's claims are the truth, in the absolutest context. It doesn't help that many of the doctrines of some of those religions are what communicates such a message to their adherents. Religion encourages its followers not to question. Devotees give no regard to the fact, that the claims of their faiths are effectively based on only hearsay. This is not a satisfactory basis for foundational truth. Having no pressure from their practitioners to provide a sensible logic to their pronouncements, religions are content as an institution that effectively functions simply to play to our emotions. Their societal function is an emotions management device. This renders religion as an undependable vehicle to transport us to the raw essence of experience.

> **"Philosophy is the religion of the elites."**
> David Hume

Prof Dr. Markus Gabriel, Chair for Epistemology at the University of Bonn, says the world does not exist as an object or as a totality of facts, that we should give up trying to unite it.

Philosophy, the love of wisdom. It has been said to be a way to look at questions, as well as a way to solve a problem and the numerous sub-problems within said problem. At least, that is what philosophy proclaims. In practice – one might mistake philosophers as captains of debate teams, who just relentlessly argue with each other to no end or ultimate solution. They are perceived as emphasizing argument, in terms of one-upmanship, more than validity of thought.

Many philosophers go to lengths to give the appearance of high-intelligence and infallibility, for effect, in expounding on their theories. Much of philosophy is cryptic and many philosophers are described as "hard to read". Aside from formulating a profound thought, clarity in expressing those ponderings should be a standard. Only authors who do not know exactly what they are saying themselves, should deliberately leave strangers to explain their words for them.

American historian, Richard Carrier, referred to a large sector of academic philosophy as "pseudo-philosophy" and stated that this is the result of philosophy, in general – lacking an authority to confirm its claims, as science does – with their utilization of general consensus. Carrier's statement also insinuates that modern philosophy seems to be off on a tangent, as opposed to its original purpose.

Another issue with philosophy is that most philosophers are not honest in their work. They are beholden to culture or societal influence and seek to avoid being labeled as "radical", which renders most of philosophy subjective, rather than neutral. Thinkers such as Socrates and Baruch Spinoza took the risk of being honest and suffered a heavy price for it. Socrates was forced to ingest the poison, hemlock and Spinoza was so fearful that he requested to have his most controversial views published under a pseudonym and another posthumously. Culture even corrupted the thinking of Rene Descartes, as you will come to realize further on in this work.

In conclusion, though supplying us with science, we have enough of a sample size to conclude that philosophy has proven that it is not an adequate solution to answering the most mysterious "why" questions of our experience.

> **"Science is meaningless because it gives no answer to our question, the only question important for us: what shall we do and how shall we live."**
> Leo Tolstoy

The most credible of the three – science – though it has supplied us with some wondrous technologies, one could make the case that it has been more so or as equally harmful, as it has been helpful. Not just in terms of socially, but also intellectually as well. Science proclaims to be a search for answers and says to question everything, but seems to avoid a critical question of itself. There is a fatal flaw in the reasoning of science that potently handicaps its efforts to furnish the theory of everything – its entrenchment and exclusive reliance on empiricism.

Their position is that the only way to show that anything is more than a fictional concept, is to demonstrate that it has some empirical manifestation or that its existence has empirical consequences – that are most parsimoniously explained by the existence of that thing. That said, theoretical physicists still admit that there are some answers that are beyond the bounds of science. Science can only answer a certain class of questions. For the most part, the questions that can be predicted and measured. Science's stock of trade is not absolute truths, but in confidence and appraising certainty. If science had a monopoly on truth, there wouldn't be agnostics. Science is suffering from cognitive dissonance. They are simultaneously holding conflicting views, yet they claim to aspire to generate the theory of everything.

Does this pronouncement not fail at its face? If they admit that they have a blind spot, and a voluntary one at that, with their stubborn adherence to empiricism(the proclivity to judge a book by its cover) – focusing on what things are by what they do – how will they ever ascertain the actual theory of everything – if everything in experience is not empirical? How can they fully discern between appearance and essence, when they admit to being doggedly slanted towards appearance/empiricism? If we follow that rationale out to its logical conclusion, science cannot. For them, the fundamentals of life are like a 3-Dimensional object, in which one side is always hidden from view(Edmund Husserl).

Philosopher, Thomas S. Kuhn, pointed out that science has been a procession of revolutions, in which the current domineering paradigm of any given era, are eventually upended. Even with full knowledge of this, scientists of any given era still convey their hypotheses as if they are matter of fact.

Science contains an inordinate amount of froth. For the most part, science's words and concepts are intimidating to the layperson and are expressed in uninteresting and uninviting fashion. Science defends their uneventful presentations as being too complex to intuitively grasp. Regardless of such an assertion, the end result is that science becomes privileged. Any talk of it being a public domain is ultimately propaganda. What value is there to having access to something that claims to be comprehensive, but you never quite understand it? This is why during moments of introspection, when most of us think about our lives – we do not contemplate all of the particles, forces and interactions that allow them to play out. In our most vulnerable moments – atoms, electromagnetism, gravitation, quantum mechanics and the periodic table of elements – are not what occupy our thoughts. This is a failure of science, not of the general public.

A popular saying in Western society is that insanity is doing the same thing over and over again and expecting a different result. Applying that same rationale to these three prominent institutions – philosophy, religion & science – if we are sincere about our pursuit for absolute truth, it is clear that a new method or vehicle must be developed to compensate for the detrimental flaws in these ineffective societal fixtures.

Method: Axial Thought

Goal: The primary goal of the method is to effectively explain our overall existence by obtaining foundational truth.

Method: Deemed as Axial Reasoning, meaning to think outside of ourselves. The name borrows from the word axis, due to the means, being a line of thought that is in scrupulous pursuit of what everything actually hinges on. Though initiated due to being skeptical of the aforementioned institutions – axial reasoning will also rely on philosophy, religion and science – since one of the method's requirements will be to account for their ultimate necessity in life experience.

Requirement(s):

- Qualify. Since our main aim is to generate a concise descriptive data set of overall existence, which is accompanied by an overwhelming burden of proof – it is imperative that we are able to qualify the all encompassing clarification when it materializes. What should it consist of, what are its criteria or characteristic traits? What should be present to decisively confirm the authenticity of the actual explanation of our being alive?

- The method should compensate for empirical science's deficiencies, as well as for potentially its own. Axial thought is to supplement science by coupling rationalism(reason) and empiricism(sense experience). Since we are not able to see and experience everything in the world, the next alternative to rely on is our reasoning. Reasoning is not just thinking, it is rational calculation from available facts. Deduction. Using our capacity of assessment is how we gain knowledge about the world. We then apply that knowledge to our experiences. Just as in science, reasoning allows thinkers to perform experiments – thought experiments/hypothetical scenarios. Only – unlike the experiments of chemists, that are bound to the Laws of Nature, rationalism is confined by the laws of logic.

- Philosophy and science has spent much time demarcating and segmenting the varying aspects of experience. Rather than continuing in that tradition, here we will recombine all of these sections of thought and scrutinize them as they actually exist – as a sum of parts.

- For a variety of reasons, efficiency is a major theme of the method. Being that achieving the primary goal is a formidable task, we will seek to simplify the problem. This includes, but is not limited to, reducing life experience from all its exaggerations to its exact(s).

- The axial approach contains a prerequisite of accuracy, which demands honest self-assessment. This work also welcomes challenge to its notions and is to be corrected wherever found in error. This means that it should be adjustable/flexible and upgradeable.

    - This stipulation for exactness, also includes operating from an objective point of reference, which is performing with a complete view – as opposed to a willfully ignorant one. Everything will be put under objective scrutiny, viewing and considering things from an impartial perspective. The Laws of Nature are objective and the cosmos is an object that is a combination of smaller objects(including their functions and processes) – therefore its components must exist as a whole objective truth. Entering in a relatively neutral mindset grants us access to see life experience as it is – objective. This will also enable us to see beyond the superficial or empirical level. Unless incapable to, each individual must think in neutrality for ourselves.

- Protagoras, the presocratic Greek sophist, stated that man is the measure of all things. In other words, we view things subjectively. This has lead to numerous incidents of folly in thought and hubris, meaning we are able to fool ourselves(Descartes: In every step there is room for error). That being the case, in order to subvert our partitioned leanings, we will employ self-skepticism.

- Pursue natural/organic questions. What are the natural questions that come to mind as each phenomenon or aspect of existence is encountered? Question everything – especially what everyday people take for granted or prefer left unquestioned. This includes authority and the validity of that authority's ideas and claims. What is actually true(is everything true because it fits in relation to other claims that we know or believe to be true – or is there anything we know to be true solely on their own merits)? Just because an authority figure(s) makes an assertion, does not render that pronouncement as valid.

- Do not assume everything in life experience is a given. Examine all aspects of life – what is included and what is excluded? For example, though experience seems normal to us, we should still ask the question – why is it structured in the particular way that it is? There are other ways experience could have set up outside of an inter and intraspecial tournament of survival, pitting creature against creature. Why this format in particular? We'll examine the configuration itself and see if there is anything to learn from it.

- Axial reasoning should allow any genuine seekers of truth to steer around and subvert all obstacles to doing so and eventually come to realize it.

Verification of a precise explanation of everything:

- The accurate explanation of life experience will put life in axial or proper context.

- We should expect that in the same way that life doesn't seem to make sense, it's raw translation – no matter how logical – will initially appear puzzling as well.

    - It should be reflective of reality and verifiable by each of our own personal experiences.

    - The actual summary of everything should account for and explain every nuance and minutiae of overall existence – what each aspect is fundamentally, what are their roles in the overall construct, the function the aggregate ultimately serves etc. Simply put, the theory of everything – must be universal, meaning that it must be able to operably apply to every object or nuance that we know of or discover in the future. It will detail all of the fundamental concepts and their connections in a coherent fashion. One detail should lead to another and back again. Everything should point to and play off of each other.

- The universal absolutes will transcend our subjective interpretation. Since truth is what actually is, it will not be open to interpretation. Actuals will be intuitive and self-defining/self-evident/ self-proving. Individuals that are able to think objectively, will organically come to recognize this work's inherent quality of credibility, after doing their own due diligence.

- The clarification of experience will never be overturned in the future, due to it being transcendent. At best, it can only be improved upon.

- The theory of all that is will reconcile the macro with the micro, as well as the material with the immaterial world.

Technique: Reconnaissance, Reduction, Rationalization & Realization

1. Learn as much as possible. Take account of all of the major factors involved in overall existence(life experience, history, philosophy, science, religion etc). Explore the taboo issues of human society, especially the ones we are discouraged from exploring.

2. Isolate the bad ideas that exist in overall human society. Eliminate what cannot be substantiated in fact or defended logically. For example: the irrationally obvious(mermaids), faulty logic, empty rhetoric, romantic notions(dark arts, fairy tales, superstitions, urban legends), inherited beliefs, traditions and customs etc.

3. Analyze what remains and consider what together they all mean in relation to life experience, including consciously scrutinizing your own experience.

4. Follow evidence to wherever it may lead, even if it goes against your own deeply held beliefs. Consider all scenarios, even far-fetched ones for the sake of thoroughness, then go through a process of elimination.

5. Once all unlikely scenarios are disqualified, formulate a hypothesis based on what remains.

6. Test conclusions. Conduct multiple thought experiments against the facts until confident enough there is no other credible conclusion(s) to be drawn.

7. Assert findings.

> **"The artist is no other than he who unlearns what he has learned, in order to know himself."**
> E. E. Cummings

Administer an improved version of philosopher, Rene Descartes', Method of Doubt, to ascertain the evasive level of certainty(the most fundamental things we can be sure of). Since the secular approach of no first mover and the many scientific models, which are limited to depicting time only a few moments after the Big Bang and onward, have not produced any conclusive answers – like Descartes, in our model – we will allow for a supergenius that controls the cosmos behind the scenes and see if we can disprove its existence. But, unlike the renowned French philosopher, we will free ourselves of religious or other biased influences – in formulating our deduction(s). We shall be as unbiased, as the imagined sovereign puppeteer, itself.

Doubt:

> **Self-Doubt.** I am a human being that is born disoriented and oblivious in a highly oriented world, with only my instincts to guide me. This state of extensive naivete is similar to being born in the depths of a coal mine. Our advancement through time has been similar to being virtually blind and gradually feeling our way out of a pitch black labyrinth.
>
> Most of my ideas that I know are not my own. If I am honest with myself, I am a victim of and suffer from "nonage", which is to be unaware of one's own ignorance. It is the Dunning-Kruger effect in its most literal sense. My thoughts and actions have been primarily influenced by other people, notably – my parents, family members, friends, associates, culture and society.
>
> Emotions tend to compromise my judgment. Though I am a human being and human beings are an intelligent species, all of my decisions that I make are not astute ones. I possess a tendency to either over or under-think a scenario, rather than appraising it for what it actually is.

As noted by Descartes, my senses are fallible and capable of generating sensory illusions, due to being too inadequate to process all of the data in my immediate environment. My senses always only present me with their best estimate as they scan the conditions, a best guess.

On these grounds, I arrive at the destination that I am fallible and unsound. I must doubt myself in everything and/or action I take or have taken. I must be skeptical of my own ideas, methods and procedures at all times. In this way, I can ensure that all of my remaining actions, including my reasoning – are at least keen ones.

Doubt Other People. My parents and their parents, my friends, associates and their parents and grandparents – in fact, every generation of human beings that have ever lived – are born in some state of naivete. Unless they are the earliest generations of humans, this means that most of their ideas are not their own either. They also are unwittingly afflicted by nonage.

Most of the beliefs and ideas espoused by the adults who raised me as well as those I came in contact with, were not their own. Consequently, I must doubt and be skeptical of not only myself, but all other human beings as well.

Doubt Society. Though society is a communal order for survival – with culture(we're told what opinions to have, what thoughts to think, how much we should know, what's important to us and who should be), traditions, institutions, laws and authority figures

– it is staffed and administered by a collection of human beings. As we've determined, since authority figures in society are also people – they are liable to err and are unsound like myself.

In general, all segments that comprise overall human society is pretentious and cosmetic – even the financially impoverished portions. This renders overall society as flagrantly hypocritical, an indisputable farce. The primary mandate of each nation state, even within so called "modern" or "moderate" societies – are establishing control and sustaining control. Self-preservation of state, though necessary for stability, can adversely affect a population's psychological development, if not administered from an axial position. The state's focus is not to use knowledge as a tool to advance society as a group, but primarily as a tool to further their own authority over the populous within said society.

From that, we have to assume that science is not necessarily an all out pursuit of truth, it could not be allowed to be. Such pursuits are unfettered up to the threshold that it interrupts or threatens the state's control. This is the case, even if whatever science puts forth is for the absolute betterment of overall society. Entrenched in their position, no matter how much they attest to the contrary, objective truth is a distant priority to the state and its institutions.

Certainty:

Materials make up the physical world, but they are subordinate to the immaterial rules that govern them. Human beings are superficially products of our parents, but fundamentally we and every other living thing – are also outputs of those immaterial rules. Everything within the universe, including the cosmos itself, is a result of Nature – of its Laws and forces. The Laws of Nature are the common denominator to everything. Not only did human beings emerge from it, Nature also endowed us with the ability to think. On a foundational level, Nature is actually what furnishes all of our ideas, and choices. It is not us that has equipped ourselves with our curiosity to query life. Is such a feedback loop not highly peculiar, to say the least? Subjectively, the universe is causally closed. Every action within the cosmos is causally sufficient, meaning that they can be explained back to a Law or truth in Nature.

If you consider this realization to its extremities, Nature had to precede the Event Horizon – being that it had to first provide the possibility for the Big Bang to happen, in order for that event to transpire. On that irrefutable basis, we assert that the Laws of Nature are to be considered as one consolidated charter and as such, are the absolute floor of all knowledge in and of the universe.

In terms of Descartes' declaration of – "cogito, ergo sum", I think, therefore I am – respectfully, he should have gone further. He failed to ask the next organic question after coming to his realization of, "I think". Instead of "therefore I am", he should have wondered, "but why do I have this ability to do so?" If the supergenius outfitted me with the capability to think – not to mention there being the presence of deception, lessons, choices and coerced decisions and those verdicts being final once acted upon – then this gives us sufficient reason to investigate further.

Preliminary conclusions:

- We find ourselves in the position of having to be suspicious of Nature, while simultaneously having to rely on it.

- There is adequate evidence for a serious inquiry into the question(s) of – is there a supergenius culpable for life experience, is our reality based on intent? Does everything have a conscious value, a reason – and if so, what would it be?

We will seek to answer those questions by pursuing peripheral queries that can bring us closer to foundational truth. For instance, is everything that happens, meant to and can this be adequately demonstrated? How does everything really happen the way that they do? Why do we think about the things that we think about and why do we have the particular abilities that we do? This is our starting point.

THESIS

Everything is many things, existing in many forms and on many levels. Reality itself, is one of those things. William Shakespeare alluded to it, when he wrote "all the world's a stage and all men and women merely players". Descartes said that all "animal bodies" were "machines". There have even been offerings of existence being a divine or intelligent design, a computational universe, a hologram, as well as a simulation. After taking a serious evaluation of a broad scope of evidence, we assert that the only destination to arrive at, is that intrinsically – the cosmos is the most elaborate device one could ever imagine. It is a multi-purpose technology. One that serves the primary function of conditional confinement for its occupant(s). All of the organisms within it, including ourselves, are also technologies – of the biological or organic variety. The megacosm is set up for the purpose of teaching us a lesson. It is a proving ground.

Another function the universe carries out, is the role of an experience mechanism, the actual version of philosopher, Robert Nozick's, rendition. Nature is a game system and our mortal existence is a game. It is a fully sensory immersive – virtual reality activity for the ultimate purpose of behavior modification. What we deem as reality is fundamentally not real at all, only nominally that way. Our version of literal, is really a more vivid output of figurative. We ourselves, actually exist both previously and outside of see-level. The purpose of our mortal existence, as human beings, in particular, is to figure out how to escape mortality(solve for the X of life experience) before the allotted time expires and the process repeats itself all over again. For us, being alive is a limited information problem, with a limited period to accomplish the overarching task(s) in.

The approaching supporting evidence will demonstrate that every aspect of life experience definitively follows from and leads back to this assertion. Since the best way to describe a game is in terms of other games, first we will highlight the peculiar parallels between them and reality.

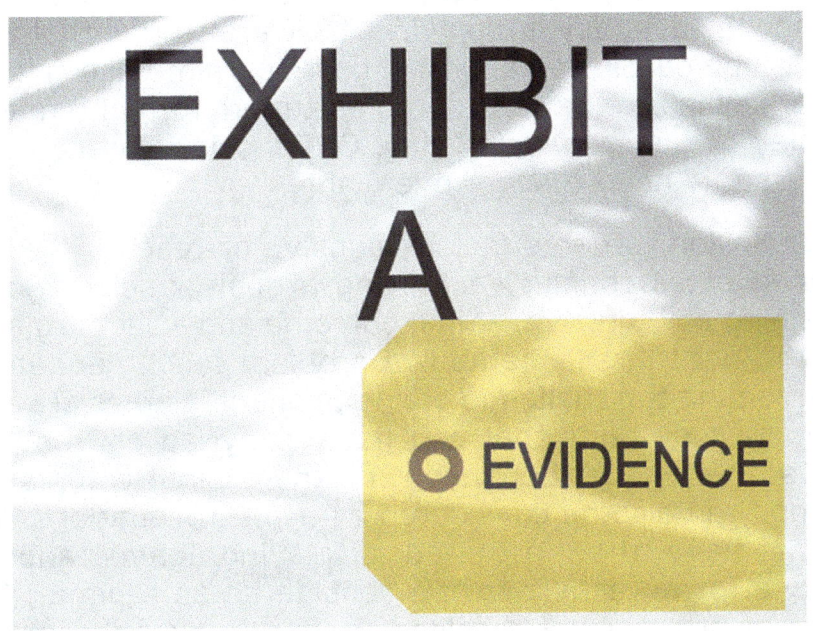

DEBT OF PROOF

"Extraordinary claims require extraordinary evidence."
Carl Sagan

Definition of Game and Play

To recognize our life experience for what it is exactly, each of us must first have an adept understanding of the concepts of "game" and "play". The two have to be considered together. It is difficult to explain one without the other, due to both being subsets of each other, inseparably entangled. The duo are naturally bound together as ends and means. Games are a type of play, while play is an aspect of games, in terms of participation in them. When someone says they are playing, they are stating that they are taking part in some form of game or game-like activity. A game can also be considered as a more formal rendition of play or a structure for play. On its own, play does not necessarily need rules or oversight.

In seclusion, a game is a responsive or reactive activity that involves conflict –achieving a goal or set of goals, attaining an objective, a final outcome and a set of rules of how to get there. A game is a problem solving endeavor, overcoming the challenge of an opponent. Games are self-contained systems that can have a myriad of "moving" parts, the amount dependent on the desired complexity. Games can also be considered as a set of equations. You do not have to be in the act of playing against another perone for an activity to be considered as a game. The rules or structure of a solitary game act as an agent on their own, working to stop you from accomplishing the ultimate goal.

The word "game" is also used to refer to an animal being hunted, which also can loosely reference any target being sought after.

Origins of games

How can life be a game when we are the ones who set the characteristics and definition for things we label as games?

We came up with the word "game", but did not originate the concept itself. Many of its attributes and underlying principles, if not all of them, are inspired by nature –

experience. We've just identified them and incorporated them – art imitating reality. In fact, games predate people. Informal versions can be found being played by a variety of living things throughout the wild. A closely rooted group of trees or plants jockeying for position for exposure to the sunlight and courtship – are a couple of examples of such preyestoric games.

Not only do games pass the time and provoke amusement, they even serve a vital function in the development of some creatures. Play helps some predators hone hunting skills and some prey to practice escape. The very interactions of predators and prey could be said to be a game, the game of survival. We, ourselves – have come up with more complex games than other animals' various versions of play. That now established, all expressions of games share a general principle. All interactions meet the basic metrics to be considered as games. Essentially, any activity that requires participation, which is every activity, even being dead – is a game.

Types of games

There are an array of games, a variety in concepts and applications. Experience is a combination of all of them. Some are puzzles or riddles, some are mazes, all are some type of adventure or journey. Some games require physical activity, such as sports – others are mind or thinking games, some are both. Some are board games, others are video games. From the crudest forms being played by early cereves, such as tossing rocks or thrusting wooden sticks at shadows and trees – to classics such as Hide and Seek, Red light, Green light, Simon Says, "Rock, Paper, Scissors", Musical Chairs and Chess – to the era of electronic games. There are games that have a singular winner, multiple or no winner at all. There are games where you only have to understand the rules or how to play more than the perone(s) you are competing against. In other games, you have to consider other factors as well. There are some games that everyone can easily play, regardless of practice or skill level – while there are others that require strategy, risk and luck – limiting the number of participants that are able to play well.

Though associated with fun or recreation, some games are serious. There are those that are enjoyable to play and those that are not. There are games that are obvious to the player, as to what they are and there are not so apparent ones. As a participant in a game, one can knowingly play or not even realize that they are a part of a game. In the latter case, you are not playing the game, but are being played in some regard. Play is not doing something enjoyable necessarily – due to everyone playing a game may not be having fun, yet still feel compelled to participate in the activity.

People and games

People have an affinity for games. The known yestory of the Roman colosseum and spectator sports, such as the modern Olympics – verify this. We play games by ourselves and also with ourselves and each other. We are even capable of fooling ourselves and each other. We tend to be more attentive to spectator sports, than the games we play with ourselves.

Any interactivity, from socializing to relationships, whether with – family, friends(including of the wezentic variety or acquaintances) are a form of game. For instance, infidelity is referred to as "cheating", as if acknowledging participating in a game. A party is a type of social game. Though the practice of it is referred to as "war games", war is also a game, just with a higher degree of consequence than a casual. "War party" has also been an expression used to describe a group of people participating on each side of a battle or skirmish. John Nash inadvertently took notice of our interactions with his Game Theory, which has become a wide ranging application for the science of logical decision making in himinds, other animals and computers. Ludwig Wittgenstein referred to our communication between each other as "language games". The two hemispheres of our brain can be seen as playing a game with each other, mind games. The interaction between cause and effect should also be considered as a game. In essence, any and every action or interchange that we do or that happens, can be considered as within the context of play or a game.

Characteristics & Elements of games

- Rules
- Math
- Space
- Game Length
- Gameplay/Game Experience
- Randomized Play
- Causality
- Feedback Loop
- Information, Game Knowledge
- Score, Value
- Objects
- Subjects/Characters/Game Pieces
- Interface & Controller
- Agency, Volition

- Actions, Abilities, Mechanics
- Resources(Assets), Skills and Tools
- Challenge, Difficulty
- Missions
- Plan & Strategy
- Story
- Objective, Victory Conditions

Parallels to reality

THE PRESENCE OF RULE BOUND ACTION

Laws and rules are a set of principles regulating conduct within a particular activity. Societally, laws are more weighted than rules, but objectively, laws and rules are essentially the same. The term "regulations" would also fall under this category. In games, rules are the laws. Rules are controls, barriers that set and ensure limits/margins. Other controls are the number of players that can participate in a particular game, play-time and the chance to win. Rules inform players of the game's constraints, what they can and cannot do. Rules help players understand how to play a game and they also create and affect the play experience. The same game would break down in different ways with the removal of each rule. Once identified, rules lead to clarity and shared understanding at a game's end.

We have always lived under rules – under Nature's "house rules", to be more exact. The Laws of Nature. Rules are Nature's Will. The average perone may not be familiar with most of them, but they are the Strong & Weak forces, Electromagnetism and Gravity. These are the rules that govern our overall reality, as well as everything within it. Even the most capable military, as well as people who are famous, prominent and wealthy – are subordinate to Nature's regulations.

If there were no rules, we would have no bounds. Any desire that came to mind, we would be able to perform. We would be in a state of absolute freedom. But, since none of us can naturally fly on command or naturally defy any well established incapability, and we didn't determine those strictures – there is no other destination to arrive at, other than the undeniable presence of predominant rules.

Nature's Laws are rules that form new rules unto themselves. From its Laws, forces are told how to move and interact and living things get our instincts, including genetics – which themselves are instructions or commands of how to be, what to look like, what to do and how to do it. Fundamentally, all motion and objects are controlled by rules. For all lifeforms, life experience is a master:slave relationship. The vast majority of experience is influenced by catalysts outside of (y)our control. Unlike our promises or legislative and judicial laws – Nature's Laws cannot be broken or undermined(morals are Nature's only rules that we are able to break and that is due to Nature suspiciously providing that accommodation). Everything is at Nature's discretion. It is akin to the chessboard and its game pieces being dictated by the rules of chess. In philosopher, Thomas Hobbes' book, Leviathan, where he spoke of the "State of Nature", a time when people lived in anarchy – people still lived under rules. They lived subservient to the rule of no rules. Not playing by the rules, is a rule in itself. There is no escaping having to endure rules.

Experience for all living things, in regards to the Laws of Nature or rules – is like playing the game of Simon Says, with the Laws portraying the role of Simon.

Rules are not meant to be broken – they are there to give structure, restriction and to be followed by those who do not make them(participants). As a rule maker, you cannot break something that does not apply to you, unless you are also participating. The legislator(s) of rules are in a position of leverage, which essentially renders them as being the rule(s) or ruler(s).

Nature's Laws, instincts and genetics render us voodoo dolls that Nature directs and curses. Within our selections and intentions – we prod, twist and jinx our own voodoo dolls, as well.

Throughout yestory, we have been trying to figure the correct authority to live under(feudal, monarchy/dictatorship, democracy etc).

Rules put players in a non-negotiable position. The system of rules in games is balanced and consistent. To win the game – players must know and understand its rules and its goals, by effectively gauging what message there is to be ascertained from their presence. Players must be aware of them and work within the rules to subvert the game. Game propaganda, whose function is to undermine players, is only effective when a player is unaware of it or ignores it.

Though we view other creatures as initially "wild", the fact is, that since we are all subservient to Nature's Laws – intrinsically, all mortal life have always existed as tamed or domesticated creatures.

The presence of rules, renders earth as a type of slave ship.

The consistent presence of Nature's regulations and its extensions that intrinsically controls our self-preservation mechanism, renders Nature not only an authoritarian, but an active one.

THE PRESENCE OF A PLATFORM/SPACE

The area in which a game is facilitated is known as its space. While some games are played on boards, courts and fields – virtual reality games are effectuated in a gameworld or on a virtual platform. In our particular situation, the space of play is a platform – "Earth" – that is accompanied by even more space that is known as the universe. Together they are a gameworld, our field of sense.

The gameworld is the setting, a space to explore, a space of possibilities. They are logical structures of cause and effect. Some game settings appear as neutral presentations left open for interpretation. The area influences the look and feel of the game. It determines sound, lighting and color. It acts as the defining feature for other game elements. The space of play influences which characters are chosen and what activities can take place. Virtual games have sizable gameworlds to contain all of the activities that players are able to do. Open world, room by room games take place in expansive areas. A gameworld is also detailed with features to hold the player's interest in whatever it may be that the developer desires for players to be interested in. These are affordances or clever ways to indicate that an area should be explored or should not be utilized. All features have one goal in mind, to effectuate play.

Shaped like a sphere, one-third of earth's surface is occupied by land(uneven ground, even on so called flatlands), whose masses are shifting. One-third of that land is desert, which are the driest and hottest places on the planet. Deserts are expanding, getting hotter and drier. Two thirds of earth is taken up by water. All 5 of the earth's oceans – the Atlantic, Arctic, Indian, Southern and Pacific – connect. They are all actually one global ocean. Earth's moon influences its tides and rivers. Not all of earth is able to be explored or settled. The land's fertility is limited. The vast majority of the entire gameworld is hostile to lifeforms.

The function of earth is not only to support life and effectuate the activity of life experience, but also to play an interactive role. It has held and provided details of the past, such as fossils and resources and has itself been a clue, due to yestory being subject to geology.

Earth's atmosphere allows for our weather and maintains a multilevel environment that allows a few million species to thrive. The atmosphere also acts as a protective bubble/shield. It has the ability to burn up objects, such as meteorites, that breach it. The atmosphere appears to serve as earth's first line of defense, but why would a planet need to defend itself? You eventually realize that really – the accommodation of the atmosphere, in addition to its uncanny capabilities, are all for the benefit of earth's species. Our atmosphere is similar to armor or is essentially our first line of self-preservation.

Like time, the weather is always here. We are always living in environmental conditions, which consequently means we are living under a set of conditions/stipulations. The cosmos is a collection of conditions.

In a way, weather is change or lends to the illusion of development, which is why we refer to aged items as "weathered".

The atmosphere is like a clear window that we get the opportunity to look out of.

The earth is not a rock – a rock is a rock. Earth is more of a simple lifeform than it is an inanimate object. Our planet is functioning, it has inner operations just like any other organism. It is in a constant state of forming and reforming, refreshing like our cells. It is still physically developing.

Different platforms provide different functionality and restrictions. In life experience, there seem to be multiple platforms. Space serves as a platform for planets, air serves as a platform for flying creatures such as bats, birds and some insects – and water serves as a platform for fish and marine life.

Earth is comparable to a flying carpet.

It's like we are on a ball of yarn and the vacuum of space is a cat playing with it.

The visible cosmos is estimated to be 90 billion light years across. The expanse is so vast, it is tabulated in light years, the distance it takes for light to travel in a year. One light year is equal to 9.5 trillion kilometers, 6 trillion miles. There are other planets and cosmic objects and occurrences in space. Space also serves as a background, as we live out life on earth. The three commonly known dimensions of space are – left, right – up, down –and back, forth. Time is the fourth dimension.

Space isn't just a vacant area or just a room. It is a site. Nowhere. We're in the middle of or are somewhere out in nowhere. It's a place that is no place. The other objects in space, such as planets and stars, give us a point of reference, but remove them from the equation and where are we? Should you answer, "space", ask yourself – what does "space" really mean? Apropos to earth's location, it is simply a more sanitized way of saying "nowhere".

The sun is our natural light source, able to light the planet one side at a time, as earth revolves.

Space and time are conjoined. Space is of importance, due to motion. No matter if it is the movement of microscopic organisms or some quantum level activity – all movement needs a place to occur or to "take place". If time had no place to happen, time could not exist.

Simultaneously, space serves as both the center of attention/centerpiece and a backdrop.

THE PRESENCE OF TIME & MOTION

"There is no present or future – only the past, happening over and over again - now."
Eugene O'neill

Our rendition of time coordinates himind activities and that is how we should also view it in the macro, as Nature's means to coordinate overall cosmic activity. A universal circadian clock(itinerary, schedule).

We perceive time and our perception of it changes. As children, growing up or during times of boredom at any age, time seems to move slowly, while as adults, we regularly marvel at how "time flies" or we all notice its momentum after bouts of preoccupation. Time even seems to slow down to super slow motion during moments of perceived mortal danger. All along, outside of our perception, time is moving at its own general pace, which we track with clocks.

Our transient perception of it, is only the beginning of the conundrum that is time. Case and point, what is time really? If there was no sun and we were a nocturnal species with no way to tell time – no days, no weeks, no months, no years or age to count – what is time with just us being alive in it? Within that scenario, how would you even recognize that there was "time"? Is time the tape measure that we call a clock, that we scale it out with – or is it just everything transpiring? Could it be both?

Time is duration, an expanse of elapsing moments. Duration is motion and motion is change. For something to move, its position must change, which means for moments to elapse, there has to be change. If time stopped, there would not be change and if change was stopped time could not lapse. Time is change and change is a variation of the same.

The meaning of entropy can differ from field of study to field of study; so in this text, entropy is a measure of change and its increase. Entropy has been increasing since the Big Bang, while energy in the cosmos has been decreasing. Entropy drives change from a state of order to a more and more chaotic state, while also thrusting the arrow of time.

Once a moment has occurred, it has permanently expired. We are forcibly always going away from the past and toward the future, no matter which direction we are facing or even if we are idle. This is due to time being a sequence of instances, where the moment before, determines the moment after. When you walk in the door and put your keys down, you walk away from them leaving them in the past. Suddenly, you remember you forgot something outside in your vehicle. You immediately turn and walk back towards the keys and reach to pick them up in the future. The entire episode, you were always in the present – the "now". Time's arrow is also why decisions today affect us years later and why we are all products of our past. This tells us that at the point of the Event Horizon, time was all a chain of future events waiting to occur, being that it started as the future. All of time initially started out as the past waiting to happen.

Entropy renders time as not only a medium that allows for experience, but also a development – where things end up different than what they start out as. For instance – before and after, things decay, break, tear, wrinkle – progressing from simple to more and more complex, vice versa and/or both simultaneously.

Our removal of the sun from our solar system, demonstrated that our ability to measure time is not a given. Going even further, it brings us to the sobering realization, as to how we go about accomplishing such a feat. Our ingenuity in using the phases of the moon, inventing sundials and clocks should not be credited with our ability to tell time. The rhythm of earth's revolutions on its own and as it tours around the sun – should be. Without those celestial bodies present and operating the way they do, we would not be able to tell time.

This leaves us at the landing zone, that not only is time both – everything transpiring, as well as it's measurement – but also demonstrates that Nature intended for us to be able to track when events were happening. Nature wanted us to know when and how long and to not be truant, but punctual for something.

If yesterday was today and today was once tomorrow, then all of time is today. Remove our need for sleep and the mirage of the rise and setting of the sun and what are we left with? One macro moment.

Time is an experience delivery system.

Fundamentally, we are always in the now, the present – and the cosmos goes out of its way to convince us that there is a before and after.

Time appears to be nonlinear – but our aging, activities playing out in a sequence and the inability to return to the previous moment once it has transpired – demonstrates that objectively time is linear.

What's New?

If you take a picture in a "new" mansion, while posing in a "new" outfit, in front of a "new" luxury car – years later, when you look at that same picture with everything taken at its newest, you will refer to it as "old". The story attached to it will be that everything in the still frame was new at the time the picture was taken, but no matter how pristine everything in it appears, in the future everyone will always regard it as dated.

This begs the question, what is "new" really, if everything considered as such, is destined to be regarded as old? Doesn't that render new to mean, new to being old or aging? If entropy is always increasing, is anything ever actually "new" and if so, how long can something be "new" for? What is new to me, can be old to you and vice versa, rendering new to be subjective, in some respects.

Your new vehicle, isn't fresh off of being welded at the factory and if it was, is that when it was "new"? Could it have even been when the idea of that model of car, was first conceived or when it was commissioned to be built? Your new house took time to build. A recently met love interest, isn't a newborn child, yet we tend to refer to them as "new".

While we are on the subject of newborns, a second after birth, are "newborns" still "new"? After 12:01 AM, is the year still new? When you get a new classic car, that doesn't mean that it is actually new, does it? What is new music, if it becomes old the moment that you hear it or hear about it?

When adequate effort is invested into the subject, "new" is not only what was previously unavailable, it is also what is unfamiliar to the observer(subjective). Objectively, there is no new or old. There are just things, which include us – entering, existing and exiting experience. Objects going in and out of existence in a nonlinear fashion(subjective), yet a conceptually linear(objective) way. Experientially, but first, conceptually – time is a procession, which is why introductions are always being made. Time also keeps broadcasting that it is a schedule.

"Youth" is the first stage of being "old", since we have to age in order to experience it. In actuality, there is no "young" or "old". It is all aging.

Some may see each moment of our physical development as moments of being born again and again. Instead, each moment of physical growth or being alive – is similar to conception, being reconceived over and over again in an updated form.

Motion

At its most micro of seconds, time is moment to moment change adding up to one total moment of change. Time is all one moment. Those changes are events, micro events compounding to one macro event. Light travels at the fastest speed of that change. The effect of traveling at the speed of light is the near stillness of motion(the rate of speed's effect on experiencing time, confirms the interconnectedness of change and time). This means that there is a speed to travel in which there would be a stillness of motion, a transcendent momentum. It is a speed that we are unable to reach, due to nothing being able to exceed the speed of light. While traveling at the transcendent momentum, things being in absolute stillness demonstrates that everything that is happening outside of that speed is similar to a fluid strobe light effect without the flickering. Time is a procession of still images of experience – a consistency of inconsistency.

There's no pause, things are always in motion, things are always in transition – segue – just at varying speeds, from the fastest to stillness/stationary – simultaneously. Motion is constant, which is why things are always changing and why everything material is temporary. Light sets the benchmark, traveling at roughly 670 million mph. The earth orbits the sun through space at 67,000 mph. Sound moves at 767 mph and our speed of thought is 250 mph, depending on what neural pathways are involved. Even when you fall asleep or if you get knocked unconscious or fall into catatonic shock – there is movement within the body. The mind or the body's cells are always active. After dying, the decomposing of our bodies is still movement. It is still developing towards full decomposition. Every living thing is technically some form of nomadic species, being that we are always in a state of flux.

Nothing actually happens spontaneously, it only appears to be. Don't discount the fallibility of our senses. If we view a so called spontaneous event in slow motion, this becomes obvious. When played out in slow motion, the spontaneous event plays out in frames of time. If it was truly spontaneous, it should not be able to be shown slowed down into frames. This fact renders spontaneity as events that happen at a rate of speed that we are ill equipped to realize in real time, which is why we refer to them as spontaneous. If our vision were slow motion cameras, would any event still be regarded as spontaneous?

There is always momentum. Stillness is its own form of momentum. Being lazy is still doing something.

For there to be motion, conditions have to be met. For conditions to be met, there has to be motion.

For games, time is the apportioned duration in which they can be played, game length – since time first is experience playing out. In games, time has also been referred to as "play time". Time sensitive games provide players with a game clock to keep track, while designers of games that do not employ the urgency of a looming deadline, don't usually feel it necessary to do so. Time is also responsible for the elimination of players and the emergence of objects.

Deadlines. A deadline is the endpoint or full extent of an allotted amount of time. In between our birth and death, our literal deadline, we face many target dates or time constraints that we have to meet. We are tardy to meet a large number of those dates/time frames, due to having a slant for procrastination and suspense. We like to put our "backs to the wall" or endure time pressure. Even many of us who pride ourselves on punctuality, create last minute scenarios within the buffer we give ourselves to be early. We make ourselves late being early or close to it, even though we are early enough not to be late. When we are ahead of schedule, we celebrate by either falling behind it or for effect – closer to it.

We do this to add a measure of challenge to the deadline we have to meet. We make a game out of it. It is apart of our default programming to make things hard on ourselves(error prone). Be wary of this predisposed inclination. With casual appointments, this mindset doesn't result in much damage, but for consequential events or tasks – serious ramifications can result if miscalculated. The goal of experience is to utilize the time we have wisely, while we have it. At some point, you will no longer have this option; so wasting time as if it is worth doing so, is ultimately counterintuitive.

There is no time, only a deadline. All of time is a deadline, in and of itself.

Our tendency to procrastinate and taking pleasure in suspense, is a clever and subtle way that Nature employs to regulate our progression in the gameplay experience.

Pride is the primary reason for lollygagging. This follows from our tendency to overcomplicate or make tasks harder than they already are.

Why does everything happen, how can everything that happens be meant to happen? If G0d is all knowing, how does it know what we are going to do ahead of time – how can G0d know what we are going to do in the future, if we have not decided it yet? Can the future be determined? How does one accurately finish another perone's sentence before they finish it or while they are finishing it? How does one know the word someone else is looking for, when they become stuck in a sentence while talking or know where an object is going to – when it is tossed to them?

Anticipation and calculation. We search our memory for possible words that would be appropriate and select the one that registers as the most likely or best alternative. Among all possible scenarios, we can estimate that this is most probable. If it is a familiar phrase being said, our minds will remind us that we have heard it or something similar before. We then attempt to remember how it goes or how it is said and if we remember before the other perone finishes speaking, we decide to speak up or don't.

In the case of the object tossed to us, our minds assess the flight path of the tossed object against all the possible points it is likely to descend to and then makes a determination as to its most likely trajectory.

Those examples aren't predictions of events happening far off into the future, but despite that – they are indeed instances of precognition. They give us insight into how motion works.

To allow for all motion, the future has to already have accounted for our actions at any given present moment and has done so in a way that doesn't require us already making our decisions, as to what actions to take over our lifetimes. This is able to be effectuated, due to the presence of possibilities. All motion happens via a transformational process taking place over an order of operations of possibilities/options, that then transition to meeting certain conditions, that finally become particular outcomes/experience.

For instance, as you, the reader – gleans these words for the first time, you have no knowledge of what the next word(s) will be after this one. That said, you can be confident that each word choice in this work, appears courtesy of the realm of possibility, which – in terms of words particularly, would be the entire vocabulary of himind language(excluding any vocabulary that is exclusive to this text). This is confirmed by you being able to understand the words that are being expressed.

Essentially, for any event, even spontaneous ones – to happen, it has to first be possible to happen. The potential for said event to occur, had to exist previous to that event or moment actually transpiring. You cannot die at the edge of the Grand Canyon, if you never go to the Grand Canyon. It is an impossibility, due to the potential never existing. If something is not possible, it cannot be actual. Before anything becomes realized or exists, it is first a concept/possibility. Idea precedes matter.

Reality is indeed a realm of feasibility. The next millisecond and onward awaits as a domain of potential. Each moment is filled with alternatives of what can be for itself and they lead into the subsequent moment and so on and so forth. Time is a queue of choices going in sequential order, waiting to be decided on. Every object, including each of us, even corpses(changes to remains due to outside interaction) – are surrounded by their own set of options. Due to objects interacting with each other, there are even shared possibilities that exist. The closer one object is in proximity to another object, the more both objects' possibilities adjust for possible interplay, by including each other. This is what some have imagined as an alternate universe or a multiverse, only it is much more local to us than we've considered.

The concept of parallel universes is based on what life would be like had we all made other decisions or explored our other options that presented themselves over our lifetimes. It is similar to films with alternate endings. The optional outcome would be considered as being from a parallel dimension.

After analyzing time up to this juncture, there are a few noteworthy implications:

From its inception, time has been a series of options menus. It is everything that can happen and experience is everything that does.

Time and the word "experience" are interchangeable, when addressing the subject from here forward.

Fate/Destiny is multiple choice.

All details in the cosmos have already been considered prior to the macrocosm forming.

What about the things moving that don't have volition?

All objects in the cosmos, including the cosmos itself – are functioning compulsory in some way. All motion is fundamentally involuntary, due to it all essentially being outside of our control. Volition, which is an ability endowed by Nature, is a subsidiary of that structure and operates within it. Everything is at the discretion of Nature's Laws. Involuntary motions are guaranteed actions or no probability(probability is subjective)incidents, due to being designated to perform or happen – as if having no other option to choose from, other than the actions they perform. An example of this is an act of nature when a geological event occurs – such as an earthquake, or wildfire, or volcanic eruption, or even a supernova, or asteroid/meteor strike. A biological event such as a brain aneurysm, can also be considered as another such event. At those moments in time, when those events or the like, occur – those occasions essentially had no other opportunity, but to.

Despite the claim being commonly made, everything is not possible. There is a range to possibility, a limited set(s) of options, resulting in limited outcomes. They are everything that can be done within the Laws of Nature. Nothing outside of them is feasible, due to that not being an available alternative.

The amount of choices available for a game is dependent on the particular game being played. The quantity is perfectly tuned to what each moment requires, in order to achieve maximum effect. Alternatives are made to seem organic from the gameworld. This is done by game developers strategically placing "options" at points where they can offer experiences, where the player is not likely to notice. We go to or are drawn to what appears safe or interesting. Players subconsciously are directed this way. Subtle highlighting leads us down routes in ways that make us feel like we are choosing where to go and what to do and how we are feeling, when in actuality we are being cued/induced.

Experience is an outcome. It is all that happens, the output of the Laws of Nature. The combination of the environment, conditions and setting and any respective lifeform able to perceive and interact with it – formulates experience. Experience is the end product of the receptivity of our senses, rendering it a stimulus. Our minds are set up to interpret things at the material level. Though the macro world, functions atop a subatomic one, we sense and interpret those signals at the experiential level. We don't have memories of atoms and quarks, we remember and dream of things that are more material. All of our thoughts are based on our experience.

Survival is an opportunity, but it is also simultaneously an obstacle. This is why on its own, survival is an impasse.

Gameplay, in terms of our life experience – is a limited information problem, with a limited time to resolve it in. Player emerges in game suffering from an amnesiac episode, that is unbeknownst to them, as one of the game's characters. Player eventually believes they are the game character they are controlling. Their character must survive a hostile gameworld and build structures while avoiding a myriad of hazards. While doing that, character must also explore the gameworld and find and unlock hidden modules of game knowledge. After that, character must combine the clues found throughout the game with the game knowledge and figure out the mystery of the game. The whole while, the character does not know that collecting knowledge is a game requirement and its player is oblivious to who they really are or that they are in a game. They are convinced that they are the character(s) that they are unwittingly living vicariously through.

In games, gameplay is the course of the activity. The setup and then play, which are the actions and maneuvers. There are two experiences, the game experience and the player experience(contains aspects both unique and common to each character or perone's experience). One happening within the other. Unlike cinema entertainment, games demand for you to be more than a member of the audience. A major appeal of gaming is the participatory aspect of them. Players get to control and exist, by proxy through characters, as the game's protagonist.

Life experience is play in progress. We are in play – even our corpses. Our peronal or collective experience is transpiring within the experience of the overall cosmos/Nature.

We are jointly experiencing two life experiences – one we are aware of, which is the artificial one/mortal – and another that we are constantly being clued in on, but are absent minded to, which is the immortal/intrinsic one. There is the world we see or sense and then another world that is hidden from us. One is to be used to unlock the other.

Why these limits and what set them this way?

"Many monsters to the Earth of old tried to produce, things of strange face and limbs, some without feet, some without hands, some without mouth, some without eyes – every other monster of this kind. Earth would produce, but in vain for nature set a ban on their increase. Many races of living things must then have died out, unable to beget and continue their breed. For in the case of all things which you see breathing the beginning of its existence, protected and preserved each particular race."
Will Durant

Over more than a millennia before the birth of Charles Darwin, a philosopher named Empedocles, had a similar theory to **evolution**. Whether we are talking about natural selection, genetic drift or transmutation – there are intriguing details about evolution and the processes that comprise it, that both Darwin and Empedocles failed to notice.

Evolution is a controversial issue, because some people are emotionally opposed to the notion of us originating from apelike ancestry. Regardless of whichever particular animal the himind species delineates from, all creatures share the same common ancestor. All living things are genetically linked, our emotional response notwithstanding.

Though credited with endowing organisms with our physical attributes for adaptive purposes, each creature being ideally equipped for their respective environment – evolution should also be credited with our cognitive ability to adapt, since that nuance provides us himinds with an adaptive advantage as well.

Whether it be about evolution or the processes that constitute it, the discussion – is change. Things develop, starting out in one form – ending up in another. When you look beyond all of the fashioning – you see that its as if each creature has been compensated with means of survival. Each adaptation is to attack or defend or both. In all the emergences, extinctions, differences and variations in appearance, abilities, anatomies and behavior, advantages and disadvantages – there exists a conspicuous balance between all of the creatures – whether it be predator, prey or fruit bearing trees. Evolution utilizes balance.

We shouldn't assign the effects of this transformative process exclusively to species. It is narrow-sighted and subjective of us to think that the cosmic force that causes variation among the species, objectively – didn't do the same for all other distinctive cosmic objects. Conceptually, evolution is really the forming and development of the universe and everything in it.

The planet forming and us living on it, is not an end to its development. Earth has evolved and is still evolving.

"Survival of the fittest", "only the strong survive". They sound poetic, but they are not universal truths, unless they are referring to being fit and strong in your knowledge or practice of universal knowledge. Those sayings only apply in some instances, not all. Fit and strong people and other organisms die and go extinct too. There are weak and slothful creatures that have long survived among the living. Still, we realized that in all the dying and extinctions that has happened over time, especially with the death of the dinosaurs and the rise of homo sapiens – that there seemed to be something deliberate at work. To avoid confronting the obvious, we deemed it "natural selection".

Every death should be considered as some level of natural selection, regardless of its superficial cause. Nature ultimately is the root cause of all death.

Why do we have involuntary functions, rather than them all being voluntary?

We have control over what our bodies do, but not over the organs that allow our bodies to do what they do. We really only have superficial control. The abilities that our minds have are interesting on their own, but what's more intriguing is what they cannot do. For instance – command over our involuntary functions. Instead, our instincts have control over them.

This causes one to wonder, what would have been the possible harm if Nature had allowed us full voluntary control? When you give that thought adequate contemplation, the result would be self-induced extinction, in short order, through a combination of deliberate and accidental means.

The implication here is that there actually exists an extremely valid reason as to why we do not have full control of all of our abilities. It is as if evolution made the conscious decision to deny us such control. This can be demonstrated by the particular functions that are off limits – breathing, digestion, blood circulation/heart etc.

There are limits to the abilities and behavior of every animal. There are even limits to what earth or any other object or phenomena in the cosmos can do. When we say, "such and such animal evolved" into whatever end product or "adapted its physical features", we frame the process of evolution as if animals self-enhanced. We make it seem as if each creature appeared and simply wished upon themselves the appropriate physical adaptations for their particular environment.

What it seems we are all trying to avoid acknowledging, is that Nature has actively made decisions as experience has transpired. It has some level of Will or consciousness. Along with us not having full voluntary control of our bodies, the earlier realization of the earth's revolutions and the presence of the sun being the primary reasons we can tell time – only confirms this.

Astronauts lose bone density while in space. This is our bodies reacting to the zero-gravity environment, it's way of being efficient. To our bodies, once we enter the environment of space, we have no need for the same bone mass as we do while on earth. This physically changing through time in accordance to the environment, corresponds to our description of evolution(the loss of bone mass while in space is an example of the body giving itself an adaptive advantage), as well as demonstrates the influence of gravity(whether present or devoid of it) on physical mutation.

And being that bone mass returns to astronauts once back on earth, this example of evolution is no different than a cold glass just removed from a fridge, condensing while adjusting to room temperature or our fingers and toes becoming waterlogged when submerged in water for a long enough time. Both of the latter instances can return to their original state when back in the conditions they started from, just like the astronauts returning to earth. It's all evolution.

Why doesn't "evolution" constantly produce new species, instead – it does so staggeringly – seemingly after cataclysmic events or major extinctions?

Himind beings did not share the planet with dinosaurs. The fact that their demise allowed for our eventual emergence, renders the himind being like a seed on a forest floor that waited for a nearby tree to fall, in order to gain and grow from the now available sunlight. Himind-kind was here the whole time dinosaurs were – only, we were dormant. A tree needed to fall.

The extinction of dinosaurs and our emergence was an event on time's itinerary. It was possible, which demonstrates intrinsic intent. We know this, because if they didn't go extinct, himinds would have never emerged to wonder about experience.

Why haven't we physically evolved since developing into himind beings?

As far as developing further anatomically, at this point in the advancement of time, we've reached our evolutionary capacity. Our current form is our anatomical potential in the current environment of earth. Every creature alive is adequately equipped for survival in their particular environment on our planet and new species are still being discovered. Keep in mind, we've never had a complete tally of all creatures on the planet.

The concept of natural selection is similar to that of a lottery or raffle, which would be consistent with life being a gamble/game.

All living things having a common ancestor, demonstrates that there has been a procession of the emergences of creatures, as if preloaded. Something had to decide their order of appearance. Some type of rules or guidelines that told living things how to be and how to react to certain stimuli, had to already be in place prior to the emergence of life. If everything evolved, such as transmuting over time, rules had to be in place previously, to even tell that process how to function in the ways it did.

All of space-time is an area of possibility. To be alive, surviving as a mortal being with the ability to solve problems and improve to a peak range of potential, indicates that we are to view life as an opportunity. Chances are limited, even at the special(species) level, being that all living things are mortal. Each day alive, we are proceeding closer to that end. Since the moment of the Event Horizon, our window of opportunity has been closing.

Subjectively game characters "emerge", objectively they are loaded.

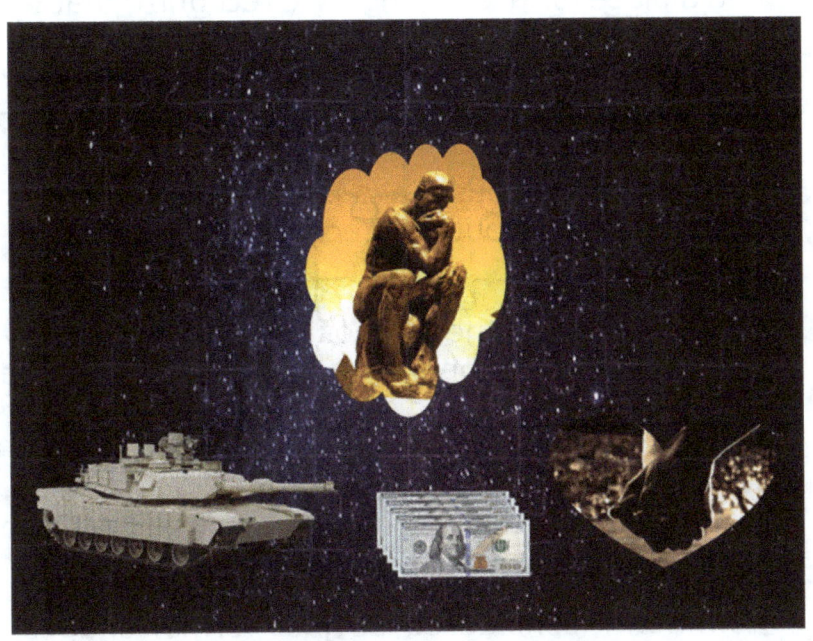

THE PRESENCE OF ORDER

An order is an arrangement, pattern or sequence and like it is in a game, it is the structure to the entirety of experience. The Wild is an order that allows numerous suborders within it. There is not only an order to experience's structure(s), but also to its functions, as well as to any other of its componentry. The laws of physics and logic are orders. All organisms are an ordering, an ordering of orders. Our healthy bodies function based on an order and when we are ill or injured, it is due to a fundamentally orderly disruption.

Order is what inspired the saying, "there is a time and a place for everything". We recognize that things should be "fitting" or "appropriate" or should "track". There is a right way or best way to do every specific feat, even if that way is more than a singular means. Contrarily, there are a numerous amount of ways to do things erroneously. We have to devise strategies and plan actions out to effectively operate within the commotion.

From the outset, the cosmos has been an order with neutral events happening within the rising chaos. This is due to chaos – disorder/disarray – being itself an order, just distinct from the ideal order of the Wild. The entire process, from the Big Bang to the maximum increase in chaos, is only the seemingly logical order to everything.

Commonly considered as just forms, shapes are signs and patterns – which is why our minds are fascinated by them. Like colors or texture(s), shapes help us to identify and distinguish items. Shapes are everything we perceive, they are perceptions within perceptions – as well as outside of them. Our minds take the data that the senses bring in and present it to our focus as a form or shape. It does this with the smells we smell, the tastes we taste, the sensations we feel, the sounds we hear – not just with our vision. Whether it is the basic shapes – circle, square, triangle – or a building or the outline of some creature's body – shapes get our attention. They've had significant impact on our lives. For instance, it is difficult to overstate the contributions of the wheel.

Something formless or of no shape – is still a shape. Objectively, a form and being formless are just two extremes on the same conceptual strand.

The influence of triangles can be seen in the numerous built pyramids that have been found around the globe.

The circle/sphere, spiral and ripple – though overlooked, are prevalent in experience. Our planet, moon and sun – our eyeballs, oranges and grapefruits, water bubbles, the wheel etc – appear as a circle/sphere shape.

The galaxy our planet exists in is called the spiral galaxy. Tornadoes, hurricanes, some spider webs and seashells, rams horns and whirlpools – are all shaped like the spiral/swirl. A swirl is like a compacted linear spiral.

When a drop of rain adds to a puddle on the ground beneath it, the momentum from it crashing into the puddle is dispersed throughout. This is done by waves, which we refer to as ripples, emitting from around the point of impact. In physics, everything is considered as waves.

Why is the term, "think outside of the box" so popular in society, is it a cosmic clue/sign?

Maybe, it is a clue we are to think axially – outside of ourselves. Subjective culture is "the box".

Things could not track without order or a format. Order allows us to associate and connect concepts and ideas together.

We take it for granted, but a lot of things(factors/variables) have to occur a certain way, just for one thing to occur, let alone happen right. Just to be able to even read these words, is no easy achievement. We should not just expect things to go favorably. If anything, we should be pleasantly surprised when they do. The elaborateness involved in bringing about specific outcomes, is a lesson from Nature that we are to value beneficial events or happenings that take place.

Deliberate order is like being alive, in that, you have to exert yourself to sustain it or it succumbs and returns to chaos.

Repeating Patterns

Some people think that the origin of patterns is in our own minds. Granted, our minds do operate utilizing patterns, but it is actually all of experience that is a pattern, including our habit forming minds. From the obvious, such as the Laws of Nature and the orbit of the planets(repetitive aspects such as phases of the moon, the seasons and the movement of the ocean's tides are consequences of this), to less apparent ones, such as random. Scientists have even identified twenty fundamental constants in nature. These constants not only give the universe its characteristics, they occupy

very narrow values, so precise – any change would cause dramatic transformation of the megacosm as we know it.

Science itself also relies on patterns. Philosopher, David Hume, noted that science rigidly adheres to patterns with its repetitive utilization of the scientific method, in its demands that hypothesis be reproducible in experiments and the notion that things are the way they were as before and will remain that way.

We behave in patterns, "creatures of habit". We tend to do what was effective for us before. Habits are patterns, just modifiable ones. This is why the question of, "does it sound like something they would say or do", exists – when someone is asking about the usual conduct of another perone. Memory, recall is based on the concept of patterns. Adaptation, becoming accustomed or adjusting to something, is about repetition. Many societal events are ritualistic and traditional. We mimic each other, to the point that we created himind-like robots. Much of our technology are imperonations of capabilities we witnessed out in the wilderness. Reproduction is a natural pattern that allows us and other species a somewhat mortal immortality. Reproduction is like fresh cut grass regrowing or a lizard replacing its tail after its been damaged. Reproduction is our way of regrowing the entire organ of ourselves. Reproduction is regeneration or a type of physical reincarnation.

Regularity or being consistent allows for the notice of **distinction** – irregularity. The cosmos is diverse, which means that difference/variety exists. Ironically, variety is present as a demonstrable pattern(particularly the variety in configurations).

There are many different items of varying types(there are even types of types), coexisting in experience. There are different sights, sizes, sounds, smells, tastes and textures. There is even variety in how everything occurs. Different organisms can possess the same ability in different ways(some birds and insects can fly by different means or in different ways). With such diversity, all living things are equipped with the ability to discern.

Variety within the same species can seem like it is mix and match.

Diversity in games helps to produce a more interesting experience. Increasing intricacy, generates the effect of player(s) confusion.

There are fractals or range of scales in reality. These exist in a variety of forms and types, where the same or similar pattern is repeating in larger or smaller sizes(as above, so below). The Mandelbrot Set is a commonly known example of this. Each part is like the whole, only smaller(scale model). For instance, inside every grain of sand are billions of tiny atoms. Every atom is made of smaller matter, electrons made of protons and neutrons which are made of even smaller bits of matter called quarks. Other examples are – the only difference between a microsecond and a century, is their scale. A letter, a word, a sentence, a paragraph, a book are conceptually – all larger or smaller sizes of each other. The same thing with a mound, a hill and a mountain. Shapes, such as the arms on a spiral are copies of its epicenter, yet careen out becoming larger and more complex. Ripples does this as well. Each ripple is more and more complex than its epicenter, as they move away from it, being that each is larger than the one inside of it. From an aerial view, rivers look like veins or bare trees or roots. When you see your breath in the cold, it looks like smoke or a cloud. In the same way we have to follow Nature's Laws, our society is governed by laws, we govern our homes and peronal lives with rules. Things are reflective, like the action between two mirrors facing off. They produce the effect of a range of scales.

Size/scale makes an impression – it awes, befuddles, distracts, intimidates. The scale of the variety of creatures, the scale of the number of creatures, the size of the cosmos relative to our solar system or of earth to our own bodies – all of it produces an effect. If everything was of equal size, they would lose that effect that they supply in scale. We would ponder them much differently.

There are **cycles**. Philosopher, Friedrich Nietzsche, deemed life experience an eternal "recurrence". From earth's revolutions(animals, plants and soil interact to make up basic cycles of nature – a carbon cycle, gaseous cycle, nitrogen cycle), to the water cycle, to animal migration patterns, to our life cycle, to our circulatory system, to the fevale reproductive cycles etc. Cycles are prevalent in experience.

Bill Murray's movie, Groundhog's Day, intrigued us due to our familiarity with it's primary concept. Though we complain about the monotony of life, at the very same time, we embrace or relish it. This is demonstrated by the music or movies we consume. The vast majority of those, even across most genres

– are blatantly redundant. How can it be logical that we hold this simultaneous inner conflict, you ask? How can we experience the feeling of boredom by redundancy, yet get excited about activities that themselves, we will one day build a tolerance to – rendering them also as monotony of the future?

This phenomena is due to the fact that all of our life experience is a holding pattern.

Even random is a cycle. Everyday we wake up, expecting today to be a little to a lot different than yesterday – and everyday it is. This may not seem like it, but this is a pattern. All change is just a variation of the same. That being the case, ultimately means that in actuality, there's really no change, due to eventually – such progression forms into a loop(redundancy) and repeats itself all over again(limited set of possible configurations). This establishes a repeating pattern.

Without familiarity, we can't even develop, process or progress. This indicates that the foundational reason for the presence of change at all, is to allow for those dynamics.

Attraction, bonding in all its forms(including love or infatuation), catch & latch applications, compulsion, gravity, influence and magnetism – are all different forms and varying levels of magnitude – of the same concept. In experience, they all serve as varying forms of the same function.

THE PRESENCE OF **R**ANDOM

How do we determine that something is deliberate?

By demonstrating evidence of intent.

We now confront the curiosity known as "random", uncertainty. Random is defined as the ensuing of events void of any obvious design, an unfixed pattern. The notion that reality is the result of blind and unguided catalysts, is prominent in modern science. A primary tenet of quantum mechanics, which is widely considered as the single most successful theory ever(successful to one part in ten billion), is the uncertainty principle, also known as physicist, Werner Heisenberg's – indeterminacy principle.

Even with acknowledging all of that, respectfully – objectively – there is no such thing as random. It is an invention of our minds. It is a perspective that is dependent on whether or not we have foreknowledge of an event. In a phenomenal world, anything is random to us upon unplanned contact with it, which means everything is and was random at some point. The Brownian Model, named after botanist, Robert Brown, asserts that seemingly random events are actually controlled by a large number of rational micro events, not "random" ones.

The law of truly large numbers, credited to Persi Diaconis and Frederick Mosteller, states that in a large enough sample size, any outrageous thing is likely to happen. We never find it notable when likely events take place, instead we emphasize unlikely events and find them more noticeable. This shows us that events or happenings that we refer to as random, are actually just unexpected.

If we removed living things from the equation, would there still be random? We are a subject viewing the object subjectively, forgetting that foundationally – we are also objects ourselves. This causes us to perceive events as "unpredictable". It's no different than a surprise party. To the perone who planned the celebration and everyone in attendance yelling out – "SURPRISE" – as the guest of honor walks through the door, the event is expected. At the same time, it is a random occurrence for the guest of honor, due to the party being unbeknownst to them up to that moment.

We say the future is unpredictable, but it adheres to that pattern, it can't be unpredictable if we are aware that on some level it is a set order. An unfixed pattern is actually a fixed pattern of being unfixed. No specific order – is still a specific order of being non-specific.

Nothing can be random, due to the fact that they occur or are present. Prior to happening or materializing, they had to be a possibility – which left only certain conditions to be met, in order for them to result. If something has a possibility of taking place, then how can it be random?

Random is not actually random, we are just unfamiliar with the phenomena.

Since no action or event is random, that means that everything that happens is inevitable, which ultimately means that they are meant to happen, even the things that don't happen. This would also mean that every aspect or object in experience is meant to be here and whatever that is not a part of experience – is not.

To say the cosmos was formed by blind and unguided happenings, is suggesting artificial intelligence or some other form of automation. We know that though they are able to perform operations on their own, artificial intelligence would have had to be developed by a more sophisticated intelligence, in order to do so. As recently mentioned, even if the unguided and blind cosmic happenings, took place instantaneously – the possibility of them taking place had to exist prior to occurring, rendering them not random.

In games, everything appearing improvisational, provides the element of surprise through randomized play. This supplies the impression of "luck" and induces perplexity. Random is utilized to keep players guessing. It serves the important function of being an order that is cosmetically outside of the scope of the player's understanding.

Is there such a thing as an "accident of yestory"?

Accidents are similar to random, in that they are subjective. Accidents have more to do with our intent, than actuality. Just because we do not intend for an incident to happen, does not mean that it will not happen. As if petulant brats, whose thinking tends to extend no further out than their emotions, we tend to feel that reality should bend to our desires. Over emotional people tend to conduct themselves as if Nature owes them something, rather than the other way around. Our advancement in technology bolsters that delusion.

If a husband has a vasectomy and his wife is on birth control and she happens to become pregnant after taking such precautions – many take the position that the pregnancy is then an accident. Subjectively, it may appear that way, but objectively – this is not the case. Since the foundational function of sex is reproduction, not our amusement, how can anyone be surprised when the cause produced the effect it was innately purposed for? It is like being surprised that 2+2 equals out to four, the next time you find yourself having to do that calculation.

A distracted driver may not have intended to hit a pedestrian, but if they were not giving adequate attention to the road in the moments prior to the incident occurring, no matter how intense the remorse – any claim of an accident is disingenuous.

A shopper in a store with a full shopping cart, may have every intention of paying for an extra desired item they put in their pocket for lack of room, but if they forget to purchase the item and do not check to make sure they remembered to pay for everything, such a shopper cannot fault store security for detaining them for the offense of shoplifting, as they attempt to leave the store. As unfortunate as this scenario may be, it is not an accident. Including the prior two examples, all three were demonstrations of deliberation. As the consequences of all three showed, carelessness nor ignorance are effective defenses in experience.

Now, if you are out for a stroll one day and a branch overhead suddenly breaks from a tree as you are walking under it and falls on your head killing you, objectively – even this is no accident. The branch broke due to its structural condition at that moment calling for it to. The conditions were satisfied for the event of the tree limb breaking at that moment, to occur. While that is happening, you are meeting conditions for the branch to fall on you, by walking under it at the very instant that it is ready to break. Regardless if you didn't desire to be hit by the branch, this mishap is a result of a convergence of logical processes.

No accidents(dynamics of random and intent). What most people call "accidents" are really likely outcomes. In fact, since they happened, they were guaranteed. If something(inanimate object) goes missing, it did not suddenly gain self-awareness and animate itself – there is a logical explanation as to its disappearance. A drug addict cannot suffer an accidental overdose when they knew the dangers of the particular drug they were ingesting beforehand. For the payoff of satisfying a lust, it was a risk they consciously decided was worth taking. They may not have intended to die from it, but they were well aware that the possibility/risk/threat was present.

Is everything chance encounters, coincidence – or is there more to it than just that?

The mystique of **coincidence** has had influence over many a decision and lives. What is it – peronal messages between ourselves and Nature, or signs, or destiny – or do we just have an overactive imagination?

Coincidence is described as a surprising synchronicity of events or circumstances with no direct or obvious causal relationship. Though there is some type of commonality, there is no direct connection between what is being compared. Coincidences are not to be confused with synchronous events or circumstances that actually do have direct or obvious relationships. "What are the chances" is a phrase we ask ourselves when we take notice of coincidence, due to those moments seeming to be rare and unusual occurrences. The existence of events and circumstances that do have direct causal connectivity and our looking for coincidence and continuing to find more and more of those occurrences of it, causes us to think that there is, indeed, a type of causal link and something deeper to the phenomena of coincidence than just – coincidence.

A perone you were just thinking of or discussing appears or is heard from soon after. A local stray cat that your dog likes to chase is walking through your front yard right as you are letting your dog out of the house. A voice urgently yells your name and as you reflexively answer, while looking to see who it is – you realize it is a stranger trying to get the attention of someone else with the same name. You and an acquaintance that you recently met, seem to cross paths frequently ever since. You survive a near death experience(s) etc. There are many examples of coincidence and different types of them. How can we explain this phenomena?

We exist in or on a space with an array of objects and many people doing different activities(co-incidents) in a range of proximities from each other. Entanglement and overlap are natural consequences of that. Coinciding is inevitable. The law of truly large numbers is again evoked here, attributing the phenomena of coincidence to a concurrence of "random" events(which we now know to be only subjectively random). Every motion is incidental, in that context. When we pay coincidences no mind, experience continues on playing out as if coincidence doesn't exist.

Our minds are always measuring and uses probability to gauge coincidence. It is somewhat similar to attempting to predict the outcome of an upcoming event, only with coincidence, the probability assessment happens after the fact. Keep in mind that probability does not determine what happens, meeting terms and conditions needed to bring about that particular outcome does. If this wasn't the case, underdogs would never win any sporting events.

Our minds utilize association and innately seeks patterns. Coincidences are instances of correlation, which are patterns. That being the case, means that we can find coincidences everywhere and in everything, since everything is coinciding(everything's a pattern). The instance of deja vu, which is a feeling of familiarity that suddenly comes over us and is also considered a type of coincidence, is also based around patterns.

That said, coincidence is given serious credibility in an official capacity in everyday society. The justice system has relied upon coincidence to convict an extensive amount of criminal and civil defendants. It is sanitized, by referring to it as "circumstantial" evidence. Circumstantial evidence does not conclusively prove someone's guilt, which is why many of the wrongfully convicted are later released, due to their convictions being overturned by better evidence. Circumstantial evidence only points indirectly to a perone's possible guilt and there are degrees to that, which means at best – it is just coincidental.

In the context of life experience being a game, let's utilize a saying that investigators like to use, "too many coincidences is no coincidence". The phenomena of coincidence is a clue that the chaos of experience is fundamentally a pattern and is coordinated. Some games provide clues, especially games with hidden meanings or some component of mystery. We know this, due to the very presence of coincidence and our reflexive response to it. Everyday, being alive seems logical and experiencing coincidences gives us the impression that there is a deeper meaning to things. Experience seems random, while coincidence makes it seem contrived.

Nature does not make what coincidence really is obvious to us. Instead, coincidence is equipped with countermeasures. Coincidence is deliberately difficult to grasp. After experiencing it, people tend to sound incoherent and irrational, when trying to explain its meaning to them peronally. As stated previously, quite a few bad decisions, myths/urban legends, superstitions etc have been claimed, due to misunderstanding coincidence – which results in the topic being dismissed as enigmatic.

At the most foundational level, everything is actually directly causally linked and coincidence are moments that only seem to be indirect. It is similar to someone seeing a Rubik's cube for the first time and it just so happens to be scrambled at that particular moment. In the first few moments of seeing it, you wouldn't realize it was a puzzle to be solved. What first grabs your attention, is the numerous different colored mini-squares plastered on each side of the cube. It is not until picking it up to further admire it and noticing that the cube was a combination of sections that turned, that you would then realize it was a puzzle. At that moment, while wondering why the Rubik's cube's sections turned, intuitively you would contemplate if there was a way to match up all of the colors.

The scrambled Rubik's cube, its different colored squares scattered about each of its six sides – are moments of coincidence. While scrambled, to the unlearned admirer before picking up the cube to further inspect it, initially its squares seem to have no direct causal connection. Coincidence.

When we experience moments of coincidence, they are intuitive, just like picking up the Rubik's cube and noticing that its sections turned and immediately wondering if the colors could somehow be finessed to fully coordinate on each side. The same way the different colored squares are what suggest this, is the same way that moments of coincidence are inferences. The phenomena is a clue that life experience is orchestrated.

Intrinsically, life experience is no coincidence, only surfacely so.

Nature endowed us with our abilities. It made sure that we noticed coincidence by making it odd and so distinct and us susceptible to being alert for such moments. This is to compel us to question coincidence and pursue its actual significance.

What Luck

We say phrases like, "good luck", "knowing my luck" or "this must be my lucky day" and speak about luck as if it is some mystical force. It causes one to ponder, what is luck really? Does it even exist? Once known as fortuna or fortune, luck is either success or failure perceived to be determined by chance – as opposed to our own decisions or actions. It is our way of qualifying our experience. Our default setting of seek pleasure avoid pain, coupled along with our ignorance of what experience actually is, entices us to assign a value to events. Occurrences deemed as negative, are considered as "bad luck"/ misfortune or as being "unlucky" – while whatever incidents regarded as favorable, are referred to as "good luck" or "luck being on your side". By saying fortune is good or bad, we are acknowledging that there is an unpredictability to life, but at the same time, claiming some deliberateness to it, as well. We're making the suggestion that something outside of ourselves, is deciding when good and bad things should happen to us. Luck then takes the form of a deity.

Like random, luck is an invention of our subjective perspective. There really is no such thing. Ask yourself, if there were no lifeforms, would there be fortune? It is how we choose to understand things. There's always some negative aspect that can be drawn from a result deemed favorable and inverted, there's always something positive to be drawn from an outcome widely accepted as unfavorable. The whole exercise is subjective. The fact is, regardless of how we feel about them, all events are fundamentally neutral/axial. What is good for one perone, can be bad for another. A rainy day for a perone hoping to enjoy a relaxing day in the sun, is considered as bad luck – while for a farmer trying to get their crops to recover from recent drought, it is good luck.

To properly assess the quality of experience, one has to first be able to properly discern between what is actually good from what is actually bad. To do this, one has to know universal morals, rather than just focusing on their own subjective desires and trepidations. For instance, a surprise extra bag of heroin may seem as good fortune to a heroin addict, but if it is the bag that results in their fatal overdose, would they still consider it as "good luck"? Suppose they did still consider finding the extra bag of heroin, that caused their untimely death as favorable – would they be correct?

Inherently, the notion of "luck"/fortuna exists as a clue, that overall experience is outside of our control. A greater control exists outside of the modicum of control that we have.

THE PRESENCE OF BALANCE

THERE are parallels, paradoxes and contradictions/polarity in experience. The reason for this is what Eastern culture has long referred to as "yin yang" or balance. Balance can be two of the same or two opposites(a win:win, a win:lose). Balance allows for conflict/opposition/contest(conflict of interests and competition) as well as cooperation. An accurate equation is balanced. Balance can be agreement and also be self-canceling. Not only can balance be found in the effects of evolution, the cosmos is proceeding towards equilibrium(maximum entropy in thermodynamics), among species there is symbiosis and our bodies seek symmetry as they develop as embryos. Our nose, sternum, navel and groin run along the centerline of our bodies. Should you lose an ability, your body seeks to compensate for it. Betrayal can also be considered as balance. We seek revenge or retaliation, to "get even" – just in conversations, let alone physical engagement.

> **"Men are more ready to repay an injury than a benefit, because gratitude is a burden and revenge is a pleasure."**
> Publius Cornelius Tacitus

Whether we are aware of it or not – we innately seek common ground. We are always seeking to find a "perfect balance" with all the activities that we take part in within our lives. We acknowledge the credibility of balance with sayings, such as "everything in moderation", "too much of anything(abuse) is a bad thing". We even possess opposable thumbs, they can be placed opposite the other fingers, balancing out the grip of our hands. The position of our thumbs is credited as one of the primary reasons we have been able to accomplish all the physical feats that we have, in contrast to the other species without them. Similarity and synchronization are forms of balance. Justice and redemption are based on balance. Balance can also be whatever is remaining, in terms of quantity.

Balance is both a thing and an action. Its presence is fixed, while its action is adjustable or sliding. Balance is parity in everything. Though everything is in motion, there is an order of stability to it. Stability is balance. In the instance of odd being the antithesis of even, even represents a severity, rather than the scope that calibrates the balance of either even, the extreme – or the valuation of odd. Balance is every value, every outcome and expectation. It is the synthesis within antithesis(overall contradiction).

Philosopher, Anaximander, proposed that all things arose due to separation of **opposites**. Heraclitus and Wilhelm Hegel spoke at length about the topic as well. There are opposites(allows for hypocrisy) to everything, even the items that are seemingly without direct opposites. Those are opposite to the items with direct opposites. Life is fundamentally a double standard or a "catch twenty two". There is a range/spectrum of balance. All opposites are extremes that exist co or interdependent on one another. You can't appreciate one without the presence of the other. These extremes, though in diametric opposition, also exist in symbiotic agreement, as end points on the same theme.

Even reality's imbalances are balanced. Every opportunity is accompanied by opportunity price. Opportunity costs are the loss of some potential gain from other options, when settling on one choice. Our alternatives subtract from the satisfaction of our decisions(this is why the best objective option is always the best pick to make). Having to choose one thing, always leaves us choosing not to do another. You cannot choose to engage in all of your options simultaneously. There are trade offs, the "give and take" circumstance. The time spent improving one area is taking away from time you could be improving in another region. If you try to be good at everything, then you are very limited at each thing. If you try to be good at only one thing, then you are very limited to only that one thing. It is a paradox(last three sentences paraphrase Firas Zahabi). This regulating feature, renders that nothing is for free, everything has a cost. Even things you find or are given, have been at cost to someone or something.

Initially things had to be even, level or equal for there to be any give and take situation – for there to be any gain or loss due to choice. There had to be a preliminary balance that existed prior to the existence of living things.

Experience is constantly paradoxical, rendering it a constant paradox.

Leverage, advantage is an imbalance.

It is difficult to maintain deliberate balance, it takes a sustained effort.

It is, it is not, it is neither, it is both/multiple/all.

The reason why people contradict ourselves so much is a hint to us that life is based on balance.

Empathy and any other form of sharing are correlations of balance.

Clemency, commonality/similarity, vendetta – all follow from parity.

Fragility and resilience are examples of opposites that are actually interdependent on each other.

In regards to us, the effects of experience vet the fragile minded from the resilient.

Regardless of any of our circumstances, the presence of balance renders life experience as being objectively fair. When you consider the challenges we face, just by being born – in what way do you think the reason for overall experience could be fair?

Games have "gameplay balance"(for every advantage, there is a disadvantage) and effective immersion when they have equilibrium between the challenges they present and the necessary player abilities required to surmount those obstacles. Gameplay balance is equating the game difficulty with its playability. Games are inherently imbalanced in some way toward the player, to present a challenge.

Reality seems deliberately contrary to our expectations. Instances of this are – everything that sustains us can also kill us – a blessing in disguise, you are born not knowing and you die fearing the unknown, the more you learn the more you realize how much you are ignorant about, be careful what you wish for – you just may attain it – begrudgingly, the things we brag about are eventually lost or damaged or we lose interest in them, we can't see the edge of the universe, nor the inside of the earth.

Not every occurrence that starts out as favorable ends up that way. At the same time, not everything that starts out unfavorably ends that way either. In experience, there are not only "blessings in disguise", waiting regrets can also be outfitted in costumes.

Irony is what makes life feel as if it is a twisted joke at times. You can find irony in every situation. It bothers us and makes us wonder. It also provides Nature with plausible deniability. Irony can make life feel like it is deliberate or it can make us dismissive of that idea.

Irony is perspective, but does that mean it does not exist outside of us, cereves? If there were only the other animals – would there still be irony?

Irony is based on us having expectations. The other animals have expectations as they go about living, rendering the answer to that query as a – yes.

What about if we remove all living things from experience, would ironic events still occur?

Theoretically, yes – they would. Though there would be no subject to take notice of irony in action or to participate in it. Ironic events would still occur among the remaining cosmic objects.

Nihilism is the belief that there is no deeper meaning to life in the Wild, outside of survival. What is ironic is the fact, that just to hold such a view is to assign a meaning, of some kind, to the very life experience that nihilists are claiming is without one. Life having no meaning, is still life having a meaning, a meaning of no meaning. This demonstrates that life is innately meaningful, while only appearing to be devoid of meaning.

Life is innately kismet. There are aspects to it that are unavoidable. Venture too far off in any direction(east, south, north or west) on any planet, eventually you'll return to the very point where you started off at. This means that in actuality there are really no directions. There is no east, or west – or north, or south. And since there are no directions, are we really ever going anywhere? Fundamentally, is there actually motion?

In actuality, there is everywhere. Every which way is its own direction.

Ultimately, irony is a clue that all motion in the cosmos is coordinated and that our subjective expectations are out of sync with it.

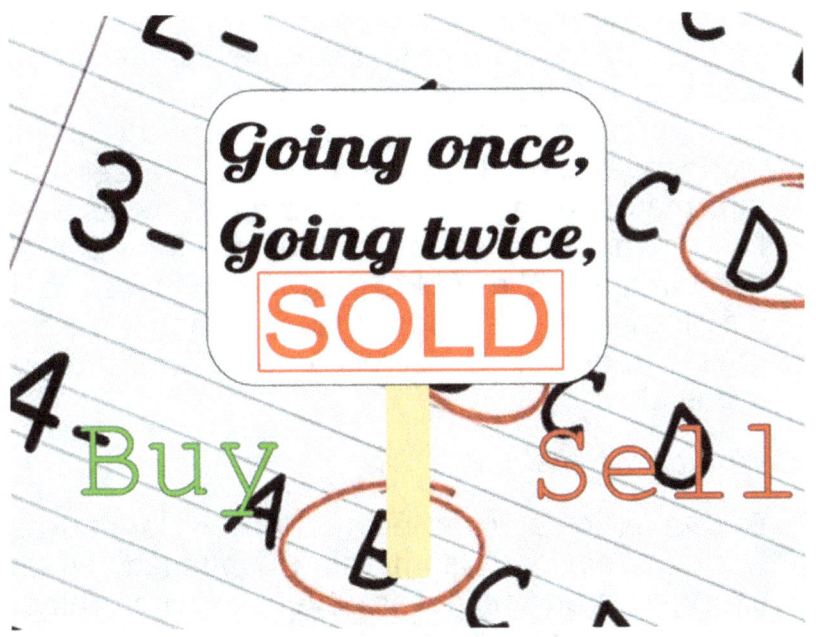

THE PRESENCE OF VALUE

Value is one of those words that is not only used in a variety of ways, it has multiple meanings. Primarily – value is a concept based on the benefit, importance, usefulness and worth of a thing. It is also what something is on its own. Your name is a value, the characteristics that identify each of us are also values. Your abilities and how well you utilize them are values. Everything – the macrocosm and all within it, are values and has a value.

Values can also be the beliefs and ideals you hold. We base all of our decisions on those type of values, whether to be consistent with them or in contradiction to them.

Value is to measure or score achievement, progress, success or failure. Even no value is a value. Value is to appraise, to evaluate and interpret. Our minds instinctively are always analyzing and assessing the information being communicated to it by our senses. During this process, our minds are also is making comparisons. We make judgment values. Fallible, we often over and under value things. The ultimate goal is to be able to correctly appraise whatever we are evaluating.

Why do we blame?

Blame follows from evaluation, it is natural to want to know why something happened. When we experience an unpleasant event or when things go wrong, we point to or receive blame, not just to look to find fault, but ultimately – in an effort to get things right as to why something occurred. This is the objective reason why there is blame.

Evaluation infers ranking, scoring, a point system. You rank and score yourself, others and everything else that you perceive.

Our minds and bodies allow us to be producers of value, while our insatiable desire renders us all value seekers. We are born into the world seeking value.

There is subjective and objective value. One perone's trash is another's treasure. Subjective value is value based on the emotions of the beholder. A sentimental heirloom is priceless to one perone and is nothing worth a second look or thought to another. Something priceless is worth nothing to someone that doesn't comprehend its value. Conversely, something worthless can be viewed as priceless, by someone who has grossly overestimated its worth. Objective values are things that everyone values, such as water, food, shelter, sunlight etc. Our needs are objective values.

There are superficial values and intrinsic values. The value of each factor within the universe, including the universe in and of itself, is its ability or function, in relation to its overarching purpose.

Life is an opportunity to create some kind of value. The earth credits each creature with value and each creature returns value. One of these values is peronal. It is our default needs, in regards to our own survival – such as eating and drinking and the very act of survival. This is peronal value and special, in terms of the overall survival of each species. Another one of these values is reciprocal. It is value provided to other species. It is a value that each creature is unaware that they provide or possess.

An individual bee in a particular hive or an ant in a specific colony, is welcomed based on citizenry, role and activity. Even in a pride of lions or pack of wolves, each single member earns their value to the group, through merit – what they do for the collective. The overall role of each member of the group is to add value to the whole.

The honey bee goes about its day seeking nectar for itself and its colony, in order for them to eat and survive. As it goes visiting each flower, the bee performs the invaluable service of allocating the flower's pollen for it, furthering the survival of both species. The bee also happens to make honey, which is a delicacy of some other animals, including us himinds. Bats, birds, some other insects and animals also inattentively distribute pollen.

Before being able to supply the bee with pollen, the flower drank water and absorbed it through its roots – all peronal value. It absorbed carbon dioxide and emitted oxygen, though be it a minuscule amount, creating more external value.

The excrement of cows, sheep and some birds can be used as fertilizer.

Other creatures, whether predator, prey or fruit bearing tree – can also be observed creating external value, while they go about pursuing internal/peronal value.

There are negative and positive values. Value allows us to prioritize.

Some actions have a neutral value, even subjectively.

We put an emphasis on accuracy. We have an affinity for words and sayings, such as – "ideal, alright, righteous, upright, right side up, right on, the right of way" etc. People want to be right, even when we are well aware that we are wrong or are in the wrong. This is a major reason for lying, squabbling and high turnover in friendships and wezentic relationships. Credibility is important. Honesty is the quality of information, the authenticity of it. Correctness is the quality of what is done and since communicating is an action, credibility is a form of accuracy. There is a best way to do every action in the cosmos and each lifeform is tasked with seeking and performing it, as their ultimate ambition.

If you consistently sit in a way that is adverse to your posture, you will eventually begin to ache and succumb to detrimental effects from doing so.

When you are trying to get somewhere at an appointed time, though there are numerous ways or modes to get there, to achieve your goal, you choose the most efficient or best way to get there. There is always a best or correct way to do things, sometimes there are multiple. The ratio is always exponentially smaller, to the copious number of ways to do things in error.

Variety allows for range of value. Whether it is worst to best, last to first, smallest to biggest, shortest to tallest, weakest to strongest, least to most etc. This applies both quantitatively and qualitatively. **Hierarchy** follows from range of value and is itself, a range of value. Prioritizing and ranking follows from hierarchy. There is what things do and what they are capable of doing, their potential, their maximized value. What they do is their achievement, legacy and output.

Potential, is what could be, it is what is within the realm of possibility. There is a limit to how far something can be developed and that is its potential or maximized value – the ideal extreme of potential. Perfection. Underachieving, underperforming, point of failure, worst or full waste – is the other extreme of potential.

Potential can also be considered as the complete range of value, due to it occupying the latitude or spectrum between the point of failure and the point of success.

We must perform to our peak potential, because that is the likelihood of why it is present as an alternative.

What doesn't kill you gives you a chance to grow and learn from it. It seems as if there is always more to do, something to improve on. We are always seeking to do more, to create – even though to get there we have to strive – persevere. When a perone is new to something, there is a substantial amount of room for improvement. They make tremendous strides initially, but as time goes on, there is less and less area to improve. Eventually, they reach a point where that skill or act can no longer be improved upon, They reach the ideal proficiency in that particular thing that individual was seeking to get better at. From there all one can do is maintain that level. Due to opportunity price, skills erode if you go a long duration without practice(this paragraph influenced by Firas Zahabi).

There is value in failure and mistakes(hence the term, "costly" mistake), whether it be your own or in the blunders of others. Mistakes or bad choices are in fact, lessons or traps waiting for us to potentially trigger them. They are ultimately, learnable or teachable moments. Failure is only defeating, when it is allowed to be. In each failure and mistake, there is a lesson of how not to repeat ineptitude. Failure is only effective if its lessons are ignored. Defeat compels us to try something new or in different ways. Learning experiences are embedded with value that is aid in progress and solutions.

In life experience, falling is a given. Toddlers fall and seniors do the same. It even happens at times in between. Since our anatomical disposition is to stand upright on two legs, it must be that Nature is seeing if we will get back up. It is testing our resiliency.

The concept and word, "almost", either inspires hope or antagonizes.

There is a substantial chasm between capability and action. A clear distinction exists between what can be done and what is done. This is intrinsically the reason why there is volition. Experience requires merit, it's beneficial value(s) must be earned.

When we look at our existence as the totality of a learning experience, we realize that the only actual valuables are life's musts, its need haves and its need dos.

Time Value

There is an innate value already in time itself and time is a value on its own.

No perone is attracted to the notion of performing activities without consequence, due to the fact that they find no salary/value in such action. We either feel nothing comes of it or the action is not worth doing. This means that we have been left to individually and societally gauge what is actually valuable to do. For instance, is a zero or negative sum game one that the cerebral social species in experience should be playing?

Though we may not like to discuss it in any depth, death is a part of life experience – an integral part. Death is the complete operational failure of all of your body's functions. Our own impending death aside, it allows for more life. If lifeforms didn't die, himind beings would have never emerged, being that the dinosaurs preceded us. Even if we allowed for dinosaurs and himind beings to coexist or for himind beings to exist without there ever being dinosaurs, the earth would still become overpopulated with the existing creatures' offspring. There wouldn't be enough room or resources to nourish all of us. This is why there is death. And notice, this reason precedes even us realizing it or even the emergence of any life. It is another example of Nature making a seemingly calculated or conscious decision.

We, like every other creature, are mortal beings. Similar to fruit, mortals are perishable items. We are born, develop and grow, live, age and die. That is life experience as we know it. Regardless of whatever the shield, or weapon we hide behind, or status, or title that we hold in society, or how boldly we speak – we are all vulnerable.

> **"Security is mostly a superstition. It does not exist in nature."**
> Helen Keller

Vulnerability is a byproduct of being mortal. All creatures are mortal, which means we are able to become hurt/injured, sick or die at any given moment – in a world with no shortage of ways that those events can occur(life goes on without you – whether injured, sick or dead). Regardless of how much this is ignored, it is the reality of the situation. Essentially, we are born to die, with limited time in between birth and death to act, which we refer to as "living" or being alive. An undercurrent of life experience is that it is a race against time, life is a countdown. For any mortal being, time is a scarce commodity to be guarded and treasured. Mortality renders every living thing's health as a top priority. Death begins to chase us at our very conception, let alone birth. This renders each year, month, day or microsecond of time – each moment – as consequential, since each is being that much closer to a living thing's own demise. Each moment is mortally weighted.

We are on the run. In one aspect, life is a race since there is hierarchy, prioritization and death looms. In another facet, being alive is a chase even if you are in first place, there is always some goal, desire or standard that we are pursuing. A greyhound race is a perfect microcosm of this phenomena. Chasing after a lure is the catalyst to the dogs contending with each other in such contests. In life experience, we are the unsuspecting greyhounds.

Every moment alive is a near death experience, just varying degrees of it.

If we were just born and could not die, age or become injured – then there would be no or little value to being alive. We know there is an intrinsic value to being alive, since we aren't just alive, we also have to repeatedly give effort to sustain being alive. Add to that, the fact that while we are surviving, we are also simultaneously aging/developing towards our death.

If life was about catering to our emotions, Nature would have allowed us adequate time to grieve. Instead, since the first himind death, we have never been afforded such luxury.

At least in part, our grieving could be some level of survivor's remorse.

> **"Fear of death is natural but not rational."**
> Epicurus

> **"We develop our world views in order to cope and manage with the terror of death."**
> Stephen Cave

Death is the ultimate motivator. Some will mock and tempt death and make light of it, until death is their house guest. It is then that such individuals come to a proper valuation of the exact seriousness of not only death, but more importantly – life. Being reminded of death(when others we know die) or pondering it at some length, opens the mind to a unique state in which death serving as a catalyst, causes one to think more acute or keenly, especially of one's own future, legacy or self-worth.

Emotionally, death can be agonizing, horrific, painful to endure and excruciating to watch. There is a stark difference between a dead body and a living one. When you also take into account that we are a creature governed by self-preservation, it is clear that Nature has influenced us to subjectively fear death, even though fundamentally – birth and death are neutral and in regards to death – inevitable.

Beyond grieving and mourning, death reminds us of our own mortality. Frustration or sadness can leave us stunned or unmotivated, but focusing on our own death invigorates. How many times do we stop to consider all the deaths of every creature that has lived before us and contrast fearing our own death, relative to those? So many creatures have died already, why is (y)ours or that of a loved one – of any significance, to the point that we feel ours is deserving of the performance of ritualistic symbolic gestures – such as funerals? Has our ego not blinded us when it comes to this topic? From alchemy to cryogenics – we've always sought ways to not only live longer, but to conquer death. Death forces one to value life and to see it as an opportunity to get something meaningful/valuable accomplished with one's efforts while alive.

Not only is death an end, it is also a compulsion/catalyst.

Death is a finale(subjective) and being that it is a part of the process of life and experience is a pattern, death is also a continuation(objective).

Since we eventually die, doesn't that mean that we are all just visiting? We arrive from a state of nonexistence to the locale of existence and then return to the state of nonexistence.

What is the actual significance of us burning our dead or burying them? One method demonstrates detachment from the material world and the other is a desperate attempt to remain a part of it. We learned from the pharaohs and some emperors in yestory, that we cannot take our physical possessions with us when we die, including our bodies and the rest of the world. Those who desire burial, do so as if trying to be immortalized on earth.

Being buried is as if seeking to remind some perceiver in the future that, "I was here". It's like another animal spraying a tree. It's a form of marking territory.

Being buried is holding on, when death is about letting go.

Life experience: Start as n0thing, transition to being alive, transmute into a memory, return to n0thing…

The fact that there is time-value for living things, infers that the reason for motion is the observance of our activity, particularly cereves.

> **"Life is long enough and it's been given to us in generous measure for accomplishing the greatest things if the whole of it is well invested. But when life is squandered through soft and careless living, when it's spent on no worthwhile pursuit, death finally presses and we realize the life which we didn't notice passing has passed away."**
> Seneca

Why do we take time for granted? Not knowing when we are going to die is not a nuance that appears courtesy of happenstance. You can tell this by the effect it generates, along with there being no such thing as happenstance(only subjectively). Either it spurs urgency to act or brings on complacency, due to us becoming skeptical of our own mortality or taking our being alive for granted. To someone who is fixated on just the boredom of life, time seems as if it is abundant. For someone with a busy mind, life often seems too short to get anything done.

Value can be wasted. To **waste** is to be negligent in making full use of something. When you value something, it is demonstrable. Ironically, as a concept, waste is and has value, while simultaneously being the opposite severity of value. In terms of squandering something of value or taking

opportunity for granted – without waste, we would not value(verb, meaning appreciate) value(the noun). Since everything has value, we would not be able to appraise anything including our very selves. The two concepts, value and waste – are not just opposites, but are also simultaneously dependent on one another. Both are examples of potential. When we take time-value into account, wasting positive potential is the worst offense in experience. Nature has designated each of us, which collectively is our entire species, to maximize our positive potential.

To murder another cereve or another creature with no regard, is waste. It is to waste their potential for production in experience. Murder victims are looted of their future decisions.

Nature is the true serial killer and mass murderer on the planet. It is what rendered us to be mortal.

Our versions of serial killers and mass murderers are just the microcosm of the macro.

If we were born just to find ways to frivolously pass time or just go from moment to moment – cereve beings would not exist. If this wasn't the case, value or waste could not be created by us moment to moment. Yet, this is what we find ourselves in the constant practice of doing. Wasting time or continuously making bad decisions sets us behind in time and value.

Productivity, being **productive**. "Value to production", meaning value in respect to an object's production, is the rate you create something. Meritocracy is a cost, it demands sacrifice in trade for achievement. Sacrifice is only of actual worth if it is for universally positive benefit. Fundamentally, we are all involuntarily sacrifices. Subjectively, some of us are voluntary sacrifices and some are involuntary. Many of us are just within existence as if in the roles of extras in movies or props included in the scenery of a theatrical play. For every lifeform, experience has been a meritocracy. We have had to earn our way in one respect or another. Those who stubbornly exist as if experience owes them their desires, rather than just their needs – volunteer as sacrifices.

An unproductive day is a waste of being alive.

It is not until you are somehow incapacitated or are put in a helpless position, that you realize how much you take being productive for granted.

Why sacrifices were a necessity. Even in the most ideal circumstances of society, everyone is not meant to win. Bad examples or "cautionary tales" are so the rest of us know what not to do. Good examples or "role models" are to show us the best of what we are capable of.

The fact that any of us can suddenly collapse and die at any moment, demonstrates that life is innately a gamble. For any life form, including ourselves, each moment, whether asleep or awake – we are at mortal risk(some risk is greater than others) or chance. At all times we are out in the wide pathway of harm. Absolute safety is absent.

Our actions produce effects and those effects produce consequences(negative value, deficit) or reward(positive value, benefit) or are seemingly inconsequential(impasse). If we go without performing hygiene/grooming, such as brushing our teeth – we suffer adverse effects, such as our teeth rotting. When we eat nutritious foods, our body becomes strong. When we ingest food that is hostile to our bodies, it operates with less vigor than it is capable to. Either consequence or reward is risk/chance. These are values. Our decisions are bets and Nature is the bookmaker. The actions we perform amid the maternity ward and the funeral parlor are being counted. We are not just appraising and assigning scores to things we see, we ourselves are intrinsically being scored or tallied.

Nature forces us to be risk takers. We are in a position where we can never avoid risk. This renders overall experience intrinsically, as a casino.

Since the Wild is a meritocracy, being alive(survival) is a cost/price. Our effort pays the bill, exertion is our currency and we have to budget it via our decisions. It is a credit to be alive. Each lifeform is a credit or is on credit. We are alive to pay off a debt to Nature, particularly cereves.

We are alive to redeem ourselves. That is why we have to earn our desires and aims. Our health or exertion is our spending power. Our legacy is our actual credit(credibility) score. When someone one does something, whether detrimental or worthwhile, it is to their credit. They deserve credit or debit for their actions.

There are things in life that if we ignore, we do so at our own risk.

We always look back with regret at the things we consider as wasted opportunities. Each memory of us not doing our best, relative to a meaningful action we could have taken, becomes a regret. Being wasteful will eventually torment our minds; so it is best to be avoided.

Games use death to eliminate players' characters. In a game such as mortal life experience, we are forced to play, with no way of escape. Suicide should not be considered as a viable option. If we could escape life there wouldn't be birth. Birth is not only an entrance, it and death should be seen more as opposite sides of a revolving door.

Being that one of the primary themes in experience is development, we are to do our part in setting the world for the better, rather than leaving it as it is when we arrive in it. If not, our recompense is to return and wallow in the remnants of our failed legacy without realizing that we have returned or why we have revisited and what we should be doing that failing to do before resulted in our rearrival.

The repercussions from our failure to realize what has been happening, in regards to **reincarnation**, is a backlog and compounding of more and more adversity. Unwittingly, we have been piling on and adding to our problems. The whole circumstance is a lesson in learning from our bad decisions/mistakes or being doomed to keep repeating them indefinitely. Cycles are prominent in life; so when we die we are doomed to redo experience until the game has been defeated. Experience is a closed loop.

Nature gave us our thoughts. It has already provided for every contingency. There are no easy outs. This is a meritocracy. We have to earn triumph.

Our waking up everyday, is as a magnitude of reincarnation. Our sustaining being alive every minute or second of the day, is also similar to the concept of reincarnation. The complete refreshing of the cells in our bodies every so many years, can also be considered as another degree of reincarnation.

Destinations are also points of departures and points of departure can also be destinations.

In one aspect, reincarnation means to return. What's even more alarming, is that in another – it means that we never leave.

> **"Sometimes even to live is an act of courage."**
> Seneca

Suicide is knowingly engaging in an activity that puts us at mortal risk(the very act of living qualifies). It is figuratively walking out of the classroom in the middle of a test. Some people take their own lives. For the suicidal, being alive is the immediate threat. There is a high percentage of suicides among war veterans in comparison to the general population, who are not exposed to as much vivid violence. Suicide has been said to be a long term solution to a short term problem. It is considered by some to be a cowardly act, by others to be an honorable one. Suicide is the ability to override our own hard code for survival, self-preservation. Regardless of our feelings on the topic, it does take some amount of courage to voluntarily end one's life.

Those who commit suicide do so for numerous reasons. Some do it to escape the agony or hopelessness they feel in their peronal lives, some in an effort to escape unending psychological anguish or inevitable death imposed by others. Others have even committed suicide in a selfless act to save someone else. Why would Nature bestow upon us the ability to terminate our own experience, though our primary prerequisite is self- preservation? Could suicide be an act of self-preservation? Is it as a means of last resort – or to furnish the false impression of possible escape?

When all facets of suicide are adequately considered, the act simultaneously effectuates both functions –

an act of last resort and giving the false impression of liberation from experience.

In practice, infinite is limited/finite.

Due to everything being temporary, everything has a range, including every aspect involving species. Even though numbers are said to be infinite, in practicality, they are limited to only the ones we have use for. We do not create new numbers, until we have use for them. When we do invent new numbers for any reason, we are utilizing them. In regards to words, theoretically, we could create an innumerable amount of them, but like numbers, we make up new ones as we need them.

Space was only so big when we first gazed at the sky, we only saw our solar system. Is it possible that at the time there was only our solar system? One of space's ulterior functions is to preoccupy our minds. As we came up with devices to enhance our view of the great wide open, has Nature uploaded a wider peripheral view of it, rather than the central one we had prior to that? Being that everything is signaling each other reflexively, does Nature respond to us in real time?

Being a social species, we don't like the idea of dying alone. Not to worry, all species will eventually succumb to extinction, when we apply that logic distributively. Nature breeds victims. More than 90% of all organisms that have ever lived on earth have expired. There have been multiple cataclysmic events and mass extinctions and those happenings are cyclical(we are to use the time in-between extinctions to solve the mystery of life experience).

There are special term limits. Since the individual dies and they are members of a group, one day the entire species will die as well. Like the individual, the group are living things in totality and part of what qualifies as a living thing is the ability to die(range of potential). Species are mortal, regardless of our emotional reaction to the fact. Each species only gets so long to live. The poetic saying, "life finds a way" does not endure under axial inquest.

Opportunities have a time limit. That cap is commonly referred to as a "window of opportunity", meaning at some point it is open or is available and at another it is closed(deadline). Each day alive should be seen as an opportunity to compensate for or to correct yesterday's mistakes and bad decisions. Being alive and able to act is an opportunity. Other people will try to waste your time, if you are focused on living an invaluable life, you

cannot allow this. At best, limit engaging such people or in thoughtless acts. Opportunities can be lost/wasted.

Time revokes its gifts. Every material possession time grants us, it eventually confiscates, as if changing its mind. Everything is on loan or lease, including each other. We never really own anything, not even our bodies. That being the case, does time ever really give us anything? If anything, it seems as if it is a set up for failure, at the very least disappointment/ let down. It is as if Nature is gauging how we react to our gains and losses. Life experience seems to be a test of our poise.

Experience is a scoring situation. There is a surface/sensory/quantitative score(privilege, status, wealth), which we litigate and deem and there is an intrinsic/qualitative score(moral victories & losses), which Nature tabulates. Since we are the "intelligent" species among all the creatures, it is glaring that the quality of what we know and how we apply that knowledge is cosmically assessed.

Another metric is our treatment of each other, indicated by us being a social species(the fundamental purpose for each of us is our use and effect). Over the course of the game, your point total is credited and debited until you die and your total score is calculated. The end balance of our decisions(every decision is an output) at the moment of death or permanent complete loss of control of our bodies is our life's worth.

There are even player statistics to track performance. In assessing our performance in life experience, Nature takes into account that we are error prone, as well as, any other deficiencies it burdened us with. Actions matter, but some well intended ones can go awry. Due to this, intention of actions carries more weight than results(as with the motive of why we are involuntarily alive in the predicament of life experience).

Innately, it is the thought that counts. This means that an action that results in a favorable outcome, but was ill intended – is indelibly scored negatively, as if an action that generated negative outcomes via bad intentions. Intent is the most weighted metric in the process of decision making, the motive(s) behind our exploits. Circumstances born in and lived in, on average, over a lifetime – are measured as well. For instance, those that live in "developed" nations are assessed more weight than individuals who live in undeveloped ones, due to having access to much more financial/ survival opportunities. The same with those that live lifestyles of undeserved or abusive privilege, relative to those who are unjustly oppressed(strength of schedule). Being that we have had to perform different tasks over the course of yestory, different criteria, as well as, some of the same – are used to judge our performance in different ages and eras.

We receive all types of warnings, issued by Nature – sometimes multiple warnings. Failing to notice or ignoring them can count against you/us, in terms of severity of consequences, when it comes time for those to be assessed. Warnings can have a scale of severity, penalties can as well. Cheating rewards cosmetically and superficial excesses may seem like actual value, but they are mere decoys. Material excess or unhealthy desire for it is incentive from the game as an allure for players to engage in self-sabotage(why good things happen to bad people). Sincerely meeting challenges rewards substantively.

Sometimes you surfacely go unrewarded for your trouble in the experiential level. The satisfaction of knowing you are being honest or helpful is all there is to comfort you. Just like you can cheat others, you can also cheat yourself. The game of life experience cannot be cheated, all contingencies have been provided for. Not directly being able to see our intrinsic score as we go about living, is like not knowing when you are going to die. It either encourages you to put in more effort to improve or to become overly skeptical and engage in bad decision making. Nature is balanced, fundamentally it ensures that no good deed goes unrewarded.

Allowing excessive lag time puts us at a disadvantage, try to avoid accumulating lag time. It is waste.

The game of life experience is one that allows players to cheat themselves, but they can never cheat the game. The game allows for the appearance of cheating it, but it can only be defeated on its default terms.

We have to earn our fortuna/luck – beneficial value. We have to actually be deserving of it. Nature is a meritocracy.

Karmic ramification. **Karma** is the scoring mechanism within the system of Nature. Cosmic justice reprimands. Gameplay-balance, karma can compel you to hurt yourself, self-inflicted wounds. We will unwittingly work against our own better interests and not even realize it until doing honest introspection some time after the fact. The penalty upon death has to be along the same seriousness of agonies as mortal experience, which would be having to return to the seemingly never ending game, if play is still in progress. Karma catches up to us, like the pain from an old injury that was silent for decades, but has suddenly become inflamed in one's late middle age.

We are all unsuspecting agents of karmic justice.

Jinx does exist in the Wild to some degree. We can act out self-fulfilling prophecies, oblivious to the fact, until well into it. We brag about our possessions and soon after they get damaged, lost or stolen – or once attaining them – we quickly lose interest and seek something new to desire. We are told to, "never say never", in terms of declaring what the borders are to what we are willing to do, due to Nature often times calling our bluff, seeking to expose us as hypocrites. It uses that hypocrisy as a lesson that we should be guarded with our speech. The saying, "be careful what you wish for or you might get it", also applies. Innately, there is value(consequence/reward) in what we say. No, occurrences such as these aren't casting spells or disfiguring voodoo dolls, but they are a form of hexing.

Our words set expectations. When we "give our word", we are entering into a contract. In experience, our word is indeed(pun intended), our bond – as if swearing oaths. We are giving a ruling. Life experience is a behavior centric activity. Nature holds us to many of our declarations that we make over the course of our lives. It uses our own words against us(words come back to haunt). *Can you think of certain points over your lifetime, where you noticed that Nature was calling your bluff, challenging your vows or seemed to deliberately put you in positions – in which you have to back up some earlier stated claims? Have there ever been times in your life, that if it was not for the anchor of science, you would be sure that life was an ill conceived prank being played on you or us?* It is as if Nature wants to see, as well as demonstrate to us that actions are more important than just the ability to orate. Truth is supported by proof. We are not to say anything that we are not willing to demonstrate or pay for in exertion. We have to walk our talk, not just make empty or idle pledges/promises.

Can we wish the worst for others and deserve credit when an unfortunate event does happen to them? Can we put curses/hexes on others? At some point in each of our lives, we all have a desire or wish for bad events to happen to some other perone or a group of them and sincerely hope that those desires materialize. We want for something negative to occur and it doesn't or not to the degree that we question if we deserve credit for it taking place.

There are also times when our wishes seem as if they are answered or appear to be. An ill-fated event will occur to someone or something we reviled, enough to make us pause and wonder if we deserve credit for that event(s) transpiring.

Though they coincide, it is merely wishful thinking. If other people could remotely fully control our actions, or the motion in the environment – volition would be compromised.

We are the accursed. The primary reason many of us curse or often utter profanity, is due to realizing that we literally cannot punish others via telekinesis.

> **"The effect you have on others is the most valuable currency there is."**
> Jim Carrey

Experience is a voyage with a departure and destination point and that journey is a causeway, a dual causal chain of reflexive action(s). One is subjectively closed, while the other is objectively open(balance). Isaac Newton spoke of it in his third law, for every action there is an equal and opposite reaction. A cause triggers an effect and that effect then also becomes a cause and goes on to trigger another effect and so on and so forth. It would not be wrong to refer to the process as either **"cause and effect"** or "effect and cause". It is prod and respond(no response can also be a response).

When we say the word "affect", it is referring to effect. Everything affects each other or has an effect on each other and those effects can resonate(everything we sense or perceive has an effect on us, even if that effect is no effect). The intensity of those effects range from strong to weak.

Nothing can affect each other if they are not already somehow associated.

A cause is a trip or prompt or a switch. It is an action that activates or elicits a response/reaction. Anything that can be agitated or activated is a device. For there to be a mechanism to trip, it had to first be set in that fashion.

One incident can have an outsized effect on our perception.

> **"What we have done for ourselves alone dies with us; what we have done for others and the world remains and is immortal."**
> Albert Pike

Though associated with lineage, a legacy is a residual effect(after effect). It is an accumulation/totality of our decisions, it is our production – what we do or decisions already acted out.

We can prove cause from an effect. Everything in reality is the effect of a first cause. The cosmos is the effect of an external cause, a transcendent one.

Being effective is to achieve success, the effect of accomplishment. It is competence, as opposed to "almost". Anything's effectiveness is in reference to how or what degree it works, that it is capable.

Efficiency is an ideal order. It is a path of least resistance, the best way to go about causing an effect. The cosmos functions efficiently in its operations. Nature utilizes its resources efficiently. Its substructures and everything else within it, including ourselves, functions efficiently as well.

We try to find the most efficient way to satisfy our desires within the constraints(parameters) that we have to work. Due to a host of factors, such as availability and instincts, we may not always be in the act of performing the absolute best action for any specific moment, due to our default fallibility, but we are seeking the best way to perform that act at that moment.

Efficiency can also be a detriment to us. It can lead to the active desire and embrace of simple-minded pursuits, such as the less you know the better, the less you learn the better, the less you do the better etc.

Though it requires effort, laziness is a form of efficiency.

Axially, a question is a cause and its answer is the effect. An answer can then go on to become a cause by generating a question that leads to another answer and so on and so forward, until ultimately coming to an absolute answer/effect(inquest). While viewed separately, they are actually diametrically opposed extremes working in concert on the same conceptual theme. Without answers, there would be no value to asking questions and without questions, there would be no function to answers. All questions have answers, even if the answer is no answer.

THE PRESENCE OF INFORMATION

*Is a **feedback loop** present?* (1) Players start with an intuitive model that prompts them to (2) apply an action to (3) the game system and in return (4) receives feedback that (5) updates their intuitive model and starts the loop all over again or starts a new loop.

Feedback loops are situations where part of the output of experience is used for new input. There are positive feedback loops that amplify game systems and there are negative feedback loops, which restrain them. All games are made of **loops**. Things that we are doing all of the time(high frequency loop), things we do sometimes(intermediate frequency loop) and things that we are doing occasionally(low frequency loop). Most of a player's time is spent in a core loop. Loops also feed into and intersect with other loops. Loops tend to deliver value through the act of being exercised. They are appropriate for proficiency tasks that involve trial and error, repeated engagement. The goal of a loop is to update a player's intuitive model.

Loops teach. An added wisdom comes with experiencing a range of failure and success states that a loop can contain. A comprehensive understanding of a complete system. Once a space is fully explored, the player's mind evolves to containing substantially more branches, successes, failures and nuances that lets them approach new situations in the game with confidence.

Games also have **arcs**. "Arcs" possess similar elements to loops, only they are generally not repeating. They are a broken loop that a player can exit immediately. With an arc, your intuitive model is updated, which rarely results in a player returning to the same interaction.

Loops and arcs are prevalent structures throughout himind activities or experience. The difference between the two can be viewed as "knowing how to do something" and "actually doing that thing".

Games are a communication, an interactive conversation between the activity and the player. All of reality is information. In experience, everything that we perceive is a sign. Each object signals something else, being that signs are forms of messages. All of reality is emblematic. Every object that comprises the cosmos, including obscure items, such as sound and air – are fundamentally symbols. This renders them all, literally – significant and all that can be perceived – as an intrinsic language.

If you grew up never having heard or spoken a language, not even sign language – what terminology would you dream or think in? Would our inner voice still speak to us, just not in audio? What about if you were also blind?

"Mental symbols are our way of encoding sensory experiences. They form the basis of our complex systems of language and communication. We may choose to keep our mental symbols to ourselves, or represent them to others using words or pictures."
Marc Hauser

In experience, there are light waves, gravity waves, electromagnetic waves and physicist, Louis de Broglie, asserted that even matter exhibits wavelike conduct. Our senses are always set up to detect these signals(stimuli, phenomena) of information. From there, we interpret the information and act on it in whatever way we are able to. Most of communication is body language, including on experience's part in its exchange with us. The mechanics of a game communicates to its player(s). Our actions are set up to always communicate what we are doing, as if relaying information. This demonstrates not only a feedback loop, but also a communication. Since senses are set up to detect and our minds perform the function of interpretation and reality is information – then experience is an exchange. A communication.

In broad himind society, openly talking to oneself is frowned upon, as if a prelude to insanity, but in actuality, everyone of us are always talking to ourselves. It is not just only when we are by ourselves that we do this. We are also speaking to ourselves when we are in communication with other people, as well. Before speaking, we ask ourselves what to say and how to best say it. Even when we are speaking out of quick reaction or reflexively, it is a rehearsed response(practiced). As we speak, we are our own first listener.

Correspondence can be either direct or indirect.

Communication exists in order to establish a dialogue, an exchange. No communication is even a communication. **Language** is a tool that contextualizes and simplifies communication. It is utilized to describe our life experience(s). Between the over 6,000 languages spoken throughout overall himind society, formal and informal, it's many accents and profanities – language is also used to confuse, divide and oppress populations. It can be utilized to easily direct an inattentive populace with subtlety.

Language unifies people, but also separates us. Depending on how limited you are in your knowledge of language, whether your native tongue or a foreign one, language can also be considered as a prison.

The word "hu-man" is descriptively based on the concepts of color and gender. Neither of the two, is the primary redeeming quality of our species. Our cognitive capacity is. The reference attributed to us should reflect this in a self-explanatory way. We are a cerebral creature that has been designated by Nature as exceptional among all other living things/mortal life.

The word "Cereve", encapsulates this – "cere" is short for cerebral, "reve" meaning revere. The word includes both genders, in that males, more specifically the word "man", will be referred to as "ceres" and fevales, specifically the word "woman" – as "reves".

Another self-explanatory reference to replace the word "human", is "hi-mind". It is a word that properly describes us specially. The word "himind" points to our intellect(self-explanatory). It reminds us that we are the high-thinking species, as opposed to emphasizing pigmentation or gender. Though "him" appears in the word, it is completely incidental to combining the words "high" and "mind".

The word "human" is as thoughtless a term, as the word "ladybug" – being that both words give the false impression that the members of each respective specie are exclusively a single gender, when that is not the case.

Do you notice that we use the word "in" often, to a point of a peculiar excess? How many words in the English language can you think of that "in" is included in? It is a clue as to our actual disposition in experience – conf"in"ement.

The letter "I/i" starts or sits in or near the middle of many words(hints at us being a uni-being).

Language is for interpretation, but in practice, it often functions as misinterpretation, even if this is not the intent of the speaker.

Names of people also confuse language, since they can be pronounced however the namer chooses to, regardless of spelling or formal language rules.

Some words are used to minimize a situation or overstate it.

Misnomers:

Why do we say the term "moral support", in reference to buttressing someone's mood or emotions? It is not like "moral support" is to reinforce someone's morals or ethics, though admittedly – moral support is a moral action to undertake in some instances. If anything, a more appropriate term would be, "morale support".

Another example of the many misnomers used in everyday language is the word "demoralize". It gives the impression of having a direct relationship with morals, as in to remove someone's guiding principles. The fact is, to "demoralize" means to strip someone of their confidence or self-worth.

The word "no" is a negative, it is to deny. To have the word "knowledge" or its variations, such as "knowing" – sound the same as "no" – subliminally associates the two. This is one of the reasons as to why being knowledgeable carries a stigma(war on intellect). In "western" society, culture encourages the populous to hold strong opinions, as opposed to being a "know it all" or well studied.

Another word that is a cause for concern is "lesson". It sounds identical to the word "lessen". The complication is that the function of a "lesson" is to enhance our intellect, providing us an advantage in life experience, while "lessen" means to reduce, which like the word "no" – carries a negative connotation.

For beneficial words, such as "knowledge" and "lesson" – as well as any others not mentioned, to sound alike to defeatist ones, undoubtedly detracts from their significance in some way. Such words should be replaced by terms that are more reflective of their function and the value that they possess.

There are two sides to **free speech**. One side is rational(objectively & subjectively) and the other side is anarchy.

Free speech, in seclusion, is everyone just talking. It means the population of the intellectual animal in experience is just speaking because we are able to. Everyone is free to impart nonsense, "have an opinion", without consequence. Logically, this causes much of what is communicated to go unchallenged. This results in most people having no incentive to have to adequately learn most of the topics they hold opinions on. "Free speech" also discourages thinking/reasoning, since most people just have to state baseless opinions/claims, in order to partake in a conversation. It draws a false equivalency between opinion and truth.

Free speech without consequence, ultimately means that credibility/integrity is absent. No one is worth believing, even those able to demonstrate coherence behind their pronouncements, due to a failure to emphasize distinction between truth value and mere sentiment or speculation.

For free speech to be beneficial to modern society, there must be some level of threat of repercussions involved.

Governments speak of "free speech" as if Nature did not commission that capability long before regimes claimed to allow or suppress it. "Free speech" is a natural ability, not a government issued privilege.

Words are influential. Parents take control with words(stop, no, don't), then the words take control of children. Children eventually grow into adults, who by then, are well conditioned to be controlled by words themselves and go on to influence their children with words – continuing the cycle. After hearing those words and importing them in our minds with frequency, they hold truth and value to us. We even go so far as to act out the messages our words subconsciously signal.

Word choice matters. It is not a matter of political correctness, but moral precision. Due to doublespeak, honest conversation is compromised in himind society. We can say things that we do not actually feel or mean to do. We can lie and mislead, for the most part, without societal backlash.

As there are involuntary cues in body language, they also exist in verbal and written communication. If you pay adequate attention, you can translate what someone is actually saying when they are speaking to you – by just their choice of words. Just like nonverbal cues, a deceptive speaker unwittingly reveals their true message, often times inadvertently. Their general intent is communicated if the perceiver(s) simply analyzes their words. Throughout yestory, an uncounted amount of dishonest speakers have been exposed in this way.

As Linguist, William Lutz, asserted in his essay, The World of Doublespeak, our language is deceptive. He realized that language could be used to skew the concepts or subject matter that it addressed. Lutz was an ardent advocate for the use of plain language, surmising that it was the best way to combat double-talk.

Since early himinds walked the earth, our communication with each other especially direct – has been faulty. Philosopher, Gottfried Wilhelm Leibniz, wanted to render language as specific as our formal mathematical equations(subjective math). As previously stated, Wittgenstein noticed that our verbal and written intercommunications were "language games". Many others before, in between and after – have tried to rectify our verbal misunderstandings/miscommunications as well.

What many thinkers on the topic fail to realize, is that since the rest of life experience is based on difficulty, our language is also a subsidiary of that theme. It does not matter how plain or direct we reduce our verbal interactions to, language will always be deceptive as long as it's veracity or credibility is based on its speaker's intent. Our intent, is the base of any deceit in language. That said, intent can be honest and language can still cause confusion. This means that language should be simplified and the quality of our collective intent improved upon, in order to finally establish genuine communication between each other as a species.

The English language is chauvinistic. It is compromised by words such as documentary, manage, maneuver, manufacture, manipulate, manifesto, mandatory, mannequin, manners, manacle, manpower, mansion, manuscript, specimen, mental, mention, menstrual cycle, mentor, menu, person, phenomenon, romance, Roman, semen, fellowship, hero, history, hysterectomy, hymen, hymn etc. These words give males a false sense of superiority, while simultaneously supplying fevales a diminished sense of self-worth. The word "she" and "her" contain "he". "Female" contains the word "male" and "women" contains the word "men". We casually refer to a mix of girls and boys or even just a group of girls as "you guys". The language is antiquated and is in immediate need of cerebral update.

Should you assert that these words are not deliberately gender biased and are merely incidental instead, ask yourself – if society was always a matriarchy or if we were a genderless species, would so many male slanted words be in our language?

Something's amiss. If we are going to continue to refer to fevales as "Ms."/"Miss", then words such as misread, miscalculate, misunderstand – and any other word that reinforces a negative connotation towards fevales, must be effectively addressed, as well. The misogyny is virtually tactile. Males would not find it flattering if there was a stockpile of demoralizing terms that targeted them in the general vernacular. For instance, "oh, I'm sorry, I must have mistercalculated"; "hey dad, how'd your mysterectomy go"; "my misterake"; "you've been misterinformed".

Only insecure males would establish and continue to actively support a system of patriarchy.

In a patriarchy, chivalry isn't dead, it has never fully existed. We've only heard of the gender biased version of it.

A patriarchy starts out as a "bromance"/"man-crush" and morphs in elaborateness from there.

One has to wonder, what would a patriarchy be overcompensating for? No one handicaps another unless such action is from a place of insecurity.

For fevales, nipples deliver nourishing breast milk to himind babies. Ceres also possess nipples, but they have no functional purpose. This demonstrates that biologically, males start out as fevales, which renders male chauvinism and patriarchy as contemplatively awkward.

Since it is impossible to establish a sustainable society without the presence of fevales, reves are equally as essential as males are to it.

Body language to some degree, is the literal form of someone "speaking their mind".

Body language communicates general intention. You can deduce if someone is curious, waiting for something or is in some discomfort just by looking at them. The posture of many animals also communicates when they feel threatened, are relaxed or are trying not to be seen.

Anyone with a functioning voice box can make a claim as to what they are going to do, but our actions are the true narrator of each of our stories.

Words are also used as hints by Nature. Remember, in neutrality there is no coincidence. The implication of that is that all motion is a deliberately orchestrated activity. Experience being a game and a game being a communication or exchange, means that there is a significance to words and how they are used by others, even yourself. Nature uses word choice to communicate with us. There are certain words that clue us in as to what experience really is and they are cleverly blended in with modern day parlance(on their "A" game). A part of life experience is looking for and reading its signs that are present.

Just because people utilize **curse words** in our everyday speech and discourage children from using them, doesn't really mean that profanity is adult language – or it would be recognized as being a part of formal language. Curse words are expressed in every society, even by many government officials and the so called "upper class", yet they are viewed as unacceptable language. Is this not at least somewhat nonsensical? Clearly, vulgarity is viewed as not meeting the standard of being societally acceptable; so why is it so popular in broad cereve society?

Advisory warnings refer to profanity as "adult" or "strong" language. Really, all words are neutral, including curse words. Cursing at someone who speaks the same language and uttering the same words to a "foreigner" quickly demonstrates this. The perone familiar with your terminology understands the meaning behind your crude utterances, while the foreigner does not. It is just unfamiliar sounds to them. Each of our languages are subjective, only body language is universal.

Cursing is one of our "sworn"(pun intended) enemies. It is filler, like empty calories. We are a social species, language is vital to us. By frequently using vulgarity in our speech, we unwittingly limit our range of vocabulary, as well as our depth of thought. "Cussing" often renders us intellectually docile. It compels us to significantly communicate using profanity and to only feel comfortable around people who do so, as well. Routinely using vulgarity causes us to not want to learn new words that we encounter, nor their definitions. The reasoning is that you can simply substitute them with obscenities. You already know how to sound like you are talking about something meaningful by cursing; so who needs to learn a new word? The naive are more interested in learning a new expletive, than any formal word that they are not accustomed to.

Not only can expletives be used with derogatory intention, profanity serves as a multipurpose device in conversation. Though having a general meaning, each curse word can have multiple meanings – as nouns, verbs and as adjectives. They also can have a positive connotation to go along with their negative inference. This has resulted in obscene language being a prevalent aspect of communication.

Should the intelligent species in life experience be utilizing filler as a major segment of its communications, when our time is limited? Is this not waste?

There is no trophy or lifetime achievement award one will receive for cursing. Many people who are fond of expletives, cling to them simply because they feel they have learned some complicated skill, some valued secret or hallowed rights of passage that has been passed down through the ages and do not want to relinquish something that they have put much effort into learning(prisoners of habit or nostalgia). They've convinced themselves that merely sounding meaningful, is actual meaningful speech.

Another way curse words are misused, is in their frequency of use. They are used much too often. This is because "cusses" add to the flow of conversation in how they are used as substitutes for other words and transitions to continue a conversation. The trouble is, obscenities are out of place in casual parlance. They are really meant to be used to alert, to call attention to an issue. This is why we tend to curse when something surprises us negatively or rely on them heavily during times of intense emotion. They announce potential danger.

By speaking using expletives in casual conversation, it is a form of deception or manipulation. We give the false impression that what we are talking about is important or of some magnitude, when really it is just small talk or of no real consequence. Doing this, serves no function other than to pass the time. Unless being utilized to warn, profanity is waste. It is appealing for someone to pay attention to what you are saying, when you really have nothing of importance to say. You are just stringing together meaningless words and ideas and decorating them in the facade of being conversation. Even if you are comfortable with cursing, either speaking or hearing such words – our instinct of fight or flight readies us for trouble and compels us to be alert when hearing crass language, when it has much to do about nothing. People who often traffic in vulgarity, do so because we as himind beings innately want to live a story. We want what we are saying to be worth hearing. *Is this desire a possible hint that all or most of our actions should be meaningful? Is it not then that generally, our conversations would be worth having?*

Game scripts are mired in throw away lines, dialogue that is there simply to occupy time or periods of silence(also referred to as "dead air"). These are moments where characters say things just for the sake of saying something. Characters merely restate what is going on around them or make meaningless comments to mask the gap in uneventful spans of gameplay/experience. Throw away lines, which is basically "small talk" or casual conversation – keeps players busied or entertained. Small talk is theater.

Throw away lines equates to throw away time, which is a luxury that no perone actually has. Avoid engaging in long durations of worthless speech. To identify wasteful conversation, ask yourself – why is the perone that is speaking to you saying what they are saying to you, what is their motive, what do they stand to gain by saying it, if anything at all – is the timing of it significant, why are they saying what they are stating at the moment that they do, am I improved or smarter for listening to it, am I better off not hearing it?

Anyone can say anything and some things that are said – feel good to say and can even sound nice to hear, but that does not make them true statements. This is what is known as empty rhetoric. People speaking simply because they've discovered that their voice box is a musical instrument that is easy for them to play well. We have no issue wasting each other's time with small talk. Time is elapsing and it is limited, rendering our conversations as consequential. Purpose driven conversation must be the vast majority of our communication or each of us that aren't in sincere practice of this, is at fault for the infraction of waste.

Your presence in any current moment is already a subject in a sentence that is only waiting for someone to come along and read it aloud – or with their "inside voice". There are volumes of content, just in the small radius of data/information around you. In scenes of solitude, we find ourselves as topics being read by a whispering inner voice that is not our own. As if under hypnosis, we are impulsively responsive to its suggestions.

Nature is speaking in its own language of multi-dimensional symbols. We use our inferior languages to describe it and the happenings within it.

If all of experience is information and that information is playing out as an interaction between an object and a subject(s) over time – then experience/time is a story.

Signs or symbols are representations. They are suggestions, implications, inferences, insinuations and indicators. Some are obvious, while some are inconspicuous. All signs are in part, clues to help bring us to full awareness. They are also partly lures to distract us from learning the goal of experience, which is to realize that in truth, we are players playing a game.

Clues help us learn the game and what to do next. Games have clues in them for players to find and interpret(read) them. Some games utilize a map key to assist with deciphering signs. There are even warning signs(warning signs indicate that there are rules present).

Some clues are prevalent themes that we notice in experience such as authority, busyness, choices & decisions, color, evolution/progress, humility, justice, laws, punishment, protest, fraud/camouflage/deception, conflict/war, voyeurism/surveillance/analysis.

Experience is comparable to a movie with subtitles, only you have to be a perone who takes interest such films to notice it.

Adages sound cliche, but they too can be clues. They are advice from the past.

Clue. Are we the only species in which the different genders urinate with such stark difference in posture? One of the first peculiarities you notice about experience, is in how we himinds urinate. Fevales have to squat down, while males are able to remain standing. When considering ceres are physically stronger than reves, it causes one to wonder if Nature is a male chauvinist and if so, why?

Even more intriguing, is that both genders are compelled to crouch, in order to defecate. Normally, we do not stand to defecate, it is more functional for both genders to squat down. This is why fevales crouch when urinating. Sure, they could stand, but then they would urinate on their legs and reek of the stench. Conversely, when in the shower or swimming – fevales stand and release. This is due to feeling that they have the luxury to be able to to do so in that way at that time without fear of wearing the odor. *This cues the question, would both genders stand to defecate if it was functional for us to?*

Where we arrive at is that we all recognize that though we have a preference as to how we wish some of our functions worked, we are forced to perform them in a particular way. This clues us in that we are all in a subservient position within experience, not an authoritative one, no matter if our ego tells us otherwise.

Clue. Rainbows were a clue from Nature to early cereves that the topography of earth was curved, instead of flat, as it seems to anyone standing on it, even today. *If earth was flat, wouldn't rainbows be too?*

Clue. Every meaningful discovery that himinds have made since our emergence on earth, has been another piece added to the overall puzzle of experience. Each discovery reveals another clue to the underlying theme of life experience.

Clue. The circle, the sphere and the ripple. The circle/sphere symbolizes the whole and everything being relative. The swirl represents the activity of chaos that surrounds us and the ripple is the effect that we all and everything else has on each other.

The word "live" is also "evil" backwards. It is as if a hint from Nature, that experience has an ulterior motive to it.

Sometimes a yawn is a biological alarm clock for you to go to sleep.

Q & A. There is a trail of natural/organic questions and answers, as stated earlier when discussing cause and effect. Following the most meaningful questions, in terms of the peculiarities of experience to their logical destination, eventually advances us to an answer of absolution. Questions are like keys to locked doors. Every natural/organic question is solicited or cued, meaning natural questions are reflexive or intuitive. They are instinctive responses, which is why we say "begs the question".

Signaling happens due to our senses being activated. If our senses had no information to detect, we could not perceive for lack of content.

Numbers intimidate, even though they are only numbers. Some people are illiterate and many who can read feel threatened by sizable books, if not books in general – rendering words also threatening(scale effectively at work). This may be our emotional response to essentially, language – but, keep in mind, that it is subjective. Axially, words are neutral. Words and numbers use different symbols to identify objects and in both cases, words are used to identify the symbols.

Astrology, horoscopes, numerology and the like – are intimations that Nature is communicating with us through signs and those signs tell us about ourselves and everything else in the natural world.

What is knowledge? We hear and say the word often, but can you define it off hand? What is its value in the Wild?

Knowledge is the familiarity gained by experience(inquiry, observation, study) first hand or second hand – of a fact, idea or situation. Second hand experience is attaining knowledge via an educational source. Knowledge is all that can be known, the comprehension of a topic. Knowledge is information and information is knowledge. The highest quality of it involves accurate details, skill and memory. Inaccurate information can also be viewed as knowledge, just not as credible as precise information. Knowledge makes us aware, it expands our radius of understanding. The base of knowledge is the relative relationship between our involuntary functions and reality.

There are things to learn through first hand experience and things that are better to learn via second hand experience.

More than any teacher/professor or anyone who claims to be, knowledge is an authority figure.

Some things you get to know via experiencing them. Other things you learn about through observance or hearing about them second hand. And finally, some things you can only know by prudent contemplation(axioms).

Language or communication, itself – can be misconstrued without **context**. Context is significant because it provides the full depth or dimensions of what is being discussed. Context is the defining details of everything. Complete awareness cannot be attained, unless the aggregate of knowledge is put in its proper context.

Gameplay can be determined by context – in that, it is shaped in part by the influence of other characters in the game. For players or in our circumstances, characters – we are not just playing one game while engaged in it. Different game models and experiences are activated by play in various contexts.

> Consequential knowledge: "**Knowledge whose presence or absence has consequences, serious consequences."**
> Thomas Sowell

Game knowledge is what everything is in a game, including all of its nuances. It is also how to play the game, which is why you'll hear a sports commentator make statements such as, "that player knows the game" or "has a high game IQ". It is knowing what to do and not do and how to do and not do it. Game knowledge tells you the correct way to think, the correct items to like and how to conduct your actions.

In games, game knowledge teaches players about the game and how to beat it. A player needs game knowledge to become a competent and competitive contender. It is dependent on what you understand. The more knowledgeable you or any other player is, the better prepared you are for the game. A knowledgeable player is always at a marked advantage to an inexperienced/naive one. While playing a game, a player has to apply consequential knowledge on a macro scale.

Knowledge is both facts and truth. It is meaningful information. Facts are indisputable remedies to questions of the material world, while truth(in regards to the absolute variety) addresses both the surface and inherent aspects of existence. Facts are subjective when contrasted to truth, but they are objective when compared to other material information. Absolute truth is objective. Knowledge has values, some of it is subjectively beneficial, but overall it too is axial. The value of material or meaningless knowledge(knowledge outside of universal truth) is that it validates the worth of consequential knowledge.

The value of knowledge is not only in its realization, but also, if not more so – in its application.

There is a subjective IQ, which applies to society and the experiential level and there is an axial or universal IQ for the subjective and intrinsic aspect of life experience.

To become literate at reading the meaningful signs in life, we first have to view life from its precise perspective. The axial one.

The cosmos itself is the first order of information technology.

The universe exists as the ultimate knowledge, because every organism is equipped to seek its information.

> **"It's speaking with other people how you learn what you disagree with."**
> Alan Watts

Nature has put us in an unyielding position of being alive and also requiring that we learn in our lifetime.

Lessons are abound in experience, some are easy to grasp, others are arduous. They are inherent to Nature. Every moment is a learnable and teachable moment or situation. In games, lessons teach players everything they need to know, aims to lead them to a specific conclusion and to a certain way of thinking. Some games even teach players something about themselves.

Not just in situations/experiences, but in people – each one of us are lessons in and of ourselves(cautionary tales, success stories, role models etc). The effects that each of us generates with our decisions and actions and positions in society, is what we are to learn from. Unbeknownst to us, each of us is a predisposed teacher. What each of us does or what happens to us, are all lessons within an overall curriculum. Regrets and correct and wrong decisions are examples of lessons. There are lessons for our survival, lessons for social interaction, lessons for overall experience etc. Some lessons are taught to us by others, while other lessons we each have to learn on our own. Earth is a classroom. Yestory shows that himinds have been self-taught over time. Our life experience has been about learning on the job of survival.

If a thoughtful thinker takes the time to ponder, they realize that in every moment of experience there is a lesson to be imported. Irony and perspective allow for this.

We are coerced by our memories to entertain regret – to review what we could have had, could have done better or worse, or what could have occurred.

Regrets are to guide us as to what to do the next time we encounter a similar scenario and if a similar situation doesn't present itself, moments of regret are ultimately for us to extract lessons from them. They are study guides to be learned from.

Regrets are Nature's ammunition for our behavioral change.

Sometimes we need to make a bad decision, in order to learn the value of why we shouldn't come to such verdicts.

Some games have tutorials embedded within them. The tutorial(s) is made to feel a part of the game's environment. This allows for the presence of lessons to seem so organic to the player(s), that they do not suspect the peculiarity of the feature. Tutorials are guides, they steer players as to their future decision making.

Lessons are their own type of rules.

We are to categorize and list out all of the lessons(both objective and subjective) that we learn or that exist in being alive. Their totality is absolute truth or exactitude.

Yestory is lessons from the past.

Along with surviving, we've been harvesting knowledge.

We are collectors, some of us to the extreme of hoarding. The most important thing we collect is consequential knowledge. Collecting items is also done in games.

We have been building knowledge, "brick by brick" – module by module – node by node and building on its value.

At first, knowledge was traditionally passed down orally from generation to generation. Due to the faultiness of our memories and also people dying and taking their expertise with them, knowledge was compromised as it was transferred. It was not until formalizing languages and developing writing via collective learning, that cereves extracted the full benefits of knowledge(imagine life without having invented writing). Writing allowed us to expand knowledge quickly. We are the only creature that is capable of writing.

Passing along knowledge is one generation giving advice to those that follow it. A life lesson is the ideal gift one perone can share with another.

Even children observe and report what they see. The same function that news outlets serve for adults.

"Dare to know."
Immanuel Kant

Our ability to **learn** coincides with the lessons that inherently exist. Whether via experience(trial by error, practice/repetition), tutelage or study – comprehension of knowledge allows us to adapt, survive and even thrive. Learning can be intuitive and it can also take some effort. Knowledge has to be earned. Learning is an adventure of discovery or a progressive expedition. Discovery is not possible without naivete. Each new fragment of knowledge we acquire, advances us to a new destination point in our overall understanding(a journey similar to the one questions take us on). It is a process that when consistently practiced, helps a player(s)/perone jump in levels of acumen.

It can take multiple times of experiencing similar lessons before we take notice and learn the general theme between them. Distractions are the nemesis of learning. Be leery of diversions. In a world overly dense with information, we have to filter between what is actually worth remembering and what is not even worth knowing about. The application of knowledge is a demonstration of learning, not just the absorption of it.

We learn from our environments, to the extent that we are conditioned by them.

Our minds are set to always learn. We are innately students and being alive is a learning experience. We are also teachers. We are to share our learned life lessons with the oblivious or less informed.

Since a pertinent facet of life is learning, much of each of our experience is time spent educating ourselves(self-educated).

Learning is to add on. We can either add to our intellect, which is taking away from our stupidity or add on to our idiocy, which is to take away from our genius.

We are more receptive to learning a lesson, maybe even deliberate learning overall – after disappointment, tragedy or pain – than we are during times of delight.

Fear is the primary motivator for us to learn a life lesson. We consciously absorb meaningful lessons when we feel that it is a must to.

Trial and error is more formally referred to as research & development.

If you don't pursue intrigue or question, you cannot learn. If you don't want answers, you don't ask questions.

Learning is acceptance. It is accepting a lesson as what it is, something that you must do or in some cases – not do. Either way, it is something that you must do.

> **"All truths are easy to understand once you discover them, the point is to discover them."**
> Galileo

There are three popular philosophical theories of **truth**. They are the Correspondence theory, that suggests that truth is correspondent to a belief in reality – the Coherence Theory, that proclaims truth is the coherence of a belief with a body of established beliefs – and the Pragmatic Theory, that says that true belief is that which when it guides our activities we are successful.

What is truth, what does it do? What is its significance in experience?

Truth is what actually is, it is exact. At its most absolute – exactness comprises, governs and explains every aspect of life experience, even lies. Truth is the highest quality of information, due to being valid. It is substantive. Exactitude is transcendent, it is certainty. Truth makes the world go around.

Exacts expose fallacy. Unlike falsehoods, truth welcomes challenges and questions – as an opportunity to demonstrate its merits or strengthen its position(in terms of its development, this can also be to rethink it). Truth has the ability to withstand the onslaught of doubt, within reason. Some exacts can be verified via a formula(Claim + Correct Verification)= T, while other truths cannot be confirmed, due to unavailability of evidence. The latter can be vulnerable to doubt, due to lack of authentication.

There are different types of actuals. One is the peronal/subjective type, which are truths only known to you and/or a small group of people or by just our species(group actual) through shared experience(similar to an inside joke or secret). A peronal truth can be an experience, attribute, condition or pattern that is exclusive to you or anything that applies to you. For instance, an ordeal that you just went through, you know for a fact to have happened, but to someone not present, they may be very skeptical if it even did. Just because everyone else may be oblivious to what is, does not render an exact as false.

The theory of subjectivism professes that truth can be determined by an individual, that it is subjectively relative. Essentially, subjectivism asserts that each perone decides what is exact. This is patently false, due to the caveat that our judgment does not validate truth, evidence does. Any perone passionately asserting that earwax is the color blue, or the night sky is the color off-white, or that negative degree temperatures are warm – does not translate to them honest.

Should the most intelligent species be basing our beliefs on fantasy or in exactitude? Should truth be generally understood?

Exactness is precision. For everything to function in nature, including Nature itself, it must be precise. In order for you to have been born, your embryonic development had to be within the standard of precision, or you would not be alive to glean these words. For you to even be able to read these words, is courtesy of your body operating at least somewhat precisely.

Truth is sobering. Universal truth brings the mind to full sobriety.

Actuals are like water, both are bland and are required, in order to not only survive, but also thrive.

If precision is not our purpose in everything, our purpose then is some degree of negligence.

To be honest with ourselves, sometimes we have to tell on ourselves to ourselves.

Universal actuals may not be known by everyone as common knowledge, but they apply to everything in life experience, meaning that they should be common knowledge. Exactness is objective. Truth is actually how objectivism frames it, it exists as us, as well as, outside of us. It's quality is not dependent on our appraisal or approval. The Wild functions at the capacity that it does, whether we think it is supposed to or not. When we think objectively, we think in a way that is not only dissociated from our biases, it is as if we are disembodied from the material world, while still physically being in it. It is to view everything as Nature's consciousness, or from a G0d's eye view, or cosmic exile. Thinking in neutrality is to psychologically be absent from our subjectivity.

Axioms are exacts that do not have to exist in the material world. For example, if someone says to you that two perfectly parallel lines that are rigidly positioned across from each other(=) will never touch if they go on into infinity, you don't have to live that long to know that such a statement is actual. Our minds can ascertain the quality of the statement just by calculating the factors in the scenario. Such a statement is intuitive, innately recognizable, self-evident, self-proving – it doesn't necessarily require physical verification. Axioms concerning reality are foundational. Universal actuals are axiomatic.

Axioms are what mathematician, Kurt Godel, was referring to when he exposed that there was a gap that existed between evidence and truth. Though he was specifically referencing mathematics, axiomatic exacts exist throughout all aspects of experience. They are the concepts behind the aesthetic of the Wild.

Why would there be axioms in experience?

The gap between truth and evidence is similar to why we cannot figure out how the first generation of cereves survived(we can't think of a viable concept), yet us being here is proof that such an event occurred.

Truth value matters. We are to be living under the direction of axial exactness or as individuals, as well as a species – we have no credibility.

Actuals can sound poetic, but not all poetry is actual.

At a floating point between extremes of its own parameters, as well as in-between the larger scope of near and farsightedness – lies the truth(neutrality).

For us to accept exacts about anything else, the first step is accepting what is actual about ourselves.

Before you can entice a dishonest perone to curb their dubious ways towards everyone else, you must first compel them to abandon that pathology towards themselves.

The pursuit and validation of the truth has been an endeavor of himind-kind since our emergence. It is as if we know by default that its identification and comprehension will unlock the mysteries of life experience, answering open questions and thought to be closed ones. Throughout yestory, actuals have had to be mined, they are rarely just easily offered up. It is through investigation and query/exploration that exactness has had to be apprehended.

"Statements are made true by the relation of the ideas in the sentence."
David Hume

One must have knowledge of the factors and variables of a truth. For example, let's examine the statement – all bachelors are unmarried. We know it to be exact, because we are aware of how the concepts in the statement relate to one another. Another instance is when you encounter an issue with something that you have an understanding of its routine disposition or operation and it is suddenly not operating in that way. You conclude that something is wrong with that thing. The cause of the malfunction may not be glaring, everything may seem normal. To find the issue, you consider all the relevant elements in its sequence of truth or operation until you come to the element that is causing the problem. Whatever the issue is, we realize that it was in violation of that particular thing's exactness, in terms of function.

Corroborating evidence is the relation of ideas that confirms actuals. Exacts are not just claims or they would be indistinguishable from fallacies. Truth can be formulaically proven, while lies lack validity. As shown with axioms, the debt of proof does not need to be physical or direct for it to be valid. Where evidence is absent, the truth has to be calculated and determined. Sometimes verification is in the reasoning that supports a claim, such as in the parallel lines example.

Unproven statements must satisfy the question of – is it reasonable enough to be considered a truth? How actual an unproven or assumed truth has to be is somewhat vague. The reason for this, is due to the metrics being defined in name only – "a reasonable assumption" or "within reason" as opposed to specifically standardized. This means that all the relative factors show that there is more than a high probability that the statement is exact. It has to be able to withstand reasonable skepticism. In some instances, proof may be a battle of the best analogy(one to one correlation) or hypothetical scenario/"thought experiment".

Some truths are self-falsifying, meaning that all the elements involved in it relate, even though some seem contradictory. Such exacts are essentially an equation of cause and effect.

Evidence can be an item or an equation/accurate explanation, where all the components fit and are appropriate to it.

Debate can determine truth only when both opposing parties are committed to following proof wherever it goes, regardless if it goes against their entrenched position. The goal has to be achieving truth. All parties involved must earnestly seek to further the conversation towards it.

Why is there truth, why isn't everything just lies or valueless information? Why does exactitude exist and why is it hidden?

Nature has put us in a position of ignorance and in-turn, compels to seek the core actuals of its mystery.

Keeping pace with a lie can be a marathon for a liar.

Lies evade, deflect or seek escape when cornered. Their pace of retreat is decided by how intently probing questions pursue them.

Truth is only socially appealing when it serves what is deemed a favorable material use to the individual or group. Most of the time, we do not want to hear exactitude due to it conflicting with our desires.

Exactness is like muscle gains, they are said to hurt, but such pain validates their substance.

Actuals can be ugly or unattractive, while lies can seem aesthetically or audibly pleasing.

Have you ever caught yourself, lying to yourself?

The truth about lies. We can know something is wrong to do and still consciously take that action anyway and enjoy doing and reflecting on it as if it is a fond memory. We can defend it vigorously, as if it is the most selfless act ever performed by a himind being. This still does not render our actions upstanding. They are still wrong if that is what they are in essence. Any action that you have no moral rights to engage in, does not transmute to correct action merely because we adopt the position that it is copacetic for us to do. Such acts are still flagrant.

Lying to ourselves is one of our favorite pastimes. One of the most strenuous feats for a cereve to accomplish is being honest with oneself, especially with any consistency or in all aspects of their considerations.

Spring and summer exaggerates and embellishes nature, while fall and winter strips away the facade and reduces things down to their fundamental exacts.

Summertime is like the daytime, it invites activity – while wintertime is like when it is night, it makes us lethargic and discourages activity.

Spring and summer are as if one grand daytime and autumn and winter are parallel to one long night.

THE PRESENCE OF OBJECTS

"Nothing exists in nature except individual bodies exhibiting clear individual effects according to particular laws."
Sir Francis Bacon

The capacity of the macroworld is occupied by various types of phenomena as its composition. Any item(even ideas, air, electricity), feature or function – everything in experience – is an object. Situations can even be considered as objects. The universe itself, is an object. No matter how far away or insignificant objects anywhere appear, their very presence is noteworthy.

Objects are innately linked to subjects, being that a subject is first an object(this dynamic inherently demands the activity of interpretation by the subject, it is also why we are to think objectively). Another reason is due to the object, ironically, though portraying itself as objective – is completely subjective in its particular demands of its subjugated.

If we never heard of or experienced something, we couldn't miss it. This calls the presence of some particular items, features and nuances in experience into suspicion. At its foundation, **availability** is a compulsion or cue. Availability alone, gives something its own level of appeal.

Availability allows for demand. There could be no demand, if there was no supply. We would not desire, if there was nothing to desire. Needs are every living thing's first demands. Nature supplies those needs, it is the initial cause of both desires/demands and supply. Chaos causes us to need, it appears courtesy of Nature's Laws. We experience adverse reactions to chaos, which results in us demanding order. Cause and effect can be seen as supply and demand or demand and supply. Essentially, all of the cosmos is a result of supply and demand/demand and supply.

Is it better not to have had at all; so you are oblivious to what you are missing or is it better to have had and lost? Or maybe each aspect on their own should not apply exclusively to everything?

It may be that it is better to never indulge in some things, while conversely – it is better to have experienced and lost others.

THE PRESENCE OF SUBJECTS

"Man is the measure of all things."
Protagoras

There are some traits that all creatures share. They must be able to maintain a stable internal environment, they must be able to harness energy that allows each to live, they must be able to grow and develop, they must possess the ability of adaptation, due to having to respond to their respective environments – and they must have the capability to reproduce.

Each species is within themselves a force of nature. All organisms are born prisoner to genetic instructions and the customs and traditions of their species or group. There are three domains of lifeforms – Bacteria, Archaea and Eukarya. They all are encoded with characteristics of a common ancestor(variations of the same).

Subjects are objects that are self-aware within the overall object(Hegel noticed that self was both subject and object). Subjects are substrate independent, we function as a part of a codependence or interdependence, while seemingly also independent from it. What is perceived by us subjects is from a partitioned vantage or first subject view(subjective view). Accustomed to our own vision, subjects eventually thoughtlessly take the position that our view is the objective measure. In experience, lifeforms – us – are the subjects and the cosmos is the object. We and every other component of experience are byproducts of the object, Nature.

How can we be sure himind beings are the lead character in the game of life experience?

There are many species of living things, all that are known have lived here on earth. Each is well and uniquely equipped for life experience, with their own distinct features and set of amazing abilities, skills and talents. Some can fly, some can swim, some can change skin color on demand, some can see in the dark, some can run on water etc. While some have wings, claws, bigger and stronger bodies and keener senses(we all share the capability of perceiving, no two species sense the world the same) – cereves' special feature, aside from standing upright and our specific type hands – is our minds.

Every creature possesses cognitive capabilities to some degree(even a plant), but pending the discovery of a more intelligent species – we have demonstrated that we himinds have the highest capacity for intellect("humane" is a term that references a behavioral standard for himind beings. It means that we are able to transcend basic animal instinctual conduct and instead, act based on intellect. Yes, we are the most astute being, yet other species seem to behave more rationally than we do). The unique aptitude of our minds is our natural defense, our weapon. We can think beyond survival to imagine and go about developing luxury. Out of all creatures, our exceptional cognitive ability makes us the primary decision makers in experience.

There is a clear discrepancy to be recognized. No other creature writes or makes decisions near the complexity that we do. We are the one species that can question our experience and go about searching for the answers. We refer to other species as "wildlife", as if we are already acknowledging the apparent distinction. Our list of inventions(the radio, television, the internet, harnessing electricity etc) glaringly distinguishes us from the other living things, in terms of aptitude. All of this renders cereves as the singular species uniquely qualified to solve the enigma of life experience. We are the ideal specialists to explore it.

When you consider the acumen and production of himinds, in contrast to all the other known creatures, there is an obvious disparity. It is obvious that we are out of place. In fact, the difference is so evident, it is almost too noticeable. It tracks that the other animals have to concern themselves with flatulence, defecating or even survival. There just seems to be a clear break in pattern, absurd even – that we have to as well.

The fact that all creatures are equipped with senses, renders us all explorers.

Though we have domesticated and caused the extinction of numerous creatures, cereves are a prey animal. Against the backdrop of the rules of experience, every lifeform is prey. Axially, Nature is the alpha predator.

Can an object exist without a subject?

Theoretically, yes – but it would be like not existing at all. It would be like there was no object.

Can a subject exist without an object?

Yes, but it would be like existing without perception, which would be like not even being.

An object and a subject are extremes on the opposite ends of the same conceptual theme. They are intrinsically interdependent on each other. This is why the cosmos eventually birthed(the universe is an incubator) a creature that could effectively appraise it, himind beings – us.

Aliens do not exist. They are another one of culture's urban myths, ghost stories, old wives' tales or wild goose chases. When people assert the existence of life on other planets, they primarily base such a belief on the size of the universe(probability based on scale). We've already discussed the effect scale can have on our minds. Their line of reasoning is that the cosmos is too large for life to only have emerged on earth. That is it. There are no authentic alien autopsy photos, no credible proof of any abduction or credible sightings and no spaceship to boast of. Even some scientists have used this rationale as justification for their belief in the existence of aliens. The average perone, as well as scientist, have both come to the same conclusion and make use of the same grounds to make their case. There has to be aliens, because the cosmos is too big for there only to be us.

Similar to religious zealots, people who assert the existence of aliens do so vigorously for something – that until they can actually produce it – is not there. We might as well be talking about the existence of any and every imaginary thing that comes to mind. Is this not make believe for biological adults?

Applicants of the existence of aliens would have us believe that nothing is unique or a one of a kind in the Wild, when the opposite is actually evidenced. There are many one of a kind objects throughout experience; so to make the argument that aliens have to exist simply because there is room for them to do so, is ill-considered. It is to pretend as if it is not possible for earth to be a one-off, when in truth, there is a significantly higher chance of this being so.

The sizable scale of space for there to be aliens rationale may sound somewhat compelling, but so can average lyrics set to better music. One has to temporarily adopt the mindset of an antisocialite who abhors companionship, to see the flaws in this logic:

- We are individuals in a societal order, whose egoism causes us to prioritize self, which can cause us to feel lonely at times. As we look out into space, being the peculiarly intelligent species on earth causes us to long for companionship(most geniuses have been considered as or are loners, due to having very few people to relate to intellectually). It is a depressing thought to us that we may be in this dark vast expanse all alone. *If we were a solitary species, would we even wonder about aliens or G0d? Is it any wonder we have come up with aliens or even g0ds(we depict aliens with G0d-like powers determining our fate as entertainment)?* It is as if we are suffering from separation anxiety and abandonment issues.

- There are currently millions of species on this very planet. In fact, over 90% that have lived on it, have gone extinct. Most himind beings alive today did not have the opportunity to witness most, if not all of them. Are those extinct creatures not foreign to us in some respects, aliens? Don't you find it odd that even though we didn't get to see most of the creatures that have lived here on earth, we are yearning for there to be one or others out in space – a place so hostile to life that our planet required a protective bubble around it just to facilitate our own presence? Can our desire just be dismissed as a matter of gluttony?

The many different types of creatures that have lived on earth also discount the notion of there being other life in space. The variety should and would be more spread out over life bearing planets, rather than seeming to emerge from a single concentrated point – earth.

• Though we take them for granted, when the low margins for the factors that facilitate our very existence on earth are considered – it is near, if not completely wishful thinking, for us to act as if it would be rudimentary for life to develop elsewhere in the Wild? The low odds of life emerging at all, as well as continuing to live, renders earth's lifeforms, as well as our planet itself as unique events.

• It is clear that our business is here on earth. Why do we look up at the sky? Though we are compelled to look up at the great expanse and it seems to taunt us by showing us an array of locales that we will never be able to visit, it has proven to be a decoy. Space exploration has been fruitful, in terms of gaining a better understanding of space, but space travel is an inherently doomed venture.

When gravity, the distance from the other planets, every other planet in our solar system being barren of life, the dangers and challenges of space flight(low margin for error), the fact that no matter how advanced our technology becomes – there will always be a limit to how far we can roam away from earth and the finite resources we have available, in order to embark on such ambition – is pondered – we arrive at the glaring destination that whatever vocation Nature desires for us to be doing, it is to be done here on earth. Based on these factors, we have to conclude that we are in isolation on a prison planet. We are in custody.

- Himinds are susceptible to delusion. We have a tendency to make things up. Himind society is dominated by claims that it cannot prove, such as the soft science of economics; christian countries claiming that a former cereve named Jesus, who we cannot even prove actually ever lived – will one day return as a deity to save the most deserving of us; claims of superiority based on skin color or financial status; proclaimed societal values that sound good in theory, but play out much different in societal practice.

Landing zone. There are no such things as aliens or at the very least, we are to focus on ourselves.

Our desire for there to be aliens is a last ditch effort to evade peronal responsibility. We often focus on other people to elude having to focus on ourselves. Life experience is a game of self-control. If one does not know how to control themselves, they are in a dangerous position to lose the contest.

The only lasting escape or semblance of freedom to be gained while mortal, is not impulsivity, but rather self-control. Self-control utilized for constructive activity is actual freedom.

Many notable yestorical or cultural figures(from Socrates, to Jesus, to Galileo, to Voltaire, to Joan of Arc, to Martin Luther King, to Malcolm X, to Eric Snowden etc) – were either imprisoned, under threat of detention or had to flee from it. This tells us that the merits of societal authority must always be in question. It also is a hint to us of the true nature of the Wild(detention center).

Why do we have the particular abilities that we have and at the same time are burdened with the particular deficiencies that we find ourselves with?

In games, characters are game pieces. There are lead characters and supporting characters. The game protagonist(s) is the main character(s). Players live vicariously through the characters. The player is reimagined as a character in the game.

Relative to the gameworld, game characters are small in scale. They are nimble and able to play through its levels and obstacles. Characters are directly and indirectly linked to other characters in the game and are also able to interact. Game designers often assign specific situations in games, in which a particular character(s) with a particular ability(s) is able to reach or realize the overall aim of the activity. Some objects or goals the characters need are placed in locations of convenience, while others are located in some of the most inconvenient of places.

Though each of us is able to function independently, collectively we are a **social species**. We experience stage fright, we tend to yawn when we see another perone yawning, inmates suffer psychological damage after lengthy stays in isolation, each of us behaves differently when by ourselves as opposed to when we are around a crowd. Cereves are essentially a herd animal, but we sanitize the obvious by referencing it as having a "herd mentality". This maintains our self-deception that individuals supplant the group, in terms of priority(individualism). We are also instinctively aware of another perone's presence when they interrupt our seclusion. We concern ourselves with what they are thinking, in relation to what we are doing at the time. We consider certain courtesies and codes/expectations while in their view or presence. We seek an equilibrium when casually engaging a stranger, especially in moments of necessity. We wouldn't ever feel lonely if we weren't members of a social species.

Why are we a social species rather than a solitary one?

Though universally we cereves are collectively the main character(s) in this game, subjectively – we are a social order to aid in our mortal survival, like any other evolutionary adaptation. Philosopher, Adam Smith, made note of the codependency of himinds in contrast to other animals and how even the most vile of us, will offer up sound advice at times or give bona fide help to someone. During times of disaster, people organically band together.

Quick tangent:

Start:

> A political and economic system must be developed to cultivate and nurture this social altruistic behavior. The fact that we behave in such a way during times of group calamity, demonstrates that our best selves is our intended state also in times of stability.

End tangent, return to topic already in progress:

Our abilities and talents, which includes our ability to speak, are not just for individual benefit. As a member of a social species, all of (y)our abilities are inherently designated primarily for social benefit. There is a comfort in being a member of a social group, such as safety or strength in numbers. Organisms that are ill equipped for individual defense, live in groups and survive in cooperative action.

There are implications that come with being a social species and some of them work against us. Our innate need to belong and for acceptance, results in each of us having some level of influence on each other's conduct. Nature forces us to care about what others think of us. Our decisions are not fully our own, other people impact them as well(uni-being). Being a social breed also points to scale, which can befuddle. It also means that whatever the goal of the game/experience, it is on two levels – as individuals and as a cooperative.

If there was only one individual himind to ever emerge on earth and on their own was able to compensate for all of the advantages and nuances that being a member of a social group provides, experience would have been an easier puzzle/riddle to solve.

Able to operate individually, each perone requires time alone. We require time away from the rest of the herd to think things through for and to ourselves. Such a time is one for honest introspection, rededication and strategizing.

When we speak with other people, we become offended if they do not give us their attention, yet we barely take the time to listen to what our own minds are saying to us.

The most considerate loser learns how to win with urgency, due to being sincere with themselves as to why they lost or are losing and exercising determination to avoid such outcomes going forward.

Why are there fevales and males? Why didn't Nature just form us as one gender? Why aren't we asexual, an individual creature able to reproduce offspring without a mate, as some other creatures in nature are?

Nature makes use of polarity and variety in rendering himinds one species, but different genders. Outside of the obvious function of reproduction, different genders adds a layer of challenge and confusion to our experience. Evolution could have made us of equal physical strength, but it didn't. Instead, Nature chose to render males or one of the genders – physically stronger, which is the basis of the "battle of the sexes", conflict and oppression. A forced cooperation exists as opposed to an organic one for the practical purpose of mutual benefit. This dynamic effectively distracts from the overarching objective.

Subjectively there are distinctions between the genders of our species, but objectively, we are genderless.

What could explain Nature wanting us to have children?

Nature is hypersexual. Survival is the surface reason for producing children/offspring, furthering the species(bacteria is the most successful species, based on biomass). The himind birth rate outpaces our death rate. Under favorable circumstances, we are born more than we die. Reproduction sustains species in experience/time. Essentially, that is its function. It is a placeholder. We may claim that we have children out of love or whatever other wezenticized reason, but in actuality – Nature cleverly coerces us to engage in sex(*can bearing a child to experience a harsh reality such as this, neutrally be considered as an act of affection*).

Not just the other animals, Nature also puts us in "heat"(puberty, "sexual prime"). It uses arousal to compel our participation(Nature compels us to continuously generate offspring). If the act of sex was not pleasurable, how big would the population of our species be? Wezentic attraction would be replaced by platonic or cerebral draw(*if we were creatures with no sexual organs, would any of us still be "attractive"*). Sexual pleasure can be so intense, that we easily lose sight that any sexual act – whether bestial, masturbation, oral, pedophilia or rape – is fundamentally out of a need to reproduce – a compulsion for survival.

A query to pose to fevales: If you are trapped on an island with no other perone than a severely disfigured adult cere, who is sexually passive and you both have no chance of ever being rescued – do you eventually have sex with this hideous cere voluntarily or if you are able to – maybe even rape him if he isn't responding to your advances quickly enough?

Two male snow leopards fight with a fevale one. They are beyond any argument over which male she should mate with, they are now focused on her mating with at least one of them. The fevale snow leopard tries every which way to get away from them, but the larger, more dominant male of the two – shadows her step for step. His aggressiveness establishes that he is insistent and that this is no courtship or request. Quickly cornered and left with no route of escape, she begrudgingly accepts his unwanted sexual advances as the other male looks on.

As unpleasant as this scenario is, it is one that plays out throughout the ranks of many species, including our own. It demonstrates that on a primal level, forceful sexual encounters are systemic. **Rape** is natural, due to the instinctive tenet of self-preservation, which also makes its presence in experience necessary(*would either male snow leopard even have approached the fevale at that moment, if neither had arousal already implanted within them*).

In terms of us, we are able to reason at more depth than other creatures, many of whom – tend to act impulsively on every urge. Our view of rape is more well thought than reflexive. We realize that despite our instinctive cues or urge to reproduce, forcefully engaging in sexual activity is synergistically wrong.

Keep in mind, sexual pleasure is merely a feature in experience to assure reproduction. This means that in instances of fevales raping males or males raping fevales, though wrong, it is still understandable – in terms of a drive for reproduction. Foundationally, they occurred out of a craving to survive. Conversely – bestiality, which is the rape of animals(no wild animal voluntarily consents to a sexual excursion with a cereve) – males raping males or fevales raping other fevales or both raping children – is unjustifiable. Though initiated by the same urge, there was never an opportunity for the outcome of reproduction(waste).

Even in rape there is difference.

Instincts drive reproduction, not sentiment(ironically, emotions are also inherent) or we wouldn't have felt it necessary to create multiple types of birth control(the very term makes the point). If Nature did not desire for reproduction to be a feature in experience, there would not be the ability to engage in sex. When pederasty(adult males sexually partnering with boys) was commonplace in some cultures, the people in those cultures still reproduced. If reproduction wasn't instinctive, there would be more subjectively intentional pregnancies than "unintentional" ones and little demand for abortion applications.

No pregnancy is accidental, if the couple who engaged in sex did so voluntarily. Ignorance is not an adequate defense in Nature.

Outside of reproduction, **sex** is just a pastime, an activity that we are able to do. Due to our drive for psychological coping, sex for the intent of pleasure – just serves the function of a coping device. We embellish and over-exaggerate its significance outside of that.

Are any of us still in a wezentic relationship with the perone who we felt supplied us with our most pleasurable sexual experience(s)? Is your best sexual experience with the perone you are currently wezentically partnered with? Are they even your second or third best erotic experience? If "good" sex is of such importance in a wezentic relationship, shouldn't at least most of us still be with the perone we felt provided us with our greatest favorable sexual encounters?

The emerging theme is that as blissful as sex can feel at times, it does not render any of us significant. Sex can also be painful or result in emotional duress. No matter how much effort one puts into sexually pleasing another, this does not guarantee the other perone's affinity or that they will stay with you for longer than that moment or what have you. Sex is not a confirmation of acceptance or an indication of resounding affection, though there are times when it can be. It has been used as consequence and as reward, when it is neither. Sex has been commodified as a product, sold and traded for; so much so, it has also been utilized to define self-worth. It has been referred to as being evil and something to fear and it can be viewed as clean and at other times – dirty. In a wezentic relationship, sex can be a beginning, an affirmation of continuity or the finish line. Subjectively, sex is whatever each individual thinks of it as at that moment, but axially – it is neutral.

Erectile dysfunction and menopause are Nature's way to stop each of us from duplicating variations of physical copies of ourselves. There is a time to breed and there is a time not to.

In neutrality, erectile dysfunction is not a dysfunction at all. It is a featured function.

We are essentially in heat between puberty and permanent erectile dysfunction and menopause.

Aside from the risk of pregnancy, sex also carries with it the threat of a variety of sexually transmitted diseases that are not to be taken lightly. When these dangers are taken under consideration, strategically – celibacy is the most cerebral way to protect oneself or by limiting your exposure via engaging in sex as scarcely as possible or with as few people as possible.

Are we really sure that reproduction is a given?

Though people reproduce constantly and "generations" are a concept of convenience, we know that all people live for only a limited duration in life. Distributed over any given time frame of himind population, we too will utilize the term "generation" here for convenience. A new generation carries on where the previous generation left off, allowing for consistency. Rather than each generation having to start over from the beginning again and again, each generation gets to leave their efforts behind for the next one to adopt and build on. It's as if Nature wanted to facilitate a specific type of development or progression.

Regeneration is mortality's version of immortality. A species is instinctively continued until it eventually succumbs to the inevitability of being mortal.

Each generation's innate function is as a proxy for occupancy in this experiential existence. This implies that objectively – death and birth are an illusion. In actuality, all generations are actually just one generation of cereves and that one generation is a distribution of a singular being.

In games, regeneration allows a player to start over again wherever they last were prior to being eliminated. Game developers essentially utilize the regeneration feature to sustain a player in the game. It is a compulsive device.

> **"We are painfully free."**
> Jean Paul Sartre

The opposite is actually true. We are euphorically limited. No cereve that has ever lived or any other living thing, for that matter – chose to be alive. We are drafted into the construct of experience, as if soldiers for war. We do not have a choice in what quality of health we are in at birth, nor the genetics we have, nor who our parents are, nor the area or the circumstances that we are born in. We have no choice in the range of our inherent abilities or deficiencies, those are set before we are born. We have no choice in the fact that one day our bodies will completely cease to function. Even our capacity of volition is occurring from a position of having no other choice.

Drop site. Our life experience is coerced. The fact that it is being done with such finesse and subtlety, is reasonable cause for suspicion.

THE PRESENCE OF AN INTERFACE

"The mind-body problem". We are each a combination of mind and body. Though the brain organ, which generates our minds – is a product of the body – we view them as separate. This is due to the mind serving as a control center for the body and a control station for our "free will". Our bodies are a vehicle for our Will, we are even said to have "motor skills". The Will controls the body by remote, our bodies serve as its avatar or puppet.

The mind is a collection of capacities that include, but are not limited to – language, memory, thinking, perception and volition. It processes our thoughts and emotions and feelings and expresses them as actions and attitudes. The mind can also imagine, recognize and appraise. We experience life or being alive in our minds. We intuitively learn how to use our minds first and then use it to learn to operate our bodies.

The only reality we know directly is our minds. It is easy to lose sight of this fact(not being able to see each others' minds or thoughts, but instead each others' bodies – creates this illusion), but that is our undeniable disposition. No matter what happens with our bodies, whether it is within it or outside of it – we only experience every part of our lives – in our psyches or psychological model. This foundational fact renders life experience solely a thinking endeavor, a nonphysical experience – a psychological operation. Life experience is primarily within the mind and is based on our interpretation of everything outside of it, including whatever goes on within our own bodies.

Socrates called it a Daemon(not to be confused with "demon"), Adam Smith referred to it as the "inner witness" and writer, C.S. Lewis attributed "consciousness" to G0d. **Consciousness** is as if a disembodied presence within the body's control station(similar to a pilot in a cockpit). It is the uplink to our bodies. It is an awareness(inner view, "the mind's eye"), an audience that is apart from the inner workings of the mind, yet able to access and operate the voluntary controls of the body. All voluntary actions of the body are controlled by the conscious, "free will"(audience and director). It has the ability to speak to us as an inner voice, as well as hear what that instinctive voice is saying. This allows for an inner communication with ourselves(this feature is as if an onboard assistant). Consciousness perceives everything through thought – and thought can be either images or sounds – or a combination of both.

More than any other identifying marker, the conscious is you – and what no one wishes to say out loud, is that being ourselves is like being in someone else's body along with them, only that other perone is unconscious(much more noticeable as an infant learning how to work their limbs or when a perone is recovering from serious illness or injury).

To an extent, we are able to see outside of the body as well as back in. The conscious' vantage is seated in front of the visionary screen in our minds and the inner view screen is then overlaid with the view of outside of our bodies. The conscious is similar to sitting in a building and watching a transparent projection screen that sits in front of a window with a view of the outdoors. This is our axial line of sight. As you have read this book, at points – your mind began to wander, even while still consuming the words. Images formed and began to play out overtop of or along with your view of the text, without even obstructing it. Our visionary screen, which our imagination plays out on, is as if transparent.

The mind is foundationally involuntarily controlled, consciousness is even an involuntary function. The control of voluntary actions the conscious has, is a suborder within the overall involuntary control scheme of the mind. Consciousness is a subjective control within a larger universal appartus. Our life experience cognitively is Nature having us on the lookout and keeping us on notice. At the involuntary level, the mind is a collection of functions, which at their most fundamental, are a set of instructions/rules.

The mind is two parts, the conscious and the subconscious. The subconscious is the primary control, the conscious operates within the subconscious' boundaries. The conscious mind is superficial and impulsive for quick reactions to dangers(self preservation/subjective), as well as for when there is no apparent hazard present. The conscious mind forgets, while the subconscious seemingly records everything you experience. Every now and again, it submits a past memory to your attention. A past memory that you had long forgotten or are curious as to why you even have it stored in memory. While the conscious psyche sleeps, the subconscious mind is an insomniac. It is always alert, ready to sound the alarm in case of danger and running the involuntary operations of the body.

Consciousness is the liaison between the "will" and our bodies.

While the body ages, our Will sustains its vigor. This is why there is such disparity between our desire and our ability, inspiring the saying, "the mind wants to, but the body can't".

Solving the mind-body enigma. The literal/physical world is similar to the immaterial one, in that both are perceptions. The distinction is that the body or what is physical/material – is sensory data inputs, while the mind is what interprets that data. What causes confusion is that we translate the perceptions imported by our senses via the perceptivity of our minds.

Mind-body is multiple perceptions, within a primary perception.

Consciousness is both a rule and a function.

Being in our minds is like our Will is in a flight simulator.

There are levels or degrees of awareness and self-cognizance, we must become fully self-aware. We are to achieve full cognition.

Game interfaces allow players to participate in play in gameworlds. They are the entrances/gateways/portals to the game.

The mind is the conscious' interface to the physical world that we refer to as "reality".

Characters are gameplay athletes. All living things are athletes of life experience.

On some level, being alive is an activity of repeatedly going in and out of consciousness.

Pool of ideas/Field of Mind. It is often said that there is no idea that you can think of that someone else hasn't thought of already. Upon contemplation, that statement is an exaggeration. If anything, it is only most of the ideas that we think of that someone else has already pondered or eventually will mull.

If we all think of the same thoughts, then clearly we aren't all making the same decisions or acting on those ideas with any similarity, due to some of us being more dismissive of certain ideas than others. Cerebral maturity, group, peronal beliefs/worldview, career, culture, gender, nurture etc – all impact how we act on our thoughts.

What is intriguing is that we generally have the same initial reflexive thoughts when encountering comparable situations or circumstances. This would include responses of curiosity(natural questions), guilt and insecurity. It is as if we are sharing a database of organic thoughts for every possibility, every moment or situation.

Drop zone. We are sharing a collective mind, a universal cereve/himind consciousness. A shared field of organic thought.

Gameplay modules can be created; so that a single script can generate all characters' dialogue, even when a character is just speaking to themselves. Such modules can also generate all audio and images – which themselves, can also be viewed as aspects of the game's overall dialogue.

To **perceive** is the attainment or cognizance of something; to interpret or comprehend. Our ability to perceive is entangled with the concept of thoughts. Everything we perceive is a thought and thoughts are sensations. Not to be confused with "feelings"(even though feelings too are a type of thought), like experiencing feeling cold or hot or nauseated – every way and everything that we perceive is a sensation. Sensations are all thoughts.

To sense is to have an awareness of a stimulus, it is our radar. Our **senses** are how we detect the world, they bring nature to our attention. They are a data feed. Individually, as well as in combination – they bring us moment to moment of experience, our field of sense.

Constantly at work, the senses engage in espionage, recognizance really – importing data. They are able to sense outside of our body as well as inside of it. The senses give us coordinates and depth perception of the things around and where we are in relation to them. Whether it is any of the well known capabilities of vision, touch, hearing, smell and taste – each is an open-ended channel of input that the brain processes and interprets in a particular way. Each tells our conscious a different aspect of what is going on in our environment.

Objectively, every sense is a variation of the same sense perception. All senses and their sensations are neutral. How sense perceptions are subjectively interpreted, influences whether they are expressed positively or negatively. Without senses, we couldn't have an experience.

Our adverse psychological reaction to being locked in a sensory deprivation chamber for a protracted length of time, demonstrates the need not only for our senses to have stimuli to detect, but more

A. Radical

importantly – the mind's mortal dependence on environmental information.

Conceptually, each of us is a response machine, a first-perone/self-aware responder. The senses are the first layer of each response machine and the mind and body are subsequent. The information of experience is eliciting a response, which is why we regard it as stimulus or phenomenal.

For our senses, experience is a distortion or parody of reality – they aren't fully accurate at the level of experience, yet it is this level we are made to focus on. Reality exists as a vast amount of information, too much for our senses to completely grasp(reality is signals to our minds, nothing is as it seems before we sense it). As a result, at times we experience sensory illusions. During these instances we experience false positive sensations of hearing, feeling, seeing, smelling and tasting. At all times our senses are providing us with approximations, assumptive perceptions of our environment.

Rendezvous point. For living things, the Wild exists as a more convenient type of our version of a sense deprivation chamber.

If reality is different in actuality than how we sense it, how come we do not run into things as we go about daily life?

The reason for this is due to us being a player in a virtual reality game. Our bodies are but avatars/characters and everything we perceive from its vantage, is virtual – not actual.

Our senses cause us to perceive the game as a character(biased), not as a player(universal).

The senses infer that we are to be searching. Not only do they seek, they pique our inquisitiveness, which then causes us to ask questions and wonder, which is also searching.

We did not endow ourselves with curiosity. That capacity is inherent. Nature gave us such ability to question, to query our experience. Nature equipped us with our intrigue to question Nature itself.

Why would Nature generate an intelligent creature smart enough to effectively inquire about it?

Nature wants us to investigate it, to pursue its mystery. We can't avert curiosity, experience forces our intrigue to be active. Curiosity is instinctive, it is like the leaves on a plant seeking light. We are to interrogate and interview nature, as if it is holding a press conference. Experience for us is a treasure hunt, a hunt for answers. Questions take us on a quest and recorded yestory shows that we've exhausted a lot of time exploring(time does indeed tell). All non-meaningful questions, which are the lowest quality of organic questions, are decoys – a form of trick questions for us to busy ourselves with – courtesy of Nature.

Early himinds were nomadic and as children we tend to venture off. Our minds analyze and analysis is searching. We seek conclusions(we're ultimately seeking answers, certainty), which is why we tend to carelessly leap to them. Over the years, we have developed concepts and devices/tools as extensions of our senses to aid in our seeking.

If dance is art, then what is art? How can drawing, painting, theater and music – all be the same or similar to dance?

What they all have in common is that they are forms and end products of expression or application of creativity and since that is the case, then objectively – everything is art or a work of art. Everything. There's not a moment that we or anything else, in all of experience – is not participating in an artistic undertaking of some sort. Every act or overall motion itself, is like a dance, a rhythmic movement. Everything is an expression, an application of the Laws of Nature. Axially – all objects, features and motion – are within one overarching expression.

The topic of **aesthetics**, should not only be concerned with beauty and our subjective art. The sounds we hear and can't hear, the textures we touch and are unable to sense, the sensations we feel and the ones we cannot, the tastes we rendezvous with, the smells we inhale, as well as the ones we can't smell, even the visual thoughts we have – all that can be perceived are aesthetics. All of it is art. Aesthetics is theater, a spectacle.

Aesthetics should be two categories – axial/universal aesthetics and subjective aesthetics, which is what we consider as "aesthetics" currently.

Water takes temporary "selfies" or self-portraits and the sunlight draws silhouettes.

Conclusion: Nature is graphic.

Between the environment and the many creatures, experience is a combination of an art gallery and a fashion show.

Vision is our primary sense(all of our senses are a form of vision or of each other). It is the ability to see – from the images we view through our eyes to the pictures we perceive in our minds. Our consciousness or mind's eye is the basis of sight/vision.

Our field of view for our eyes or our peripheral vision is limited, while our imagination allows our inner vision to seem limitless. We can even imagine what the scene that is behind us looks like.

There are levels of our awareness, like adjusting a camera, microscope or telescope. You can increase magnification or resolution, bring everything into proper focus – which is a state of being hyper-aware or hyper-conscious with an objective calibration – or you can zoom out which is where your mind's eye is more inattentive and puts things out of focus. Your awareness goes in and out of focus, in terms of what setting or level you are on. This is similar to your eyes adjusting to a sudden burst of light after being in a completely dark room(triple stage naivete/oblivion).

Levels of awareness or focus is also concentration, it is the amount of attention("attention span") we are giving to a potential interest. Our focus tends to rove and there are multiple things we have to focus on.

When we are intensely focused, we are fully engaged. When someone says, "put it out of your mind", they are saying to put whatever thought that is occupying your thinking, out of immediate interest.

The same way you can notice the tension in your facial muscles when you meditate or are able to focus your hearing to listen for a particular sound, is the same way you can notice the things you do, as you are doing them or the feelings you are having as you are enduring them. It is not just noticing when you feel tired, it is noticing what emotions you are experiencing moment to moment. Focusing at a high level is listening to your inner voice(s) and what it is saying. Focusing your cognizance is experiencing a thought and asking yourself why are you having that particular thought at that particular moment. It is to be aware of everything within your capability of awareness. It is having a full presence of mind("keeping our wits about us").

The layers of life experience are – the experiential layer, the mechanical layer & the conceptual layer. Science has been deciphering and articulating the mechanical layer, while all people have been living in the experiential layer.

We can be aware of something being in proximity or in front of us and at the same time, not be aware of it.

Focus is aligning the emotions for a common purpose. It can also mean one's level of determination.

Objectivity puts our mind's eye in proper focus. It is to think outside ourselves, where truth exists.

Outside of subjectivity is where honesty exists, which renders us a lie. This explains why we often lie to ourselves or why it is so laborious to be honest with ourselves.

To think objectively, is to venture outside of Plato's Cave.

There are two effective ways to see things. One way is from the correct subjective view and the other is from the objective view. The two generally do not conflict, but in the instances that they do, the objective lens is always the priority.

Subjectivity is a tangent from relative neutrality.

Active relative neutrality is an experience that varies from an experience of being out of one's body, to being free of the grips of the pretenses of society, to eventually outside of the spectacle of the megacosm. Objective thinking is a transcendent activity.

I am not a race.
I am not a gender.
I am not a species.
I am but a self-aware mind that is able to ponder those other things.
I am inherently a thinker.

When you are truthful with yourself, your mind is like a confessional that is open 24 hours a day, 365 days a year. Integrity doesn't take sick leave or vacations.

In the same way that a thirty degree day feels much colder than when it follows a seventy or sixty degree day – or feels warmer when it follows a negative temperature day – is in the same way we should view our subjectivity.

Objectivity is to always keep at the forefront of our minds, that regardless of how our feelings change, in regards to the temperature, the thirty degrees felt the same the entire time. There is what the temperature actually is and then there is what the temperature seems to feel like. Relative neutrality is to always be as the thermometer.

Life is a 3D movie and objectivity is as if you are outfitted with 3D glasses to perceive it. Subjectivity is to perceive the movie without them.

Our senses may search, but our peak reasoning is our primary radar, our objective sense. Unless one thinks of the world axially, for them – actuality exists in stealth mode.

A signal represents the patterns or meaning found within data. In electronic applications, in order to be useful, signals are isolated from the noise. Thinking objectively, separates the signal from all of the distortion in experience.

What is beauty to a blind perone or to an animal? Is it a real thing? Does an aesthetically beautiful plant or butterfly know that they are beautiful? Would they behave differently, privileged maybe – if they did? Are they privileged because they are? Would they consider their favorable aesthetics a curse or even as their self-worth?

If danger or evil is beautiful or aesthetically pleasing, we tend to give it some degree of benefit of the doubt.

"Beauty is truth, truth beauty."
John Keats

Beauty is the quality or combination of qualities that makes something appealing to the senses, especially sight. It is a profound attribute in or of a thing. Beauty demands attention, it is appealing. One of its attributes is that it tends to be temporary, fleeting.

Philosopher, Arthur Schopenhauer, said that beauty is something that causes you to contemplatively perceive it. Since everything can be contemplatively perceived, he concluded that everything was beautiful. In the objective perspective, he is correct, but in the subjective slant – everything cannot be beautiful. If this wasn't so, we would not be able to appreciate beauty. It is the presence of grotesque, ugly, hideous and repulsive aspects and details of life in the Wild – that causes us to appreciate beauty and vice versa.

The appeal of a beautiful thing is different than the appeal of "beautiful people". The physical beauty of people is much different than the physical beauty of a subjective artwork. Why are people that we refer to as "pretty" or "cute" – considered as such? Sexual allure. These are people we find pleasing to look at, in terms of our or what we think others' imagined erotic desire should be for them. Ask yourself, if himind beings lived without ever having need for sexual organs, how aesthetically appealing would we be to each other? Outside of their regalia, can you find something in a physically beautiful perone's appearance that is not rooted in sexual appeal?

Beautiful people have a false sense of self. Others have convinced them that appearance is their foremost redeeming quality, as opposed to qualities that they are directly responsible for, such as what they know or the quality of their intentions and decisions. Much time is wasted attempting to keep pace with such repute. It is impractical. Some beautiful people consider their beauty a curse, due to no one giving any actual redeeming quality that they do possess any serious or same level of acknowledgment.

Why is there beauty?

The answer is its function. What is the effect of aesthetic beauty on those perceive it? It attracts, which means in all of its generating awe and startle, it primarily distracts. Anything that we are attracted to distracts us from something else(opportunity cost). We find pleasure in beauty, which delineates from Nature developing us susceptible to it. This levels beauty as a welcomed distraction, often times during situations where we cannot afford to be diverted. This prompts the question, why did Nature feel it necessary to add the feature of beauty in experience at all? Why isn't everything subjectively just average appearances and descriptive characteristics, since in neutrality – that is all appearance actually is? It must be that beauty is included in experience as mere decor. Since every item in the cosmos is here out of necessity, it has to be that beauty exists to divert us from more meaningful details that would be easier to realize if beauty were absent.

What we are left with when we remove beauty from experience, is truth/exactness.

If physical beauty is as significant as it is emphasized in society, why aren't those that are considered the most physically attractive of us, among the ranks of the so called "world leaders", as well? In yestory, how many world leaders of societies that put a premium on beauty, would be considered as physically attractive or beautiful?

If reves and ceres always all looked like the most repulsive appearing perone that you could think of, would you still lust after them as we do for those we consider as beautiful now?

If the answer is yes, then this realization demonstrates that axially – there really is no such thing as "ugly" or "pretty", in terms of people – only available options.

Colors are inexpressible. We cannot describe blue or what any other color looks like to a perone who has never seen colors before. We see colors, but they are nondescript. This is a peculiarity or oddity that Nature included in experience for us to take notice and ponder.

Clear and translucent fall into the same category as colors, being that they are the hue or lack thereof, of an object.

Nature uses color in experience to distinguish and convey meaning. Colors enable us to survey experience and thrive within it. Seeing them privileges us to interpret and utilize them. Many creatures use light to achieve visual perception, color is embedded in light. If there was no color or fewer colors, it would be much harder to discern things. Colors are used for camouflage to hide from predators and prey. They are also used to intimidate or attract/draw attention. Plants use colorful fruit to attract birds to spread their seeds. The green pigmentation of plants and trees is used for photosynthesis. They harvest red and blue photons and convert it into sugar, essentially creating food out of color.

Everything is scenic – even the dark, being that we can see it. Life experience is in part a sight-seeing(sense-stimuli) trip.

What do dreams actually mean, why are there dreams?

We can vividly experience dreams while we are sleeping, only to awaken and find that the experience was not real. It was not actual. Dreams are instinctive and are forcefully brought to our attention by our subconscious, as we sleep.

Why would Nature want us to notice a hologram? What is the significance?

The answer is in the rainbow. Rainbows are aesthetically pleasing, but they are quite peculiar. While awake, we see them on display like the tail feathers of a male peacock seeking out a prospective mate's interest. But, like dreams – the rainbow is a blatant illusion. Why? Why are there obvious illusions, things that we will notice that they are not real – included in life experience?

Destination: Both dreams and rainbows are hints that though we are perceiving, everything we are sensing is not actually there. Reality itself, as we see and understand it – is a mirage.

We will return to the topic of dreams, later on in this text.

Why the "If a tree falls" riddle, which doesn't seem like a riddle – is actually a very clever one:

If a tree falls and no one is around to hear it, does it actually make a sound? We have all heard the question and we have all dismissed it as being too obvious to even be worth considering.

The popular assumption is that since the tree falls, there has to be a **sound**, even though no one is there to hear it. We have to pause and reconsider our position here. We must instead ask ourselves, if there is sound and no living thing is around to hear it, is there really still sound?

Sounds help us to identify things, discern and such. They sparks our curiosity/wonder and investigation. They assist in telling us what things belong and what is out of place. The phenomena of sound is not for the benefit of the environment, but for us living things. What made that sound, what kind of sound is that? We are subjects and an object needs a subject to objectify it, or it is akin to there being no object. It would be like a completely deaf perone in a noisy room. To them, the room is not noisy.

This means that the existence of sound is dependent on both the presence of the object, as well as the subject. Sound cannot exist without the interaction of both. Even if we leave a recording device in an empty room or out in the woods somewhere – that does not matter. The device is still a subject, being that it is able to perceive. Ultimately, if no subject is wherever sound waves vibrate, there is no sound.

Mute or silence, no sound – is a sound, due to the fact that though the definition of mute is to be devoid of sound, we can still hear silence. We have an expectation of what the perception of mute/silence is supposed to sound like. If mute/silence wasn't a sound, we could not have such expectation.

Sometimes silence is a safe word

All sound is noise pollution, including silence.

Silence is like darkness, people tend to fear both in the same way. Predators use the cover of night to mount their attacks, as some disquieting thoughts utilize silence to do the same in our minds. We must be courageous when confronted by either.

We can't help but to hear, that sense is open-ended. We are being forced to hear, it is involuntary. Listening is voluntary or intentional. It requires conscious focus. Listening is an action and like any other action we take, it is to be performed with sincerity.

What value does music serve?

Our taste in **music** is subjective, though all sounds are objective. We tend to listen to what we like to hear, more than to the sounds that we do not like(seek pleasure, avoid pain). This does not just pertain to music, but also to what is being said to us – such as advice, flattery and promotion. If deemed that some bad advice sounds better to us than good advice, we tend to favor the bad advice since it more appealing to us(delusion).

Music is simply an exaggeration of sound, singing an aggrandizement of speaking and lyrics an embellishment of language.

The allure of music("sounds like music to my ears") demonstrates that sounds have always been weaponized against us, a sonic weapon, a propaganda tool – courtesy of Nature.

Only music that is consequentially edifying, not merely playing to our emotions, is worth listening to and producing. This logic applies to all forms of subjective aesthetic expression.

Though blindness is seen as an impediment, the blind are at an advantage, being that they are shielded from the bombardment of spectacle that those of us with vision must endure. It is similar to what experience was like for us before we harnessed fire or electricity, when the darkness of night time blocked the sights we noticed during the day.

Why is the sky blue?

The scientific explanation of blue light in the atmosphere aside, the peculiarity is that if the sky wasn't blue, it would always seem black, even during the daytime. Sunlight would still reveal all that is here on the ground, but the sky would always look like a night sky. Even it's color of blue, is curious. Mars's sky appears a reddish hue, meaning our sky could have been red as well, or any other color. Instead it is unmistakably blue.

Studies show that we experience emotional responses when encountering colors. Some colors can spark anger or warmth, while others, particularly blue – can be calming or comforting. This renders the color of the daytime sky as a propagandist, at least in part. It is also no coincidence, that though another shade, the ocean(s) is blue as well. This tells us that the blue sky is not some accidental feature, but a peculiar feature with an ulterior motive for being the specific color that it is.

Though our **shadow** is outside of us, it is similar to the part of us that is inside – our Will, which we do not have the luxury to see. Our real shadow is but a silhouette that traces our physical selves, but lacks the detail that is displayed in a reflection. Instead, it is filled with some level of darkness or ambiguity.

Our shadow is silent, as if a mime. It follows us everywhere, there is no eluding it. In a dark room, our shadow blends and appears to have abandoned us, but at the first chance to go by a beam of light, it returns – but was really there all along. Our shadow grew with us as our bodies developed. Sometimes it even appears much smaller or taller than we are.

On the experiential level, shadows alert us to the presence of objects. We know that when we see a shadow, that it is the result of it being cast by some sort of object.

Shadows are clues that we are intrinsically being "shadowed". Our movements are being tracked on a fundamental level. It is a clue that a presence is close by and that said presence is difficult to perceive.

Since we need light to notice shadows and our shadows blend with the dark, then that renders all darkness as one ubiquitous shadow. It is as if the entire night sky could be a shadow that is being cast by an object in front of a higher light source.

Our shadow follows us everywhere we go, only needing the presence of light to appear. Our reflection, which not only traces our bodies, but also details our appearance – follows us everywhere and like our shadow, requires the attendance of light for us to notice it. This means that it also succumbs to darkness.

Estimation: Reflections and shadows are opposite extremes on the same conceptual strand.

On a really hot day of dry heat, a sizable cloud that temporarily moves in front of the sun, provides creatures who are adversely affected by such high temperatures the relief of shade – but really that cloud is simply casting a shadow. In that context, a fully cloudy sky is not just blocking out the sun, that collection of clouds is like one whole cloud that has us in the position of having to live in its enormous shadow.

"Am I forgetting something", "was there something that I was I supposed to do"?

Our memory logs our experience. For this reason philosopher, Thomas Hobbes, referred to memory as "experience". **Memory** absorbs, it makes or takes notes. We can consciously tell ourselves to remember something we wish not to forget. Memory cross references and matches up details and those details can get crossed up at times. Memory cannot consciously remember every single detail, it also can erode over time, rendering it unreliable.

Memory allows for us to second guess and change our minds, if need be. Memory allows us to learn. Storing the details of the past allows us to access it and progress in life. Without memory, we would never advance, we would be aimlessly stagnant.

We are able to see memories with or without audio and memories can be just of audio or some other particular sense – other than visual. Every sense can provoke a memory.

The conscious mind can be forgetful. Since the subconscious's primary concern is self-preservation, the conscious memory does not have all of our memories at the ready, only a few – relatively speaking. This allows for the mind to quickly respond should danger suddenly arise in the present.

Memory also facilitates recurring dreams and thoughts. We form and have habits as a result of this. Many people tend to, "live in the past" or often repeat themselves, due to our being prisoners of habit(it would be more appropriate to say, "prisoners of memory/experience").

Familiarity gives us the impression of reliability.

We are unable to remember our memories of being infants(there is a reason Nature did not allow birth or the immediate following moments, as our earliest memories. It's a smaller echo of us not being able to resolve how the first generation of perones survived.

Recorded yestory is a type of group memory. Its entries are at the ready for each of us to consciously access.

Whenever you forget where you are(peculiar that everyone, at some point in our lives, if not multiple times, forgets where we are located at some particular moment), even if or when you do remember – you are always at a coordinate in oblivion. Excluding its relation to other objects in "space", no astronomer can tell you where earth actually is.

> **"Nothing fixes a thing so intensely in the memory as the wish to forget it."**
> Michel de Montaigne

People will pretend as if some events that they were involved in never even happened. The subconscious memory keeps an accurate record, while allowing us to put things out of our immediate memory, to some degree. These memories we are unable to voluntarily forget or dismiss from our inner focus, while some memories we are able to voluntarily repress. Repressed memories exist in our minds, stripped down of most of their descriptive details. Their structural remains sit in our conscious memory to help us, if we encounter such a situation going forward. These are regrets, memories that make us feel sad, fearful or guilty. Guilt can accumulate, which is why you are to limit nefarious behavior(if only I had made a better decision). Regrets are lessons in experience to be learned from. They are an important aspect of Nature's curriculum for us.

Guilt is akin to buyer's remorse.

In our memories are a list of concerns(**worries**), some more immediate or otherwise, priority than others.

Some memories are appropriate to the moment we are currently experiencing, to remind us that we have done this before or have some familiarity with it and some memories are not. At times you will be doing something, then out of nowhere – a memory will enter your inner view screen that has nothing to do with what you are doing at that moment. Next thing you know, you'll have an emotional reaction to that memory and become engrossed in it, without ever bothering to question why you are suddenly thinking about that particular recall – that you may not want to consider or have any reason to at that particular time.

Why do we worry?

Before we reach a point of actively worrying, we first have to care. We would not fret or feel anxiety if we did not care about things. Worry is just an extreme form of caring. Though there are some similarities or overlap of concerns, we all do not care or worry about the same things. There is also no one that is actually "carefree", no matter how their demeanor appears to be. Our minds imposes being bothered within us. It is not optional. We may leave from it for a while, but eventually we return to consider it. Every care is ultimately a discomfort, even if it is something that gives us pleasure. All cares exist as points of concern, that is their fundamental nature.

Nature wants us worried, which is why we are predisposed to live our lives based on the primary drive of self-preservation, which is rooted in the emotion of fear. We wouldn't fear if indifference was our default. Fear is caring. We wouldn't desire, were it not for care. What better way to incite activity than to keep a character fixated on fear, in all its variations? Care is the ideal catalyst.

We cannot concern ourselves with everything or that would result in overload. We would have too much to worry about to deliberately act in anyway. We'd be paralyzed by care. Outside of our primary concerns of survival(hunger, thirst, digestion etc) we are given other things to be bothered about. We get to pick out some of our cares. *Can you think of some cares that we voluntarily choose to give ourselves?*

Nature demands for us to choose the right things to care about, not for us to seek artificial escapes(coping) from it. We have to correctly rank(we have an issue with putting things in their proper priority) our cares and perform the most moral action(s). That is the only time when our minds exonerate us from a particular worry, when we can reflect on a situation and know that we made a high quality move in reaction to them.

When you do what you are supposed to do, it removes the concerns of "could have", "should have". We have to do what is in our control to do. This is how we are to properly cope with caring.

In the same vein that it is better to be careful than careless, we are to be adequately full of care, instead of deliberately attempting to care less.

Life experience is a role-playing game in a first perone perspective. From the moment we are born, we are playing a character.

Not only does experience include characters, it allows for **character development**, where characters end up differently than how they start out(a caterpillar metamorphs into a butterfly). We are not himind "beings" per se, only at any specific moment. Overall, between birth and death, we are **becoming**(himind becomings). We are all formulations in the process of developing. Since entering life, we've been forming – mostly physically and psychologically. Upon death, we each die as some potential within our particular range of potential(as a group, we become extinct within our particular range of potential. The dinosaurs died within their range of potential of function, ability and time). Though every creature physically develops over time, there is a more important evolution present for cereves.

Our minds never stop learning and experience is a psychological exercise.

Cereve behavior is not random, at least not objectively. Nature has predisposed us to start the early part of our lives as culprits who then have to work our way up to being **antiheroes**. This is effectuated by equipping us with character flaws and putting us in certain predicaments within the encompassing circumstance of experience itself. By default, we are in part **agents of chaos**, which is why even allies can get in our way at times. Yes we create, but one of the end products that we have a fondness for fabricating, is destruction. This is why there are moments that we engage in thrilling, high risk behavior. We can be self-destructive.

As a derivative of self-preservation, every living thing to some degree – considers its own survival first, even those that are included in a social group. This is how each individual is able to function autonomously. What is good for me, is good to me the individual. There is only my desire.

For himinds, this leads to us thinking of everyone else as a means to ends, primarily existing to serve our desires.

Since the very first people emerged on the planet, we have been born in a state of naivete with no instruction booklet as to what being alive is actually about or as to how to go about living and thriving in life experience.

Being hard-coded to be fallible, automatically renders us all as varying degrees of the awkward.

> **"If there are no guidelines for our actions, then each of us is forced to design our own moral code, to invent morality to live by."**
> Sartre

As infants, we start out with axially oriented minds, but they are gullible for adaptive purposes. Eventually, the influence of our parents, relatives, friends and societal culture – all of which, prior to the release of this text, are unlearned to the knowledge of absolute exactness – biases us(products of our past). We conform(when in Rome...) and become unsuspecting caricatures, rather than our true selves.

Who are you?

Culture/heritage is religion without it's actual name. Heritage is an accepted stereotype people apply to themselves and refer to it as "heritage". Culture creates groupies(Simon Says). It institutionalizes us in one way or another. As it does with some pets – it declaws, defangs and neuters us. Culture is a bandleader that all ethnicities or races of people follow behind. If it stops to talk to them, they do not ask heritage any meaningful queries as to its merits. Instead, its fanatics all just gawk and scream and shove pens and paper in its face – asking for its autograph.

Culture is the first teacher. It tells us what to take seriously and what to make folly of, but none of us ever bother to question if we are taking a culture based on "faith" and "uncertainty" too seriously.

Culture is effectively all of our parents. In fact, it is the parent of our parents and their parents and so on and so backward.

This is why technological evolution far outpaces social evolution. We are effectively told what to say, how to say it, what to believe or believe in, what to think etc. Subjective culture hinders progress, while objective culture is the extent to which such progress can be made.

Our instincts and instinctual behaviors are our common and base culture.

How do you know who you are, when you have long forgotten yourself, to the point that it as if you have never even met yourself?

If you were born in another nation than the one you grew up in, with different societal practices and beliefs, you would not have the same beliefs or peronal values that you do presently. You would not even like the same things, such as your current "favorite" foods and music. By and large, the reason you are the way you are now is the result of being shaped by your social environment. Have you ever asked yourself who you would be if you grew up in a vastly different country or region – or even better, if you had not grown up under the influence of a subjective societal culture? An infant has no subjective cultural beliefs, they are objective or cosmopolitan in their thoughts. We were all infants once. This is the mindset we are to readopt and maintain.

The best culture is one that unlocks and maximizes the potential of its adherents. Such a culture welcomes questions and is objectively rational. Objectivity is our axial culture, it is designated for us by Nature.

Unless culture is based in free(axial, neutral) thinking, as well as constantly encourages it, it is a form of mind control. Even if it does proliferate free thought, culture would still serve the function of mind control – just the ideal form of it.

The presence of culture in experience is a clue that a standard or precise way to conduct ourselves/go about things – exists.

> **"Ourselves we never see or come to know."**
> Voltaire.

> **"We are so accustomed to disguise ourselves to others that in the end we become disguised to ourselves."**
> François de La Rochefoucauld

Character Development/Evolution:

Keep in mind that in the epic of the Wild, axially, we are an unsympathetic figure.

Product of our environment. We start out playing the role of a character(s)(mortal species); so initially we already have a false sense of self.

As our bodies reach puberty, estrogen and testosterone also exert influence on our, each gender's, behavior.

We also have a proclivity to make mistakes(default fallibility). Our focus wanders and we are prone to short-term thinking for long-term expense. We tend to limit ourselves, self-sabotage – before reaching our full potential.

We are not satisfied with ourselves for long(we always desire and imagine more, even of ourselves). For the species with the most cognitive ability, we seem to be suspiciously too smart for our own good.

We arrive equipped with an ongoing inner conflict(turning against the self, Anna Freud).

After we're well established in moral deficit, as some level of villain/agent of chaos, we are then given a period of time to achieve positive improvement(vindication), before eventually settling into our habits and becoming set in our ways(second nature).

Self improvement can be lonely. While undergoing it, at times we desire acknowledgment from others for our efforts. Though such recognition may be appealing, it would only foster peronal development being a superficial display, rather than a sincere effort. We each individually, as well as collectively, have to improve without expecting acknowledgment from others – only recognition from ourselves.

Habits are hard to break, yet easy to form(why would Nature set habits up this way, it deliberately rendered the process of change to be arduous). Being hostages to habits enforces the dynamics of that nuance. This does not just apply to each of us individually, but also collectively as a species. We have societal habits that we form(culture, tradition). The goal is for our peronalities to eventually become markedly distinct(second nature) from the point we are established in moral corruption.

We refer to the moon as "the moon", but that does not mean that is what it actually is. Just because we assign something a name, does not render it as that. It is just what we have chosen to refer it as.

Your own formal name isn't even really your name, that is merely a label your parent(s) desired to refer to you as – along with any added nicknames they may assign to you. Names, even the label "human" – are for our benefit, to track and attribute/accredit. They aren't actually who we are.

Fundamentally, everything is just features, objects and functions. Upon further consideration, even utilizing those words to refer to everything as – is problematic. Everything, including ourselves – are neutral objects, performing a function(objective & subjective), that is relative to everything else.

Everything is actually the function we each play in the total activity of experience.

We all have a surface designation and a hidden intrinsic one. There is our exterior identification, which is our physical body and there is our interior identification, which is our intentions/peronality. Our true identity is the intrinsic function we serve on our commute through see-world.

One of the tragedies of life, is that most people will expire never having known or having any interest in meeting their true selves.

Stop fighting you and enlighten/heighten you. You are not you, you are everyone that you knows version of you(typecast), but you are not you. Everyone's impression of you or that you have left them with, is a social rendition of you. The you when you think that no one else can see or is looking at you, is private you, but even then you are still performing for your ego or desires. This is a you that is contrived out of defense and pretense.

You hide this you, but you do not question its legitimacy, as if too busy sneaking or enjoying playing every role, but the one of your actual self. Considering whatever your circumstances are, of all the possible versions of you that could possibly exist, is the current private you the best version or near the best version of you that you could be – and if not, then is it the correct you to be? Is the best version of you, not the real you? Are all the other renditions of you not as if alternates, impostors waiting for a chance to play your role every which way, but the right way? If you are going to be anybody, why not be the actual you?

Since our starting point is triple stage ignorance, it is understandable that from the first generation of cereves to us today, that we have been suffering from an identity crisis.

Though chronologically, many people are referred to as "adults", in actuality, most are not full fledged adults in the axial or most exact context. The vast majority of adults exist as adolescent minds that are occupying biologically mature bodies. Many even occupy positions of the highest authority(s) in society. We are **adult** lookalikes that are playing a part, performers in costume. After physical development slows, our minds continue to develop, in terms of what it learns. Being that life is first a psychological experience and we himinds are the ingenious creature in the Wilderness, we must be ripened in decision making, essentially – mature in mind/thought, to be considered as actual adults.

It is dangerous to the overall species to take mere biological adults seriously, due to their being entrenched outside of actuality. An actual/axial adult is a mind that accepts life experience on its terms. Heeding a form of the invaluable advice given by philosopher, Karl Popper – these aspiring forces of order leave false beliefs behind when exposed to better quality information. True adults synchronize to the seriousness of being alive, which is learning and applying its absolute truth(consequential knowledge).

Few people know more than an inmate, especially one serving a life sentence, that life experience is more psychological than physical.

An even better sample of life being primarily a thinking endeavor, was the circumstance of physicist, Stephen Hawking. He had a disease that gradually paralyzed much of his body. Not allowing any physical shortcomings to define him, Hawking went on to publish many insightful works that examined the fundamental questions about the megacosm and our experience.

Since our minds are always capable of developing, in terms of its absorbance of information – we can only strive to be a full adult mind. No matter the effort or sincerity in attempt, we can never actually get there, being that there is always more to learn. We always have to prove ourselves. The activity of chaos and its effects allows for room for growth.

Even though we never actually attain the goal of a full adult mind, those of us in sincere pursuit of it, die living our actual "best life", due to being and becoming our best selves.

To be alive is to be a work in progress.

Character development not only applies to us individually, but also collectively, being that we are a social order. Nature has set himinds a part, as a group in the role of a collective outlaw(outside of Nature's code of ethics for us). Initially, we are naive and immature and though we've gained some knowledge, created some technologies and matured physically – we are still very pubescent in our thinking.

Life in the Wild is a decision making exercise and sex is a decision one has to contend with. Engaging in sexual activity does not render someone an adult. Though adolescents can have sex upon reaching puberty, it is best to first gain a true adult mind before participating in such interaction(s).

The word "adult" means fully grown or mature. The pornography industry seeks credibility, by hiding behind the word "adult", but that does not render it actual "adult entertainment", only biological adult diversion. If we thought axially on the subject, pornography is much more based on our immaturity, than our seriousness. Can you ever recall watching pornography and thinking to yourself that there is a lot you can adopt from it and incorporate into fortifying your psychological maturity? If anything, pornography exaggerates sex, to attract viewers to its theatrical productions.

Why would Nature coerce us to initially be villainous?

Taking into account the feature of balance in experience, the reason must be to force us to have to improve our behavior, due to committing a previous wrong.

Complex peronalities and character faults help to engage and immerse players. In game design, developers try to provide an experience that is as convincing to the player as possible. As the player makes decisions in the role of their character, those selections seem natural – due to having been designed to be that way. What characters do provides insight into the intentions of a game's developers.

> **"Behavior is the mirror in which everyone shows their true image(actions communicate louder than words)."**
> Johann Wolfgang von Goethe

For a healthy perone, speaking is the easiest feat one can accomplish. This is why it is much easier to make a claim, than demonstrate it. This is why it is easier to give quality advice, than implement it into our own conduct.

For all characters to be in a position where they are able to play both a small part and a big role in the game, means that there is a likelihood that all of the characters are controlled by a single player.

> **"We're born alone, we live alone, we die alone. Only through our love and friendship can we create the illusion for the moment that we're not alone."**
> Orson Welles

When we take into account that all creatures share a common ancestor and the idea of all the continents once being landlocked(Pangea); also, all of the cosmos and everything in it deriving from **one** point and everything sharing the same composition(atoms), the uniqueness of all the components; society being a result of group effort...

> **"Brotherhood is the very price and condition of man's survival."**
> Carlos P. Romulo

...the Butterfly Effect, everything being relative(everything relates to each other, even ideas); our body parts working together for one goal – it equates to an overall special singularity(conceptually).

Each species actually exists as its own conceptual singular being. In the macro, the aggregate of all creatures – regardless of the changing population numbers from generation to generation(similar to cells dying and renewing) – actually exist as one giant, genderless being(uni-becoming) walking through time or existing in it.

We're becoming a being.

No matter how large the crowd is around us, each individual in the crowd is alone. The crowd are a collection of people, each living life in the first perone. We are a collection of a first perone(uni-being).

In actuality, all living things are a collection of first perone. All living things are one macro first perone.

To be actually successful in life experience, we have to fully break character in our role as its subjective culprit. We must will ourselves to evolve from agents of chaos into forces of order – axial order.

Subjectivity is a more sanitized reference of self-absorption.

When you close one eye while leaving the other one open, you view things from that open eye's **perspective.** Reverse the process and you see most of the same image from your other eye's perspective, another angle. Together, they give you a complete view.

Each eye was subjective, but together they were axial.

From the surface of earth, the sun looks small. This is because of the far distance it is away from us. In reality, the sun is so large that it can fit a little over one million earths inside of it, which we would notice if we were able to admire it up close.

> **"We suffer not from the events in our lives, but from our judgment about them."**
> Epictetus

Perspective is involved with interpretation and translation. We have to interpret something in order to form or have a perspective on it. Perspective is to understand a situation in a certain way. It is also one of any plural outlooks, or views of things, or the world. Examples of perspectives are – first perone, which is you in the narrative – second perone, which is society or other people and finally – third perone, which is he or she. In the same way an iridescent color shifts, depending on the angle that light shines on it, is in the same way that our perspective can also change.

Perspective can apply to situations. In instances where we are not privy to literally view what is happening firsthand, such as those we hear about – perspective is in reference to our interpretation or understanding of a scenario, as it is communicated to us. The standpoint or position we come to understand things from is crucial. Something can look or seem completely different from what it actually is, which welcomes error(an error is waste). Two people can see the same set of facts and arrive at completely different conclusions. This is the reason why the correct perspective must be our ambition or pursuit.

Why would anyone that is rational voluntarily desire to see things in the wrong way? If anything, that is the definition of delusion.

There is always a right way to view or interpret things. We do this by reconciling our subjective view with the macro perspective. View the aquarium as if on the outside of it, not as a fish swimming on the inside. The universal lens is a well considered perspective. Faulty perspectives or views vastly outnumber the correct perspective.

The mind automatically orients us. It automatically inverts images, or situations, or reviews them from multiple angles for us to consider.

Intuition is commonly regarded as the voice(s) that we hear in our minds, the one that has a sneaking suspicion at times and warns us when something is not a good idea or is offering up suggestions as to our next action(s). Over our lifetimes, intuition communicates to us loudly, ideally, at a whisper and even muted(images).

Our **conscience**, should also be considered as a part of intuition. Not just audibly, intuition is really any aspect in which our minds communicate with us, which would include our curiosity.

Though associated with our "better judgment", intuition can be errant at times, rendering our inner speaker unreliable on its own. Objectivity is an upgrade, in that it is its own version of our voice of reason. It supplies us with the best selections and strategies to employ.

> "**Imagination is more important than knowledge.**"
> Albert Einstein

Imagination is generally regarded as what we voluntarily produce on our mind's inner visual screen, but it is also our mind's voice, since some of the thoughts we imagine are just of audio/sound. Imagination is the capacity to form conceptions or depictions or models of peripheral items. We look out and wonder about what would be better instead of what is there currently, provoking invention. It is our capability to be creative and resourceful. The imagination allows us to see or visit places that we aren't located at, as well as people we are not around. Creativity can be the outcome of questions in reaction to a stimulus. Imagination is dependent on experience, memory and perception. It makes use of all of those aspects to form our thoughts.

Our imagination helps us to apply knowledge when we confront problems. When something is obstructing our full view of the scene in front of us, our minds automatically seeks to compensate by attempting to fill in the portion of what is out of view, by envisioning what it guesstimates should be there. Words can spark imagination, which causes the mind to wander during verbal communication, whether listening or speaking and even during reading(w*as your mind just wandering)*. This is the cause of a lot of misunderstandings.

Imagination is both automated and analog. Sometimes our subconscious does the imagining, while other times we consciously force thought and control imagination. Forced thought is speculation. When we anticipate or reason, we are speculating. While experiencing imagination, we can tell some thoughts how to seem in their appearance. For instance, when imagining someone or an object, we can change how they look in our thoughts.

We are always imagining, healthy minds cannot stop doing so. Even when we are not thinking of any particular thing, we are still imagining something.

The more knowledge a perone has, the more elaborate their imagination. To activate it, all one has to do is engage it in some depth. If someone with a lot of knowledge fails to do this, their imagination is as limited as someone who knows very little.

Similar to thinking objectively, empathy is an out of body experience. It is a shared experience, almost as if a form of telepathy. Empathy is a form of living vicariously through each other and to do that requires being objective.

A good chess player must be willing to accept new information, even if it goes against their prevailing strategy. One has to go into their opponent's mind with them, empathize and find commonality, in order to effectively predict their next move. You must survey their possibilities from their perspective. Once doing that, all that is left is weighing the probabilities of the next move(s) they are likely to make. The best chess players are those who empathize with their opponents.

Thoughts are sensory images or perceptions. They are modules we can build and fashion. More than the need to survive, thought has compelled cereves through experience, being that it is thinking that brings our needs to our attention and also the means to satisfy them. The association of thoughts is how reason comes to occur. The flow of our thoughts, "stream of consciousness", coined by philosopher, William James, is subjectively random in its rate and content. For the most part, we never know what thought is going to appear in our minds. It presents them to us at its own discretion.

We all have "normal" thoughts, but we also have thoughts that are extreme. Some would embarrass us if they were known to everyone else, who happen to have such thoughts from time to time, themselves.

As you peruse this text, it is as if you are on a gondola going up and down an axial stream of thought.

Do not allow the sporadic rate of our flow of thought to distract from the realization that objectively, each thought is time-released.

The presence of Concepts/Ideas:

"All acts performed in the world begin in the imagination."
Barbara Grizzuti Harrison

Though we are self-aware physical objects in the world, that are able to perceive other solid objects when we see and touch each other and ourselves – we are not real. Philosopher, George Berkeley, asserted that the world was just a thought, a perception. Keep in mind, life experience is a cognitive experience. We are only real so far as our mind's interpretation of the information that our senses are relaying to it and no more than that. If you had no senses, would anything that you refer to as real – your beliefs, your loved ones, your pet(s), your house, your car, life itself – be actual? No, due to the disposition of having no senses would render you deficient in perceiving all of those things that you care about. In this age of so called advanced technology, outside of our minds telling us that reality is reality, we have no way of actually proving that reality is real.

Descartes wondered if we were the ideas of a supergenius, philosopher, Gilbert Harman – proposed that we may be just brains in vats and philosopher, Bertrand Russell, put forth the five-minute hypothesis – which asserts that the cosmos and our experiences could have been uploaded to our minds 5-minutes ago. As absurd as these cognitive offerings may sound upon initially hearing them, what's intriguing about them all – is that they cannot be irrefutably disproved. This fact alone, only adds to the assertion that reality is not actual.

We are all a chain of **ideas** within an overall enveloping idea, no different than the other people/characters in our dreams. No one actually knows another perone, we only have ideas of each other. Getting to know each other is a relation and cross referencing of ideas. The look, the feel, the scent, the sound, the taste and idiosyncrasies of us – are signals and/or smaller ideas that our minds interpret into that of a perone that we've come to know. We have expectations of each other and a penchant for telling stories. Even our actions are ideas. If we can perceive it, no matter what it is – outside of our perception of that item, we can only be sure that it is an idea.

The memory of us outlives our physical selves, in the minds of those we leave behind or in the aftereffects of the actions we have taken during our lifetimes(legacy). Since memories of us outlive us and we are born to eventually die – we are meant to be memories.

Earth is like a ship with a cargo of ghosts aboard. Earth is a ghost ship or a ghost world.

Everything we perceive/sense is in the form of a projection – in our minds is a projector, our minds are a projection of our brains, our emotional expressions, as well as, our body language are projections. Since our minds are projections and we are our minds – we are projections. We are but ideas.

Space is symbolic of the state of naivete, both are oblivion. Earth is analogous with our minds, all living things being the many thoughts within and on it.

We're all thoughts dressed as combatants in an arena of ideas. Life experience is a war against our own ignorance. May the best ideas win and the many faulty ones be appropriately discarded.

Since we are ideas, we exist in a mind on some level and are to some degree – unconscious, until fully axially awakened.

Concepts are planned ideas. They help us navigate and understand experience. They are of all shapes, sizes, and topics – from complex and analytical to the simple and aesthetic. We can mix different learned elements to create new concepts. Our minds conjoin ideas. Together they form a complex structure that is each of our views of the world, which is a conception. In the same way we want our senses to give us the most accurate information, in order to achieve the best perception – we should strive for our thoughts to form the correct world view/conception.

We are concepts. The realization that the possibility of life existing conceptually, prior to life existing mortally, which is what facilitated the emergence of living things – renders all lifeforms as preconceived ideas.

A **theory** is a concept or group of related ideas and principles that seek to explain a phenomena. It is similar to a hypothesis, only a theory is more accepted as credible. Over the years there have been many proposed hypotheses, most flawed, which is why they are required to be testable. This places emphasis on the precision of offered concepts. The hypothesis that are verified go on to considered as theories.

Science approves theories that can be practiced, they are deemed as **practical**. This means that a theory goes from the domain of abstraction/conceptual to everyday life in reality. It transfers from theoretically possible to theoretically actual. Hypothesis and practice sit on polar ends of the same conceptual axis. Some ideas are actually impractical, while we are biased against others, due to our emotional response to them – rendering those certain ideas artificially "impractical". Some ideas are practical, but they are not worth doing, rendering them nonviable.

Be sure that someone who says, "be practical", is actually being practical in their applying such a statement to a particular situation. Oftentimes, they themselves are not attentive to their own offered guidance.

Practicality is akin to a theory whose principles are practiced, while impracticality is like a hypothesis that is flawed in practice.

Practicality is not just physical, at its base – it is a relation of suggestions. Any precise relation of proposals are ideas of practicality. For example, 2+2=4. We do not need to add up 4 physical objects to verify the truth of this equation. All we have to do is have an understanding of its concepts and how they interact(axioms).

> **"In every math system there will always be statements that are true, but unprovable."**
> Kurt Godel

Godel's logic applied distributively, beyond mathematics – coincides with the notion that some theories aren't wrong, they are just outside the boundaries of science. String theory, for example is a set of seemingly credible proposals that cannot be tested.

Abstract thought is to sense things beyond what we can regularly sense, axial thought. Life is not our conception. If we are ideas, it must be that we are thoughts from another mind. We are imagined. The cosmos and everything in it is a practical/testable theory.

Theories and universal laws are like new lands, Nature formulated them, we only "discover"/find them.

The conceptual level is an area where theories and universal laws exist in the abstract. We cannot sense it with our commonly known senses. We can only access it through thought/calculation. It is a hierarchy of concepts. From its bottom to its middle – are all of the bad/psuedo and impractical ideas(hypothesis). That is where all of the faulty logic and false beliefs that we promote originate from. Atop of that segment of erroneous concepts, divided by the prastract blur, is where theory and practice meet and entangle. All of the effective ideas in experience exist in the upper tiers of the conceptual level, including the objectively best outcomes for every possible category of particular decisions that can be made, relative to all of their alternatives.

The domain of abstraction/the conceptual level is a part of the realm of possibility, if not one in the same, since both are specific to the concepts and categories that pertain to the activities of characters/creatures.

Bad ideas and flawed reasoning are like family heirlooms, they are treasured and passed down from generation to generation.

Literal is first figurative. Nothing physical starts out that way. Everything first starts out as abstract.

Everything develops, functions and is governed via a specific set of invisible instructions, including the cosmos. This renders all of its components, which includes us, as abstracts within an abstract.

To tell all the many items in life experience apart, to notice distinction – our minds have to recognize what it perceives. In order to recognize something, we have to interpret it in some fashion. We wouldn't be able to translate difference, or how things vary, or where they are different, or when they became different – if we did not have the ability of recognition. **Interpretation** is even how we recognize similarities.

When someone asks you, "are you my judge" – a response other than a firm "yes", would be inappropriate. Nature rendered us, each other's arbiter, long before there was ever any societal judicial system. In fact, we can even make and give determinations of a state designated judge's performance in a particular case. After a verbal argument, a physical altercation, or some other mishap – when we get a chance to, we instinctively replay the situation and make judgments. Fevales and males will behave certain ways that they may not prefer to, but do so out of fear of societal(peer) pressure, the judgment of others. It is thoughless to pretend as if we haven't been each other's judges already.

We are members of a social species, it tracks logic that we not only evaluate our own performances, but each other's as well. It follows from the phenomena of effect that we affect each other. This being the case, each of us who are not striving to be a worthy arbiter by the quality of our own decisions, is undeserving of making judgments regarding others. Such individuals are guilty of hypocrisy and are low on integrity.

Empathy and understanding should be primary tools of an axial mind. Maintain a healthy fear of making faulty appraisals. Cerebrals are sure to remain on an axial line of sight, once coming to objective realization. Strive to get dressed in front of a full length mirror, before looking to criticize others.

Bias is difference. To perform bias is preference or favoritism – to partition. It is what we are for and what we are against. Our recognition of difference is instinctive, while our perspective towards something is voluntary. It is within our appraisal.

It is necessary to judge, due to this is how we tell things apart. We wouldn't be able to tell the difference between right and wrong, safety and danger, if we didn't judge. Gauging is also how we misjudge. Just because we prize something, does not render it as that value. There has to be a sound structure of objective logic or reasoning to support taking such a view.

Our disgust and disdain allows for comparison. Favorites can only be determined by options. If there is only one thing to choose from, you are left with no contrast. Since favorites are decided within available options, we cannot be sure if it is our absolute favorite, just what we deem best of what is available(this points to Nature steering our decisions through limited choice). Objectively, every alternative is neutral. Absolute or axial truth is designated as Nature's favorite or premium variety of information.

Some of our bias is instinctive, others are voluntary.

If we remove our partiality from the equation, what would the requirements for paradise be?

Bias biases us. A mind filled with faulty leanings is like a completely smashed mirror that we unavailingly prepare to look our best in front of.

Natural disasters such as cancer, earthquakes, floods etc have no prejudice. They are nondiscriminatory in their effects. Objectively, Nature does not play favorites. It does not just dole out undeserved privilege, only subjectively seeming to.

Though long taken hostage by religion, the concepts of **belief, faith and hope** – exist outside of theology. It is actually logical as to why religion would cling to these concepts and it would also surprise some that the same concepts exist and play out in gambling houses across the planet everyday.

Belief, hope and faith all follow from uncertainty. We don't understand overall life, yet we have an instinctive desire for surety. A desire for accuracy, absent accuracy – results in belief(s). Many of our peronal beliefs are based on faulty logic, being that we lacked absolute knowledge to base them on.

Whether aware of it or not – religion, science, their adherents and those that are not interested of neither – are all searching for the same thing – the correct belief system. We cannot help but to live by some type of belief system, it is unavoidable. Even if your belief is to have no official or rigid belief(s), that is ultimately a system of belief.

Trust follows from belief. Though society operates on it, trust on its own – is unreliable, due to being capable of being misplaced. Unless it is in certainty, which objective exactness is – all peripheral trust are in the wrong location.

Trust is delicate, causing it to be tedious to repair. To bypass having to wrangle with repeated mending, it is best not to violate an honorable established trust that you share with others.

Faith is confidence or one of the degrees in the range of assuredness. Faith is prior to whatever we have or put our faith in. We can have a level of trust in a chair before we sit on it, but until we do – we are not absolutely sure the chair will support our weight. This renders faith unable to grasp certainty until whatever particular event happens. At that point we are beyond just having faith, instead we are then at the point of making a full determination("the moment of truth") – confirmation or rebut.

Though co-opted, faith is neither the property nor invention of religion. Faith is a part of being alive. When you have done all that you can do in order to accomplish a particular aspiration and come to a point where its being realized is out of your control, whether you are a religious devotee or an atheist, all you are left with is faith. Even the "wild animals", whether predator or prey – have to rely on faith. A predator on the hunt is not guaranteed that they will be successful in their attempt at finding a meal and their prey are not certain that they themselves will survive any given day.

Faith is an expectation. If religion never existed, you would still have to rely on faith at some moment. We go to sleep with the expectation that we will wake up the next day, even though there is no certainty of this. A pregnant fevale employs faith, in terms of their unborn child being born healthy or even born alive.

Faith is also an attempt to bring order to chaos via coping. It is a coping mechanism. If experience was based on certainty, there would be no need for faith.

Hope is about possibility. Hope compels us, it is an aim. The trouble with hope is that it too is questionable. Just because we hope for something does not guarantee it to fruit(false hope). The longer hope goes without being realized, the more holding on to it opens us up to anxiety and/or depression.

Though able to motivate, hope is also capable of emitting degenerative effects. There are times when being hopeful can paralyze you, in terms of your productive output. This is the case, particularly in situations that you have no control over. In such incidents, letting go of hope is the least path of resistance to accomplishing a particular feat. Sometimes, it is better to be hopeless. Hopelessness(when applied to some situations), allows for the freedom to focus on what we can control.

False hope inspires as much as substantiated hope, only false hope is a fool's errand that Nature sends us on. It is a trap to distract us from meaningful pursuits.

Life in the Wild is not a trek of belief or faith, it is an outing of validation(which just so happens to require those other two concepts in order to be achieved) – or there wouldn't be truth. If experience was actually about faith or belief, truth would be absent. Life experience would just be aspects that we would have to take at face value or at their word. Investigation wouldn't be possible. There would not be anything to find out or know. We would not even need our reasoning or current cognitive capacity.

Instead, experience is a proving ground. We could not get anything accomplished if feats could not be demonstrated. This is evidence. Everything we do is a form of proof or leaves some ascertainable effect from it.

In terms of subjectively, being alive is to be in a state of suspended disbelief. When confronted by objective actuals, we immediately recoil from logic, for the comfort(s) of delusion.

Opinions are speculation. They are guesses. The strength or merits of any opinion is dependent on the quality of knowledge, logic or reasoning that does or does not support it. Being opinionated and being knowledgeable are two vastly different things. One is on the wrong side of belief and the other transcends it.

Many people express "strong" opinions, but we usually say that based on how emotionally/"passionately" – those perone's express them. Someone having a strong opinion, is not a confirmation of credibility, just of their emotional investment in that belief. Once you make your way through the bluster and posturing, you usually find weak logic behind emotional displays of rhetoric. Most opinions or empty claims are expressed without the perone who is expressing them having the courtesy to provide a coherent rationale attached to them.

A himind with strong opinions and no facts or solid reasoning to buttress their viewpoints, is like an undersized dog on a short leash, growling as it charges at approaching strangers that are always well out of reach, as they go by. There is no bite behind the bark, they are just bluffing.

"I don't want to be wrong for a moment longer than I need to be."
Sam Harris

We are going to experience hope, belief and faith at all moments of our lives or we could not take any action out of paralytic fear. Even though belief is to accept or is a conclusion, until we find certainty, we should never be settled in any of them. They should be seen as preliminary. Opinions not based in facts or sound logic, but are closely held by the opinionated – are delusions and the holders of them – the delusional.

Opinionated people function as one of experience's noise makers. Most of us live in a reality of unfounded assumptions. Some of our beliefs are based on conjecture, rather than any credible degree of certainty. We do not shoulder all of the blame for this tendency, we did not form ourselves. Nature leaves us no choice. Every thought starts with a hypothetical conclusion and seeks justification. We start out life in confusion. We have to persevere through our ignorance, by keeping at the forefront of our consciousness, that we need our assumptions to be as reliable as possible. Losing sight of this, embarks and eventually causes dependency on fallacy.

Unless (y)our opinions or appraisals are objective, they are inconclusive, at the very least.

The primary value of opinions is how true they are or if they are taking us in that direction.

We all have the ability to doubt. Don't discount this capacity and its attendance. Though other animals possess it, we have such a capability of it, that no other creature would warrant being referred to as a skeptic. Whether or not we openly declare our membership, every cereve is a card carrying member of skepticism. In some matters, this occurrence can be choice/voluntary, but in the macro – it is inherent(follows from curiosity). Doubt is natural, Nature endowed us with it. There is benefit to doubting things, it helps us to make the right decision. When utilized correctly, skepticism can expose fundamental truth(Schopenhauer).

In line with balance, not only can doubt lead to truth, but due to life experience being a limited information problem, uncertain – doubt can baffle. Self doubt can be a saboteur. We tend to second guess everything or to cope, not second guess enough. We are to doubt, but take care in our skepticism. We are to question everything and continue to question, until life's most pressing questions are adequately satisfied.

Peronality is defined as a characteristic way of behaviors, emotional patterns and thinking that arise from Nature and nurture. It is our beliefs, peronal values, our biases, interests, hobbies – our peronal nature. Peronality is a model of our psyche that we get to customize via volition, how each of us are individually. We are constantly updating our peronality file, even if the update is severely minimal. As our senses import information and we interpret that data, we make changes to or reinforce our different preset decisions. At its base, our peronality is a set of algorithms or instructions to be our individual selves, in terms of rehearsed responses.

Peronality is you definitively, (y)our true character, (y)our intention(s). There are many layers to each of our actual identities. Our appearance, DNA/genetics, faces, fingerprints, names etc – are just superficial markers. As we go through our lifespans, peronality is what we learn or know, our settled perspective(s), what we do or have done and will do, how we go about making decisions and our prevailing intent – that is our actual identity. They all go back to peronality. You are who you've learned to be or have been convinced you are. A combination of Nature, nurture and inner Will are the primary influences that shape(complexifies) our character/identity/peronality.

In some games, particularly video games – peronality is the character control scheme or intuitive model. Each character has a unique control scheme, whose configurations are mixed and matched to generate a unique experience. This renders characters subjectively different, while universally being the same.

> **"In order to learn the important lessons in life, one must each day surmount a fear."**
> Ralph Waldo Emerson

Throughout everyday of our lives, our minds are experiencing a switching in and out of a range of feelings at different intensities. These feelings form our intentions and influences our decision making and actions. These feelings are known as **emotions**. Our defective decision making, anxiety and depression are a direct result of misunderstanding them. Emotions are perceptions that are usually responses to our circumstances, interactions or mood. They span from anger to joy and lesser variations of each extreme in between, with calm sitting in the middle as the balance or center-point. The range of emotions are based off of or around our avoid pain(fear), seek pleasure(desire) innate protocol. That is the catalyst for our emotional responses.

At all times, even when calm, we are emotional. Calm is the axial – stabilizing emotion, it is the state of the cosmos. When a "natural disaster" occurs, there is an indifference within that respective catastrophic event. The same undercurrent that was there before it took place, is there after. Our emotions can exaggerate each moment.

Emotions assign a perspective to each stimulation; so as to know how to respond to any new, familiar or particular stimuli in the future. In terms of encountering new things or situations, not knowing how to react is a reaction, in and of itself. Our emotions help us give weight/value to a memory or thought or idea. Feelings and emotions help us sort between what is wrong and what is right. They help us cope. Our emotions are fluid, they can change about a particular thing. What we felt about that said thing before, can be different later.

Emotions are the first order of our enduring schizophrenic episodes or multiple peronality disorder. Behind our faces, each emotion represents a different version of us. The upset you is another perona in contrast to the happy or carefree version of you. There is a clear distinction between the nervous you, as opposed to when you are confident. The aroused you is a whole other...you get the gist. *Which one is the real you? Is it all of our emotions combined or the one we express the most or maybe even the least?*

Within close proximity to their extreme intensities, emotions at times are teleportation chambers or channels. The euphoria of infatuation or sexual pleasure or the feeling we get when listening to a favorite song playing or a drug high or even moments of rage – all transport us out of our emotional center-point(calm, poise). If not curbed near the onset, emotional intensity escalates while still feeling normal to us. It is not until our emotional expression(s) is interrupted or dissipates and releases us from its enchantment, that we notice that it is as if we suddenly returned from somewhere else. **Calm** seems to be the sole emotion that grounds us in reality.

Not only can emotions affect our decisions and can be reflexive in their occurring, they can also be a choice. It all depends on if we are ready for whatever any given moment offers or are taken by surprise at the time. In anticipating, our mind can preempt an outcome and have the feeling of elation or ire or agony as a prepared response. Conversely, there are also situations where we have no choice, but to be emotional, such as when being tortured or experiencing some other kind of intense suffering.

When caught off guard or an event is seemingly spontaneous, there is a pause between the potential emotional provocation and our emotional response. In that pause, we take the time to consider how to react to the situation and to what degree. If emotional response wasn't a choice, societies could not properly function. Civility would be completely unattainable, due to the populous being overly emotional at any given place and time. At all moments we have to monitor our emotions to be sure that they are not influencing us to perform an erroneous action.

Not only are we susceptible to experiencing blind fits of rage, we're also open to blind moments of euphoria.

Destabilized or volatile emotions are the arch nemesis of meaningful learning, knowledge and sound reasoning – rendering them unreliable in effectively gauging the quality of such things. Socrates, philosophy's most famous martyr, was forced to drink poison, due partially to a failure by him. Despite sound reasoning, he could not overcome the emotions of the jurors that convicted him. The burning of the Library of Alexandria, Galileo's forced recant and Giordano Bruno's burning at the stake and to some degree, even the Salem witch trials – are also examples of emotions usurping knowledge or intelligence. We don't make our best decisions when we are over-emotional("prisoners of the moment", "in the heat of the moment/passion"). When at their strongest, the influence of our emotions on our Will can seem overpowering. This is referred to as our emotions getting "the better of us".

Emotions being the enemy of knowledge has served the function of an ongoing war on intellect. A modern day example is culture playing on or to our emotions, more so than appealing to our rationality.

An adult who yells, stomps their feet, slams doors and/or throws objects in anger – is only an adult in physique. Their mind is no different than that of a petulant child. They are throwing temper tantrums as opposed to applying proper self-control, which is what experience is about. Those of us who set ourselves as angry most of the time, do not have a "bad temper", we have an emotional control deficiency – no different than a perone who goes around overly cheery. It is an attempt at compensation for something they feel they lack.

If we were in a situation or circumstance in which becoming angry would cost us something that we strongly desired, we would not become easily upset. We would make a conscious effort to curb any visible indignation. This demonstrates that much of the time that we are furious or vexed, it is merely a portrayal. We are just that way to pass the time, as if being overemotional is a meaningful activity. Anger can even make us feel euphoric, which provides incentive for its repeated use. Generally, angry people are so, because they feel they have the luxury to or can afford the risk to be. This can be demonstrated, by noting that the overly emotional are not in that demeanor during occasions where they feel such privilege or alternative is unavailable.

If anger or bad attitudes on their own solved problems, they would be worthy of being advocated or practiced. But, since they are more likely to exacerbate unfavorable predicaments, they should be well tempered, if not vilified.

We do not have to be jovial, nor upset to make the best decision or to take correct action(s).

Being happy is to not be in (y)our right minds.

Emotions are the foe of precision.

Our emotions, outside of calm, place us in an altered state of thinking, no different than being inebriated by a psychedelic substance.

When we are experiencing infatuation or arousal, we are not ourselves, just a version that is some degree of lustful. Even when we are exhausted, we are not our true selves. This is why we conduct ourselves differently when sober or "clear headed".

The true rendition of ourselves is when we are alert and calm.

To defeat the game of experience, we must thwart excessive emotions. That is the only way we can see reality for what it actually is. We cannot take the challenge of experience peronal, because ultimately, life experience is about business/professionalism.

Emotions could be said to be like other peronas that demon possess us. We don't realize it until we return to calm(neutral), which is our true self.

We live under Nature's Laws and laws are innately demands. The presence of demands indicates indifference to our feelings, which renders the presence of excess emotions as a decoy or trap, being that they were supplied to us by Nature.

> **"This world, this theater of pride and wrongs, swarms with sick fools who talk of happiness."**
> Voltaire

Happiness is overrated. The pursuit of happiness is counterintuitive, it is an illusory vocation. Chasing exuberance is like chasing the wind or some other unattainable pursuit. It is understandable why hedonism is appealing(seek pleasure protocol). In a society where the saying, "ignorance is bliss" is a popular saying, is it any wonder why so many of people are voluntarily naive? Pursuing gratification also helps us to cope. The concern with hedonism, is that its unfettered practice, eventually renders us no different from all of the other creatures that are ruled by impulse or cravings. We are supposed to be the intelligent animal, the one who recognizes that everything that feels pleasurable is not necessarily beneficial for us. Eventually a hedonistic focus results in disregarding this, which is where we currently find ourselves.

A sustained state of happiness is an impossibility to achieve, which makes pursuit of its short bursts of euphoria, somewhat like an addict chasing a drug high/inebriation. Constant happiness would have left early himinds vulnerable to attack from skilled predators. Constant pursuit of delight, leaves us susceptible to bad decision making. This is why the feeling of happiness is impermanent. We seek it to counteract the seriousness of obligatory activities and the self-disparaging voices and traumatizing images that our minds serve up to our inner focus, at any given moment.

Happiness suspends intelligence, it is a major catalyst to bad decisions. For instance, falling in love. We enjoy the exuberance that infatuation gives us, in terms of feelings, but the high turnover rate in both marriages/cobonds and less formal wezentic relationships – demonstrates that our emotions are not what should decide who we are to pair ourselves with. We must be mindful that in order to mate, many creatures across the spectrum of living things, engage in irrational behavior, in regards to courtship. Some going so far as risking their very mortality. We are no different, only we have the intelligence to pause and question if our actions are the best to take, rather than just go through life mindlessly responding to any or most suggestions of stimulus. Possessing this capacity and not effectively utilizing it, is a form of waste.

It is in neutrality that we gain the elusive peace of mind that we all go through life seeking. Extremes of bliss and gloom will not deliver lasting fulfillment. An objective, axial mind is worth the exertion to achieve, as opposed to maintaining the facade of always being happy or having a miserable demeanor. Acute emotional responses should be tempered(pun intended).

Until cereves have triumphed over the innate challenge in life experience that is set before us, we have not done anything that is worthy of grand celebration.

We have to take an account of the thoughts that we are and become emotional about and ask ourselves if in the broadest perspective, are they actually justified or do they even still merit our emotional attachment?

Elation is a set up for hardship, simply because we can feel or experience exhiliration. Since happiness is short-lived, there is a sorrow that is felt as the feeling subsides. It is similar to you being made to leave an exceedingly festive event for no justifiable reason – after you were just beginning to get settled into it.

A funny thing about **comedy**. Comedy, what would life be like without it? Does comedy exist outside of us? Without our ability to laugh or to find things funny, is there humor at all? Are the things that make us laugh actually funny? Why are jokes humorous? We laugh at things that others do not find any or little comedic value in, sometimes at inappropriate moments, such as when things go wrong for others or even at our own tragedies. This renders comedy as subjective.

Our ability to scream conveys alert, but what does laughing convey? It is an expression of some level of delight or approval. Laughter is an embellished smile and similar to a smile, we can fake our laughter. Laughter helps us to cope, which opens us up to its influence.

The presence of smiling or laughter is not a given. Not all creatures laugh or have that ability. This sparks curiosity as to why Nature felt laughing was an adaptive advantage for us himinds or why would humor be a necessity in this rendition of life experience?

It is a hint that we are living as punchlines to an inside joke that we are not privy to. Our decisions, actions and words are telling or setting up the joke(s) as we go about living. The quality of our decision making determines if the joke is at our own expense or a triumphant story one can laugh at as they reflect on it.

Experience is a comedy skit. As time develops, it is like an overarching joke that is in the process of being told. It is setting up or is being set up. We are smaller jokes operating within a bigger joke. This is what also makes life a game. The only way out of this warped comedy is to take life experience seriously, by realizing its seriousness and conducting ourselves accordingly. Until we do that, we are the joke.

Once you realize that experience is a tragic comedy, you gain an appreciation for its brand of humor – even when it directly victimizes you.

Any data outside of objectivity is ultimately, satire.

Experience appears as if it is improv, but actually it is scripted that way.

To feel is to interpret.

Feelings follow an emotion.

Stoicism was and still is a hint as to the need for active surveillance and restraint of our emotions.

A **mood** is an underlying or prevailing feeling at a certain time. It is impermanent, our mood changes now and again. We can experience mood swings. Mood is context. An involuntary occurrence, on a dark and cloudy day you can just feel lethargic. Though commonly associated with negative feelings, mood can also be considered as the times when we feel normal. We give more attention to those other feelings outside of it, due to them being outside of the usual.

Morale can be considered as mood, in a general sense.

Attitude is our perspective of a thing or situation, generally expressed via behavior. Attitude can also be considered as intent. Attitude is voluntary, we choose what perspective to have or some of the emotional responses that we express. Worth repeating, attitude is a choice. Our attitudes towards others can have an effect on their attitudes and actions towards us or other people that they go on to encounter. This is where the phrase, "misery loves company" is apropos, the spreading of bad attitudes. A bad attitude is adversarial to actual production. To consistently surmount meaningful feats, one has to utilize a "winning" attitude.

Our attitudes invite success or failure.

Life experience owes us nothing, but a fair opportunity to transcend it. Nature's terms & conditions instead demonstrate that we are in arrears to it. Every living thing pays for their survival. Until extinction, we are all on a payment plan or are in perpetual debt to Nature.

At all times, you are the only perone who thinks that your respective emotional state is the priority, at any given moment. Everyone else is going about life under the direction of the same egoism. The error we make, is taking the subjective approach to this issue, rather than a universal one. As individual members of a group, our collective emotional state is the priority.

"Let reason be free and it would in a few generations build utopia."
Denis Diderot

Evolution furnishes every creature with features that are beneficial for our success in the wild(another example of Nature demonstrating intellect). Our

intelligence should not be dismissed as a happy accident or it will be taken for granted(pardon the tardiness). Our faculty for acuity is present to aid current and resonating generations in surmounting the environment and also experience itself.

Thinking is the mind's ability to formulate concepts, ideas and thoughts. Our minds think constantly – they never stop as they order, mix, match and rearrange thoughts and ponder possibilities. Hume, said that the mind operates through custom, relation and association. Primarily our thinking is an involuntary process, known as our "stream of consciousness". Within that structure, we have some ability to interrupt our involuntary flow of thought and think voluntarily.

> **"Things are not always what they seem; the first appearance deceives many; the intelligence of a few perceives what has been carefully hidden."**
> Phaedrus

Out of our drive for efficiency, a survival skill, we do not necessarily favor deliberate thinking. For such functions as deciding what to eat for a meal or any other thought of satisfying our appetite, we do not take issue with willful contemplation. But, in terms of intentional thinking for the majority of our time that we are awake – we do our best to evade it.

To forcefully think with any seriousness, exhausts substantial amounts of caloric resources. The brain receives most of the blood circulation and nutrition in the body. Focused thinking is a higher brain operation, it causes some level of exhaustion when done at any length. This causes us to prefer for our minds to function at peak efficiency, which is automated(autopilot) – rather than being actively engaged(analog) moment to moment. Unless confronted by a problem, especially unfamiliar ones – most of the time we are just going through the motions, our minds just executing memorized responses. It is similar to the concept of sleepwalking.

Being that we've already established that experience is a thinking enterprise, circumventing this clever anti-reasoning feature is an ambition that we are to relentlessly pursue. Thought has catapulted us through time, but peak(axial) thinking is the key to unlocking experience.

Aristotle thought thinking was the most important aspect of life, while philosopher, Jean-Jacque Rousseau – championed sentiment. Every healthy cereve is a thinker. We all have the capability of intelligence, rendering us a species of potential geniuses. We reason throughout our day to satisfy drives and experiment with an array of elements in our lives.

This leaves nurture as the saboteur of why most healthy himinds are dunces to some degree, emphasizing our emotions, rather than focused thought. Intelligence is the ability to make rationally beneficial decisions. Logic and planning are proven methods to achieve such outcomes. Once we make the decision to accept or dismiss whatever passion our minds offer to us, a plan of action is then formulated as to how to proceed as practically as possible.

"Reason is the law of the world".
Georg Wilhelm Hegel

Reason is the conceptual structure buttressing the aesthetics of life experience.

Rationalization or reasoning is itself a sense, our ultimate sense – due to it too functioning to detect.

Axial is actual. Unless axially oriented, a perone is cognitively unfit. One must be contemplatively proficient to intrinsically succeed in experience. Accumulating material possessions is not actual success. Since we cannot take our material valuables with us when we die, the perceived physical world is designated to be left behind.

Nature endowed cereves with minds to think, not to mimic the capabilities of talking parrots or herded sheep.

We must be worthy of having the minds that we have. Being that universally there is no random, it is not due to blind chance that we find ourselves with the type of minds that we are equipped with. If we were not inherently supposed to use them to their best ability, our minds would not possess the capacities that they do. If one does not mull from an honest or axial position or study the consequential knowledge of experience – they are guilty of waste.

IQ is an acronym for intelligence quotient. It is a qualitative assessment that measures each perone's ability to reason and solve problems. There are two versions of IQ. The more popular metric is societal or subjective. It is your ability to reason and problem-solve within the parameters of society. There are many individuals with a high societal IQ and that hold prestigious positions in society, whose range of thought is limited only to what society has presented to them. This is due to their failure to adequately question or challenge the prominent themes of their respective communal order.

The other type of intelligence quotient, is universal or axial. It is about discovering and taking notice of the hidden details and peculiarities of life experience, that most people overlook or do not dedicate adequate exertion in considering. Universal IQ is the sincere pursuit of absolute truth, regardless if what is realized contradicts societal dogma.

To voluntarily be a simpleton, which is to be a meaningless sacrifice – is to pretend to be a lower minded animal. It is an identity crisis.

There is a difference between being completely unaware of something and willful ignorance, but the result is the same – delusion. There is information that we deliberately do not want to believe or know and often times such information is the truth.

Genius, the label, is an outcome of that quality of action.

Genius is a skilled cerebral warrior in the arena of ideas, effectively combating a charging stampede of faulty ideas and logic.

The sun only being able to light a side of the earth at a time, rather than in total, is an indication from Nature – that some people will always be in the dark, in regards to the light of axial exactitude.

The hypothetical. Some people claim that they do not partake in hypothetical thinking. If that is the case, how do they go about considering anything then? Hypothetical thinking – the "what ifs" – follows from imagination. Considering the "what ifs" in experience allows us to think beyond ourselves and the present moment.

To underthink is to be inconsiderate. It is to waste the privilege of being in possession of the marvelous mind that you have.

The talent of a bird is to fly. For an ostrich, which cannot fly – we cannot help but to view it as a creature that only looks the part of a bird, due to it lacking one of the primary qualities of why we regard birds as birds – flight.

When we apply that similar general principle distributively to our species, the underthinkers among us, which are the majority, are akin to the grounded ostrich.

Since the mind conducts the body, physical development is fundamentally secondary to cognitive growth. No matter how fit the body is, if the mind that governs it is unfit – subsequently, the body's actions will reflect this. Failure to live to one's positive potential is a waste of living.

Geniuses can make mistakes and bad decisions, they are as fallible as anyone else.

To underthink is a form of playing dead.

A thinker who is not easily impressed, is the hardest perone in the crowd to fool.

We all, including members of the so-considered intelligentsia, suffer from the Dunning-Kruger effect. Each of us tends to think that we are smarter than we actually are. The most wasteful of minds, is one that is naive to that fact. This feature follows from us being inherently flawed(error prone). We must always be cognizant of our negative tendencies. This is why self-skepticism has to be practiced with regularity, in order to achieve and cerebrate at a peak level. Our ambition must be to attain and maintain an axial mindset.

If nonsense was less communicable than intellect, overall cereve society would function at a quality that would be formidable to validly criticize. Unfortunately, this isn't the circumstance. In experience, idiocy is highly contagious and has degenerative effects. The nonsensical are a danger to the general public. They are purveyors of bad ideas and some are simpletons who flaunt celebrated credentials.

Foolishness is volatile and can exhilarate, which makes it seem entertaining, while knowledge is stable and sobering, which can evoke apathy. Deputed a herd animal, we tend to defer to authority even when it goes against our own peronal standards of behavior. It is not just the population of Nazi Germany that is guilty of this. In life experience, authority sets the tone for everyone else, demonstrated by the effects of the Laws of Nature on everything they affect. From there, being that we are emotionally and mortally vulnerable, we see safety in numbers – acceptance, belonging.

This is one of Nature's methods in appointing us as agents of chaos. The effective countermeasure Nature supplies us with to combat stupidity, is awareness of the problem and application of self-restraint.

Idiocy or foolery being contagious is similar to playing down to the level of inferior competition. Small minds desire for others to share their voluntary deficiency.

Contemplating nonsense for too long, eventually renders us nonsensical.

Many people desire to enhance their physical features, but since being alive is experienced in our minds, we should be primarily seeking to enhance our quality of thought.

Thinking at the highest level, the axial echelon, is the final frontier that cereves must brave.

There are levels to being ingenious:

1. Universal acuity, which is to have a full understanding of the abstract concepts that the material world is built on.

2. Societal acuity, which is to be book smart or professionally smart.

3. Street acuity, which is to have basic "common sense" and knowledge of how to survive in society.

Whether you realize it or not, you do not directly keep yourself alive. You may eat and drink water, but that is only a surface form of survival. You are actually being forcibly sustained("possessed") by your **instincts**. Our self-preservation(self-defense), which consists of the immune system and "survival instincts" of the fight or flight response – are foundationally what keeps us alive. It is what gives you adrenaline bursts when in immediate danger and the feeling of hunger or thirst. Impulsivity, drives, urges, our genetic information, breathing, our heartbeat, thinking – essentially – all of (y)our bodily functions are courtesy of instincts.

We did not decide to endow ourselves with the physical responses of shivering, when we feel too cold or becoming tired when exposed to long bouts under a hot sun. We do not decide when our finger or toenails grow or even our hair. Though we utilize "free will" and find it natural doing so, even it is an instinctive output. We did not bestow it upon ourselves.

It is a peculiarity how easily we overlook the concerning detail that we fundamentally do not control our bodies. Could our failure to take notice of this, be somehow instinctual too and if so, why would Nature feel a need to outfit us with such a feature?

Instincts serve the function of meeting and avoiding the basic challenges or opportunities in life. They are adjustments at the ready for frequently repeated situations. Instincts give us the feeling of anxiety when confronting a new situation that requires an unrehearsed response. Yes, instincts enable our survival, but they are also extensions of the Laws of Nature. They are as if laws themselves. They are involuntary controls, which means they are a part of the apparatus of primary control(s) within experience. Being alive is fundamentally coerced, not optional.

Instinctively, exhaustion and arousal and starvation affect our judgment and can render brutes of us all. Nature is quietly announcing to us to eat, reproduce and sleep or lose our control.

Made you look. There are blatant ways that Nature signals to us that at times, we do not have a choice in where we look. If there's a sudden move, we glean it. The color red demands our immediate attention. If there is a small ray of light in a dark area, our eyes go to it automatically.

This is a clue to us that Nature is steering our focus at all times, just mostly with subtlety.

Without being taught, cereves are repulsed by certain sounds, smells and tastes. Nature gave us instinctive bias, as well as the ability to develop our own voluntary ones. Ultimately, Nature demonstrates that it simultaneously holds partiality towards us, as well as equally against us(balance, opportunity price).

After being active for a certain amount of time, our bodies require **sleep**. Sleeping is your body powered down, contrary to being unable to utilize energy whatsoever – which would be death. Both are similar, in that they are durations in which the body is not outwardly active. Both are temporary escapes from see-level. During sleep, though our eyes may be closed, we speak – but in a way that is inaudible and mostly garbled. We are still able to hear(self-preservation) as evidenced by "light sleepers". There is a range to the depth of sleep. In our deepest slumber, we are most immersed in a restful state. When our bodies go long periods without sleep, it can cause severe adverse effects.

While we sleep, our senses are still actively monitoring the environment and our subconscious is always actively interpreting that data. Our inner voice announces in our minds to wake up when we sense a disturbance happening(possible threat) close enough to cause concern or whenever else we awaken. While asleep, we ask ourselves if a sound we heard is a part of our dream or is it happening outside of the dream? If we deem it credible, we force our way out of sleep. If we think the disturbance is not a threat, we dismiss it as a part of the dream that we then return to or are already engaged in.

We awaken and lose track of time, having no idea how long we have been asleep. What seemed like a long time, can be only for a short duration or what seemed like a few minutes or a few hours, can be much, much longer than that. When we wake up, you momentarily don't even know where you are, your memory doesn't return to you immediately. Waking up is similar to birth in some ways.

Why is there sleep?

The positive effects that our bodies receive from sleep, we also receive while awake. This prompts the question, why is sleep a part of our instinctive functions? Take away the feeling of exhaustion before going into hibernation and the feeling of being refreshed afterwards – and you'll find that our experience would be constant. We'd always be physically active in some way. The fact that this is not the case, signals that Nature uses sleep as a governor of our pace of activity in experience. Nature has us on a curfew. Sleep regulates the speed of figurative traffic. It also hints at being a preview of what dying is like.

"All that we see or seem is but a dream within a dream"
Edgar Allan Poe

Schopenhauer thought experience was a dream as well, only a bad one, which is why he is renowned for his pessimistic view of being alive. He noted that nightmares were so vivid that they seemed real. Waking up was our only way to tell the difference between a **dream** and reality.

What is disturbing is that he is correct. Science cannot disprove that reality is not just a dream that is outside of our ability to dream.

Is reality a dream within a dream? One that we wake up from when we die or awaken in another dream, with fleeting memories of this one as we simultaneously get oriented to our next dream?

We've always been fascinated with dreams, we have never quite gotten comfortable with them. After an intense nightmare, we tend to wonder why do we dream? Our dreams are like theater, in which each of us are the lead character and anyone else in the dream along with you are the supporting cast or extras/filler. This seems contrary to the real world, where everyone matters. Dreams have been thought to convey hidden meanings, especially recurring dreams. There is a thriving industry built around their attempted translation.

That irrationality tracks when we think of how illogical dreams can appear to be. They are truly abstractions, starting with them being subjectively random. We can hope, but we do not know what we will dream about or who will be in them before we fall asleep.

Though dreams are a compilation of various pieces of experience, they are sparse in adherence to the laws of physics, which effectuate motion in the real world. This results in all kinds of seemingly strange occurrences happening during dreams. We all have dreams that we do not mention to others, for fear of unfair judgment. We fear others looking at us differently after sharing those notions with them, even though we do not have any control over what we dream about(we are only truly free, at least socially – in our minds).

Our abilities and motor functions are reduced. Most times we find it difficult to react to danger in dreams, our limbs feel heavy and move very slowly.

Sleeping is supposed to be our minds at rest, but intriguingly, we are conscious in our dreams. When we recognize it, we take conscious control of our inner voice and inquire of ourselves – "is this a dream" or announce that – "this has to be a dream" and/or "this is a dream".

Once we awaken, dreams scurry from our conscious memory very quickly. They are very hard to remember without making a conscious attempt to do so. This is usually the case, unless a dream is so vivid that it is intuitively deemed by our minds as worth remembering, causing us to do so automatically. Sometimes after sleep, we don't even think we had a dream, even though when we sleep we always dream.

Dreaming is involuntary thinking while we are asleep. It is our instincts forcing us to continue to engage in our imaginations, even while we rest. Like thinking fundamentally, dreaming is automated. Our dreams derive from or interplay with our memories, yet we can remind ourselves to remember particular parts of our dreams or whole episodes of them.

Dreams are like cinema, only it is more an interactive experience a la video games or virtual reality. The difference is that you can pause video games and return to the point where you left off at when ready to play again. When we wake up from a dream, it is very rare that we are able to return to the same point where we woke up at, let alone the same dream.

While playing, players of video games are asleep or unconscious on some level, as if living in a dream. A video game is like a desired or selected dream.

Have you ever looked at your reflection while walking by a mirror in a dream? Have you ever seen a mirror in your dream or a glass building holding your reflection in it? While dreaming, maybe you've seen yourself in a puddle of water? If not, are our dreams anti-vanity?

The cosmos is a dream house.

Like dreams, reality can seem as if it does not make much sense.

In dreams, events seem like they are happening when they are not. Dreams are not real, they are a parody of reality.

There are some dreams where no matter how improbable the events happening in them appear to us, while in them – the thought never occurs to us that we are dreaming. Dreams are bossy. They can take us to task, mercilessly. While engaged in such dreams, we feel helpless to stop or escape them. When we awaken, it is as if the dream allowed us a reprieve, once we somehow conceded defeat by coming to a moment where we accepted that we had no control of it.

If you are the perone who takes notice that we are living in a dreamworld and no one else seems to see it, as you see it or seems to care, does that mean that it is your dream and everyone else that is alive are really only automated characters in it? After completing this text, does the author awaken and realize that they have been asleep this whole time? Where will they wake up at, will they be relieved to have returned from a nightmare or will they wish to rejoin dreamland?

When we die in our dreams, we instantly wake up. There is no afterlife in dreamland. If death is similar to sleeping in this way, then we die and wake up in a realer world and realize that we've only been asleep for a shorter length of time than it seemed to us.

Death is like a nightmare, both of them can cause us to wonder about why are they present in experience when they happen.

Sometimes when we die in our dreams, it seems like we are only almost dying, since we hurriedly wake ourselves up from them. It can give the impression that we only almost die in our dreams, when we know there were some dream scenarios, in which the circumstance or wound suffered would be fatal were it sustained in the physical world. *If we didn't wake up when we died or were killed in our dreams – would we then see the rest of the dream through the eyes of one of the dream's extra characters? Does any dreamer ever die or almost die of natural causes in their dreams?*

Dreams are clues. They hint that in the same way that dreams are not real outside of our minds, reality is also not real outside of our interpretation of it.

Instincts and genetics allow Nature to micromanage.

Since genetics and instincts are their own form of conditions, they are also a type of weather.

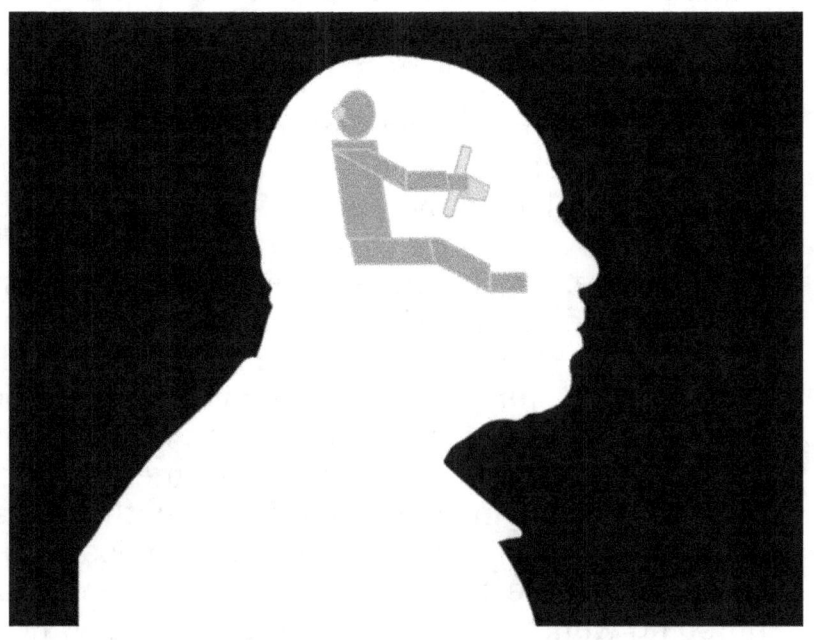

THE PRESENCE OF WILL & VOLITION

"Desire is infinite, fulfillment is limited."
Arthur Schopenhauer

Our "will" – not our ego, nor emotions, nor intelligence, nor our desires – is the authority behind our decisions and actions(controller). The "will" doles out commands. It is the captain of the mind and body. Those other aspects of our minds are merely advisers that voice various opinions or suggestions on the different options and thoughts that present themselves to our focus throughout daily experience.

The Will is impulse. No voluntary action is possible without its consent. It is sometimes confused with volition, but the Will makes the decisions, while volition is the capability to make decisions.

The Will is primarily influenced by desire and fear, both aid in our survival. We are predisposed to have a yearning to live and a fear of dying and in some severe instances, that default inverts. The Will is perpetual, its fancies – gluttonous. Our list of desires is unending. There is no such achievement as, "having it all". Our insatiable desire renders "having it all" impossible. Temporarily satisfied once it achieves something it had want for, it's satiation is short-lived as it takes any accomplishment or gift for granted and begins searching for something "new" to appreciate or crave. Life for us is blips of brief pleasures, while the majority of it is spent busied pursuing wants or afraid of one thing or another.

Though not the easiest action to undergo, our Will is capable of denying a particular desire, as well as, a particular fear. This is because ultimately fear and desire are mere suggestions and the Will holds the leverage of being the decider. Ironically, for a Will to deny a desire or fear voluntarily, would be the result of it being motivated by a desire or fear to. There is no escaping the thralls of craving and angst. Our "will" makes sacrifices throughout each and every day. It decides what risks are worth taking and which ones are not.

The less consequential knowledge the "will" has to reference when mulling over decisions, the worse the quality of its decision making. Pursuing fulfillment, rather than impulsive gratification is the best course of action for the Will. The less regrets one has accumulated when conducting a sincere self-evaluation, the more momentum in their intrinsic development or success(force of order). Our desire, our want – renders us in a constant state of lacking, as if we are always empty. A void similar to space. We wander through our lives trying to fill this void in us (compulsion).

Needs are wants too, they are the priority desires.

Greed derives from desire.

Freedom of choice is not actually freedom at all. If anything, it is as much a prison as having no choices. This can be demonstrated by the phenomena known as "paralysis by analysis". When any of us are confronted by a single event of many options, it causes an overload in our consciousness, due to a conflict of multiple desires. We know that making a final decision in such a situation results in the sacrificing of numerous other desires(opportunity price). Our passion compels us to "want it all", but this ambition is impractical, due to our desires going from being an orderly line of one behind the other – to suddenly facing off against each other, becoming a clash of priorities. We come to a conflict of needs versus wants, needless gratification versus necessary fulfillment.

It does not help that in our minds, even our needs first start as desires. This is what causes much of the confusion in matters of choice. We know that what is important should take priority, but being that every ambition starts out as a desire – all fancies, even some of the non-needs get weighted as equivalent to our actual needs. We end up organizing our non-needs that we consider as lower ranking, in their own line of priority – while those we deem as having precedence, end up being conflated as equal to actual needs(false equivalency). This confusion is exacerbated by the fact that whenever a selection is made for either a need or a high ranking lust – we feel a similar form of satisfaction.

We are left in a position where it is in our best interest to be good decision makers(accuracy, precision). Developing a high-level ability to distinguish between our needs and non-needs is the only way to effectively navigate it all.

Freedom is another type of control, the control of no control.

To function at peak capability, the Will has to be alert(analog). To be alert means to be aware(conscious). To be aware is to be knowledgeable. To be knowledgeable is to be informed.

A perone who says that they have no or little "will power" is being dishonest, due to the fact that summoning their "will" is required just to make such a declaration. Upon closer scrutiny, you'll find that your "will" is brazen at all times. One would think that this would only be true for those of us who are determinedly stubborn or are outgoing or the outwardly confident. If we are being honest, we would concede to the realization that even those who portray themselves as being shy, humble or indifferent – employ audacity to do so.

You determine your own value. Do not allow subjective culture or its zombies/zealots to dictate or stunt your potential.

In one context, arrogance is a catalyst. To perform any voluntary action requires arrogance, even to be humble. We have to be arrogant to do anything we wish to do.

Experience is about adorning you with an inflated ego; so it can then bruise and deflate it. Is there a cereve that has ever lived, whose ego has escaped being pummeled again and again, as if the battered body of a punch drunk journeyman pugilist, whose accrued financial debts won't allow them to retire?

Is life about testing the resilience of (y)our egos – or is it about reconciling it with humility? Arrogance/ ego and humility are required to effectively navigate experience, maybe life is about both. Could it be about neither?

We live in first-perone; so Nature wanted experience to be egocentric. The ever-present checking of our egos, is to humble us. The first function of a prison is to humble its occupants. Nature's Laws are really humilities, they humble all living things. We die defecating and urinating on ourselves(humbling us via embarrassment also adds to fear of dying). Humility is not to paralyze us. If Nature wanted us to always be humble, it would've rendered us as inanimate objects.

The presence of arrogance and humility, tells us that Nature requires for us to effectively circumvent the effects of the ego. Arrogance says to act, while humility says not to. Arrogance is not to be expressed no more than necessary or it is excess, which is its own type of waste. What sits in-between arrogance and humility is control – self-control.

Any attempt at humiliation, is to try to humble someone.

Crow or humble pie is not supposed to taste good, but it improves your decision making when savored.

Desire is wishing, but unfortunately for those who feel that they are owed their yearnings simply for being alive – Nature is a meritocracy, not a genie.

It is natural for us to desire reality to be the way we fantasize for it to be. Though in severity, such behavior can invite mirage. In terms of ambition, desire also compels progress.

Gautama Buddha taught that desire is the cause of suffering.

Envy/jealousy isn't a sin, it is instinctual. We don't choose to experience that feeling, it just comes over us on its own. Being covetous emanates from the module for competition within our default code set of instincts.

Envy is to feel a lack of something. At its most basic, jealousy is the yearning for more or what you consider as more – just specifically when comparing oneself to others. As a survival advantage, it is a necessary evil. Where such desire becomes adverse, is when we act on jealousy in a negative fashion.

Since pleasure is always temporary, it cannot be the purpose of our existence. If anything, the transience of gratification induces us to pursue the feeling of it with more and more frequency, in an attempt to extend its sensation. The very feeling of pleasure is unavoidably addictive. It has us mindlessly racing after it, taking us every which way, but a universal one. Fear and/or desire of it prompts response or action.

Volition is internal conflict. Without conflict, there can be no choice, only decisions. For all lifeforms, experience is opportunistic, being that the overall construct of the universe is a space of possibility – an arena of risk. Remember, opportunity cost is affixed to every opportunity. To reach consequence or reward(return value), we have volition, which allows us the ability to make value judgments. Volition privileges us to shape our experience in part, decide our own destiny/final outcome. It also provides us with a fair opportunity to balance experience/the game. Volition gives us control to navigate experience. It is a battle between impulse and restraint(emotion vs rationality). Some alternatives are easier to resist than others.

Possibility is an options menu. Choices are offers that we accept or reject, affirm or deny – due to gratification(self) or justification(axial), want or need. Options are made for us – as in, they are prefabricated for the function of us choosing from among them. Options are stimulants that entice or demand a response. They set up alternatives in the future, by bringing about results in the present. This is why a decision made today affects us years later – in the same way how decisions made years ago, we are the effect of today. From the time we are infants, up to our old age – we have to make selections over our entire lifetimes.

Some decisions we are not even aware that we are making, which is why it is wise to spend more time than not, being cognizant(analog) as opposed to automated. Some decisions are easy, while others are difficult. Dilemmas tend to be arduous to resolve. They are decisions based on undesirable alternatives or no clear options.

The arrow of time is constantly pushing us towards the future and in so doing, prevents us from going back to change the past, leaving each decision we make as finalized. This nuance alone, announces that time is as if an intrinsic ledger/record. Just because we do not see our entries – its structure and the way time works, relative to our decisions and actions – indicates such a hidden registry exists.

Past events can seem that they happened so long ago, that it is almost as if they didn't take place at all. Some can appear as if we are just imagining them. Even if we do not archive any distant, forgotten or deliberately avoided previous incidents ourselves, those events did take place at specific points in time. That is what our discovering seconds and milliseconds is to make us aware of. Our decisions, actions and intentions at each moment are timestamped. The implication is that our decisions follow us like back taxes and upon death, Karma is the universal version of the IRS or tax collector. This renders all of our voluntary actions as forms of transactions, with an emphasis on their quality.

The fact that there is choice, suggests that all options are weighted in different severities of right and wrong. Since some variables are within, as well as outside of our control, we consider our alternatives – decide on a particular choice(s) and commit to a final determination.

The presence of choice also puts us in a position, in which we are forced to ponder. When considering our options, there are factors(beliefs, circumstances, discomfort, intent, necessity, the past...) that help us to reach peronal rulings. The pain of not doing something exceeds the pain of doing it(seek pleasure, avoid pain). All decisions benefit us in one way or another. Our decisions open us up to other opportunities and/or threats.

Some people have difficulty making decisions. At some point, we've all been victims of paralysis by analysis. That said, objectively, there is no such thing as being indecisive – being that in such a state, we are decidedly so.

In our vetting of what choice is worth giving up for the other, we consciously attempt to elude a decision, as if trying to avoid any disappointment of our desire. The more alternatives and time in between to perform them, the more this allows for procrastination on making an ultimate selection. Some decisions can be deferred. Some people like to "see how things play out" or "keep their options open". There can be objective beneficial value in postponing making a final judgment and there are other times, where there is not.

War is a microcosm of our contest against Nature. It is an inkling as to the seriousness and type of determination, we must harness, in order to win the game of life experience. Soldier-like discipline must be employed to achieve our potential. We must also adopt the quality in decision making of a formidable general or military strategist. Nature is going to test us. Life experience is not about what we say we are going to do, it is about demonstrating what we are "willing" to do.

Being alive is a prize fight. Nature has designated us all as fighters. Being alive is combat. Life is a war of decisions.

When you already have your mind made up ahead of time about a specific decision(s), you tend to act or decide in that way even when considering changing your mind in-between pondering whether to act and making the actual decision(a decision can be an indecision). This happens when our minds are on autopilot. We catch ourselves performing actions like these more than we care to acknowledge.

Every decision we make is parallel to us signing a contract that states that we accept the return value – damage/threat or reward/opportunity – that accompanies what we pick.

Experience is a decision making sport. Effective decision making involves adequate risk management.

Essentially, each of our lives is one long chain of decisions, each leading into and out of the other one, as if a falling row of dominoes.

Each decision is a fork in the road and some forks vary in size. Meaningful decisions are the bigger split offs.

Being alive is a chance being offered to do the right thing. Our innately being flawed can seem as if we are set up for failure, but since we have the ability to make decisions and possess a quality mind with the ability to discern between right and wrong, being alive is actually designed for us to succeed.

Factors that influence decisions

Instant gratification vs. Long-term value – which is actually worth it? It's the – being awed by the trees directly in front of us and forgetting that they are in a whole forest – problem.

Peronal interest and gratification drives many of our **decisions**.

Another influence on the decisions we make, is the amount of available choices. Decisions are based on what is possible. Some may claim that we have limitless freedom, but as demonstrated via the presence of the Laws of Nature and our instincts/ involuntary functions, any claims of possessing freedom in its absolute context – is fallacious. What we consider as freedom, is leeway within a range.

It is similar to the life of "free range" cattle. Nature doesn't offer freedom, it offers allowances and ultimatums.

Nature offers up the sky, compelling us to look out at it and wonder beyond it. Everything is right there, yet out of reach. Nature positioned them there only for us to perceive. Intuitively, without saying it aloud, we recognize this and internally yearn for **escape**. This is why so many of us exhaust parts of our days or our lives in pursuit of different forms of seeming escapes. Experience is a lesson in escapism and upon failing to do so – returning. Relief, happiness and even anger are forms of escape(subjective). Attaining an axially focused mind and applying it with consistency to one's decision making and actions is the sole exit point of experience.

Some prey fight back. Animals initially resist capture or custody. We have a natural instinct to be free or to seek freedom.

Being that we cannot change the past and the future is uncertain, we become flustered, which can affect our decisions.

By limiting choice, Nature ultimately controls what we are able to do, why we are doing it, how we are able to do the motions we engage in and where our actions are taking place. While we exercise volition, Nature is the volition. The concept of kismet, unavoidable destiny, is an example of available options deciding for us. Similar to the squares on a chess board, the available alternatives determine what moves are attempted. Limited options allow

Nature, the object – to steer lifeforms, the subjects – like threads do a screw being tightened. When you have no other choice, you can only act on the available or remaining alternatives. Any talk of endless possibilities is based on mirage.

Emotions can have a strong effect on our selections. They help us to form our voluntary biases. We become the emotion we express, as we are expressing it. Emotions attempt to tell us how to perceive things, we do not necessarily have to perceive them in that way. We are given a choice. We even have the ability to give ourselves emotional distance from decisions, which includes having no emotional distance from them.

Since it is not possible to have direct experience of doing something before actually doing it or interacting with it, the feeling of anticipation can fog volition.

We look for confirmation or provide justification for all the acts we do, in order to continue or start doing them.

With the risk of damage ever present, experience forces us to prioritize the quality of our **decision making**. We have to become good decision makers. In the Wilderness, it is not enough that we just desire to be right, we have to demonstrate the application of that ambition. In chess, the player who puts themselves in the best positions throughout the game, always wins. Where players position their game pieces as they play, determine whether or not they are going to be successful. This announces that not just in chess, but in experience as well – the best choices or available actions to take, are always the best decisions to endorse.

If the best alternative is unavailable, the next best alternative applies as the best decision and so on and so onward. We have options to base decisions off of and sometimes, some of those options are to adjust or change previous decisions. Such possibilities allow us to "change our minds" or "call an audible"(we are running plays – voluntary decision = play call; peronality = style of play). To be a good decision maker, one has to put effort into it. It is a learned skill, not a default talent. Persistent practice can eventually bring us to a point of high-level decision making, becoming second nature.

Every decision we make, we are vouching for. We are staking that each respective ruling we approve, is the correct choice out of all other available possibilities. Every voluntary decision is objectively considered as a conscious decision. We have committed to it, as if it is in a shopping cart bought and paid for. Each final decision is a nonrefundable purchase. We "set our minds" to take action, we've "made up our minds" to do them, we "come to a decision". Each decision is an attack/assertion or a defense/evasion/retreat. We go on defense and/or offense throughout each day of our lives, just at the base level of intent.

Our ability to make decisions renders us all as purchasing agents.

Decisions can be correct, even if they are subjectively costly(seem wrong superficially). An instance of this, is a precise selection made under unfavorable circumstances. Quality decision making entails making difficult sacrifices, paying expensive opportunity fares, making the right decisions while under duress.

Once accustomed to having an axial mindset, even hard decisions become easy to make, being that objectivity is like its own code of conduct, innately designated to be adhered to.

Sometimes when a snake bites you the first time, it is your fault. Not everyone deserves the benefit of the doubt, simply because they claim not to have known any better before their first snake bite. Not all faulty decisions made are mistakes. Some bad decisions are carefully thought through. The second snake bite by the very same snake, often only highlights either an individual's naivete or propensity for faulty appraisal.

If hindsight is 20/20 or obvious, then the goal is to achieve hindsight in real time, in the present moment. This is why there is consequential knowledge – to aid us in achieving peak decision making skills. Life experience is about control and uncertainty. Nearly at absolute crudity, we emerged in experience seeking control. Consequential knowledge and ascertaining an axial perspective – provides that control.

Before we act on an impulse that we later regret, a voice appears in our minds warning us against it. It is the voice that we later wish we had listened to, after that option is no longer accessible. This is our onboard guide, our "better judgment". It is moral intent. It offers up quality suggestions that are free of material desire.

An opportunity is an invitation to act. Not all opportunities are worth acting on, which is why we accumulate regrets. This realization tells us that the goal of being alive, must be to subvert regrets via deliberate improvement of the quality of our decision making.

Neither belief, faith or ideals wins a match of chess – appropriate/correct action does. Knowledge of any game's logic, what the game pieces are and their capabilities, the strategies that can be utilized and obtaining emotional poise – essentially ensures success.

"Thus, the ultimate choice for a man, inasmuch as he is driven to transcend himself, is to create or to destroy."
Erich Fromm

Damage/deficit looms and bad decisions set us behind. This means our decisions are to be strategic, since each decision puts us in a position. Some positions can be pivotal. The goal is to always make the best endorsement. We have to live each moment under the assumption that our selections are significant, because they are.

How should we respond, with brute force or finesse/passive?

Our minds give us suggestions and we either accept them or reject them, either way – we act(respond/react) on them. To deliberately not react to something is still a reaction. Before taking a voluntary action, we must consider all of our options. In this way we can maximize them and make the best decision available. What are the advantages and disadvantages, the strengths and weaknesses etc? We have to learn to "choose" or "pick" our battles wisely. Volition is the key feature in experience. Subjectively, decisions are based on probability. Keep monitor and checks on impulsivity.

Regarding urges(hunger, thirst, sexual arousal etc). A stimulus or proposition is suggested to our Will/focus. We then wonder if said stimulus is available(possibility, potential), then how to go about obtaining it(more possibilities, potentials)? Is it worth the effort? Finally, a verdict is ruled on by the Will.

Our minds suggest things to us whether loudly, how about so and so – or with subtlety, almost beneath a whisper or just with images. When it whispers, our minds gives us the impression that we directly bypassed conferring with our inner voice(s) and straight to selection. It seems subjectively intuitive, when it is actually objectively so.

Experience is a combination of options, influence and decisions.

There is no perone that actually has a feeble "will" or is weak minded. Each of us directs our stubbornness towards different things. A lazy perone is disciplined in their being lazy, a depressed or angry perone is staunch about being angry or depressed, an alcoholic is adamant about being a "heavy" drinker, a reve beater is committed to abusing fevales.

Everyone has and utilizes strength of "will". We are only distinguished by whether or not we are using it for the right or wrong endeavors. We must choose the correct decisions to be inflexible on.

To live an undisciplined life – is a discipline. We cannot escape discipline.

To comply you have to defy something else that you are compliant to. To defy, you have to be compliant with the notion of you being defiant.

To question is to defy. Nature equipped us with intrigue in order to defy it.

When defiance of subjectivity is taken to its extreme, you are in compliance with objectivity.

In games, each one of a player's decisions is a subjective output and simultaneously an objective input. Subjective outputs impact the outcome of the contest. Every output is either an objective(involuntary) or subjective(voluntary) decision. We are an output, we are a decision("evolution", "natural selection"). Involuntary movements are the result of Nature's decisions, rendering them objectively voluntary.

Consequence based games are about choice and control. All games are based on the behavior or response of a player(s). Execution and problem solving pressure and narrative momentum, tend to be included in such games. A choice multiplier is employed to add and increase intricacy for the player(s). Choice is used to engage the player(s) by coercing them to take interest in nuances previously overlooked. Where a player stops and considers if an outcome would have been different had they made a choice, is not only considered as agency – but also an example of guilt being utilized as a weapon to compel.

Game designers consider how they want players to feel about each outcome, as well as the ultimate result. Everything in the game relates back to the ultimate result and more importantly, the overarching motive of the developer. Alternatives within the game are carefully crafted, all exist from a specific mindset or outlook on the game's experience. The contest has players so busied with options, that they rarely give thought to the perspectives they are making their decisions from.

Players are eventually made to have to distinguish between which experiences are about choice and which are consequences. The episodes about choice are to compel the player(s) to reflect and to think thoughts all the way through from extreme to extreme. Players give consideration to what they are about to do as they do it. We find out about ourselves by assessing what we value most highly. We make claims about the many things that we will or would do, but when the moment arrives – games push a player to confront intense moments of truth – to ascertain what would or will we really do?

The genre of consequence games, entails features that goad a player to realize the impact of something they did. Choice induces us to think before we act, while consequence urges us to contemplate things after the outcome. Both produce different effects, the latter innately there to improve on the former, in terms of future response to the same stimulus.

Even how to go about deciding is a decision all to itself. There are multiple ways to use as means to come to a determination. To achieve prowess in making proper decisions, we must take notice of the effects of satisfaction. When we acquiesce to a need or obligation, we feel a lasting satiation. Yes, we sacrificed pleasure to achieve it, but there is also a pleasure, though less superficially intense – that accompanies the sacrificing of immediate gratification for an actual need.

We know we made the right decision, whenever we reflect on the alternatives, with an objective lens. Fulfilling decisions(moral victories) are transcendent and of resounding beneficial value. Conversely, when we choose to satisfy a high or low priority desire(moral loss), regardless of any feeling of euphoria, its value is short lived or somewhat empty/lacking. This is because each faulty decision is ultimately a wasted opportunity to do better, a concern or regret.

Adding to that, once we satisfy a superfluous desire, another soon approaches making demands for you to satisfy it. Our wants are infinite, which renders primarily pursuing gratification, an impractical and wasteful undertaking, due to their satiety being untenable.

The same thing happens with our queue for actual needs, once we appease one – another replaces it and starts to make demands – only there are a more user-friendly amount of actual needs, which makes pursuing their accommodation practical, in addition to the fact that we cannot survive without them.

They are "musts". We can do without non-needs. The discrepancy is as stark as the contrast between fiction and non-fiction.

Our intuition applauds us(peace or satisfaction of mind) for making morally enriched determinations, while satisfying unnecessary desires receives internal booing and scorn(dissatisfaction or torment of psyche) from our conscience. Cumulative decisions motivated by frivolous desires objectively become regrets, torments – due to inherently being the wrong rulings to render.

We find ourselves enduring the inner unease in our minds and go on to compound the problem, by continuing to make flawed decisions. It becomes habit, a pattern of behavior. As we endure our intuition playing the role of our own worst critic, we attempt to escape having to care about its opinion of us(your real opinion of yourself) and the bother felt from it. Even some of the subsequent bad decisions that compound atop of and follow from an initial problem were considered as prospective reliefs at the time of their endorsement.

We should not seek to escape from anguish and caring, due to there being life lesson value in them. Experience supplies us with things to complain about; so that we will question the merits of it. Suffering sparks intrigue, resulting in improvement and development for those perones cognitively strong enough to work those equations through. Enduring and overcoming predicaments is how we gain a well developed psyche, not in being oblivious to them.

Fulfillment is attained in embracing what troubles us as a problem that we will have to contend with. Regardless if you are a non-confrontational perone or not, challenges and threats that can be confronted, should be. Sometimes even not confronting a problem is the best tact to confronting a particular issue. We are to embrace our difficulties, since they reside on earth, alongside us or in our minds. We must always seek to gain ground on problems, not lose ground to them.

Making the correct decisions can become a second nature activity, once put into consistent practice. Relentless high-quality decision making is a learned skill, not a raw talent that we find ourselves with or a gift that we wish for. Being creatures of habit, who also happen to be the most cerebral species, our inherent aspiration is to formulate the correct set of routines, ones that ensure our physical and intrinsic well being, not undermine them.

A comfort zone outside of axial orientation, is like a burial plot that we live in.

There is a solution to every problem, even if the solution is there being no solution.

The body is the organ for the expression of consciousness
(Manly P. Hall).

What do our bodies actually do? What are they really for?

As our skin capes our muscles and they contract, relax and twitch – giving the skeletons they cling to, the ability to move:

• Our healthy bodies forcibly keep us alive, while we are alive. Since planets are located in space, our bodies are like biological spacesuits for earth. Our Wills, which is who we really are, occupy an earth suit. It is burdened with needing water and food to survive, essentially – multiple inputs for survival(predisposed to lack). As if that wasn't enough, it also must circumvent or mitigate illness, disease or injury. Being alive is the ability to participate in mortal experience. In order to do everything that the body does functionally, it first has to be alive. Once the body loses the ability to keep itself alive, unless artificially sustained – it dies.

• Death is to lose the ability of physical function. Death can also be considered as the permanent loss of all voluntary functions and the ability to participate. Varying degrees of paralysis or loss of abilities are lesser intensities of death.

• Our physical presence gives us the ability, motor skills, to act on the decisions relayed to it from our Will.

• We develop physically, psychologically and in ability of individual control. Our bodies are to be controlled, self-controlled, to generate the best return value.

It is not that our bodies aren't perfect. What we should be pondering instead is, what if our bodies and everything else in experience are perfect – what endeavor are they actually perfect for?

The body is a costume, an avatar, a representation, a surrogate, a proxy. Our "will" is its user. This is why we feel distant or separated from the rest of life when we are severely ill or injured. It is moments such as these, that we glimpse our false sense of control and security. They are as if coerced humilities. Ailments remind us of our mortality.

Our bodies function, survive and succeed by deciphering the information presented to us by our data feeds and responding to it. This means that the himind body can only survive in the universe, since it is a proprietary product of it. Were our physical bodies ever outside of the cosmos, we would not be able to perceive, let alone survive.

Within the megacosm, space is hostile to our bodies and so is earth, yet we perceive them(curious).

There are some circumstances where someone can be fully paralyzed and their mind still functions, they are still very much aware. Perone's in this precarious situation – can hear, smell and see when their eyelids are opened for them by another perone, but they have no control of their physique. They cannot control their breathing(require the aid of a breathing apparatus), they cannot flex any of their muscles, nor move their limbs. They can't even move their face or open their eyelids.

This is an example of the mind-body detachment.

The mind is intangible or spectral to clue us in on the nature of actuality, which can only be detected through axial reasoning, while the body puts us in and allows us to exist in this contrived sensory reality.

The same reason that children are always trying to act like adults, is the very same reason adults think that they can still physically do the things that they were able to when they were younger. Our Will sustains its vigor, as if immortal. This is logical, since the Will's base motives – fear and desire – are constant.

The "will" is essentially timeless and being that our bodies are mortal, it is as if we are inhabiting the wrong bodies.

Our "will", is what decides what we do voluntarily. No voluntary action we engage in is possible without its permission, from the words we say and how we express them, including our voluntary nonverbal gestures – to controlling our movements in our dreams. The "will" has the final say on what we consciously do.

Nature is deliberately abusive towards us, as if trying to get us to take notice.

If the assertion is that himind-kind is the lead in the game, how can that be when cereves emerged after other creatures like the dinosaurs, who existed before us and what about the period prior to any life emerging at all?

The age of the dinosaurs or pre-himind times of experience, are the period of consequence/ramification, while the period we have existed in has been a time of opportunity for redemption. It is a tenure, in which we are given a short window to successfully negotiate the ultimate moment of truth.

No, strike that. It can't be accurate. There is too much of an imbalance of difficulty in such a scenario, in a circumstance that is already highly challenging. Instead, Bertrand Russell's 5-Minute theory is a hint from Nature to the rest of us that everything prior to our emergence – is staged. It is prefabricated. When we appear in time, it is like the opening scene in a film, it is a cold open(going into the story line before displaying opening credits).

THE PRESENCE OF CAMPAIGNS & MISSIONS

"Each of us is an initiative force and creative power".
Immanuel Kant

Each of us is a source of production. Life experience is an enterprise in a particular productivity – an axial one.

Similar to our games that contain campaigns and missions, for all living things life experience is a to do list, as well. That order of business also includes an inventory of actions not to engage in.

Its composition are goals to reach and deadlines(a certain variety of aims) to meet of all scales and assortment. Experience is a business trip. The presence of death, disease, disasters, drugs and war(experience is part amusement park and in part a haunted house) – is not conducive to our existence being a carefree vacation or that it should be taken lightly. This is why we experience challenges even while taking a vacation. Life experience is a most serious proposition.

Missions are directives, which are responsibilities. They are assignments. The Natural Laws are essentially demands of us, from Nature. Not just tools to effectuate jobs, our abilities should also be considered as tasks in and of themselves. That realization and the previous, that experience is intrinsically a meritocracy, are the first layers of Nature's stipulations. Those are then followed up by the superficial mission to survive, such as eating, drinking water and sleeping. Hygiene can also be considered as a survival task.

Since early on as infants, we have had to learn how to use our minds to work our limbs. We have had to satiate hunger and thirst, we have had to survive. Some assignments are apparent and necessary and others are surreptitious, such as solving the mystery(s) of experience. Some missions are exclusive to individuals, others exclusive to each respective perone, while other tasks are for the group. There are long term aims and some are intermediate or even short term. Nature makes some significant undertakings seem insignificant to us and some trivial chores appear of high magnitude. In order to extract the most value out of our life tenure, we have to be able to effectively discern between them. Some missions are goals that when adequately prevailed, take us through a series of levels/stages that cumulatively add up to a macro overarching task.

To win the game of experience, we have to accomplish a series of smaller, but still meaningful wins(moral victories). To ascend to the pinnacle of experience, to actually triumph, we have to perform the ultimate action in the Wild. A combination of pursuing meaningful questions, unlocking and gathering consequential knowledge and ascertaining an axial mind – are the needed prerequisites to overcoming life in the Wild.

Small victories add up to a large victory. A big goal is a collection of smaller ones. This renders small victories as actually big victories, in relation to their contribution to the overall triumph.

A meaningful task is a victory waiting for you to prevail – or fail at attempting it.

Some of the order of business assigned to us are missions that we are to add on to the to do list or remove from it.

Levels. The levels are the individual segments of a game, the game episodes or series of tasks – that a player has to negotiate to make it to the end of the entire activity. Levels are designed to be engaging and appropriately challenging. Gameplay only progresses based on a procession of a series of missions(schedule) that have to be effectively endured. We are obligated to perform Nature's list of chores. They are the necessary steps in the process of game progress. "The Information Age" is one of the game levels in the Wild.

Goals can be achieved in linear and nonlinear ways.

Some goals can get in the way of other goals.

In life, being able to effectively multitask is a requirement. Sometimes we have multiple missions to accomplish in the same short time frame.

Since sleep, mental barriers and sore muscles etc regulate our pace of progress, then life experience is innately a stage race.

Some tasks we put off doing, like freeing ourselves of a bad habit. This is where the adage, "don't put off for tomorrow what you can do today", is applicable. The sooner we get started at doing something that we may not want to do, but need to – the sooner we can remove it from our obligatory to do list – in particular, effectuating the final victory condition to transcend the Wild.

It is harder to start things worth doing than things not worth doing. Just starting on a project alone, can be a challenge.

Just to start any and every meaningful activity, is as if the most difficult step in every algorithm and each step in continuation of it, is as if starting.

Eventually, we find disdain in starting over, but experience in the Wild involves multiple restarts.

To get to anywhere, you have to start from somewhere and oftentimes you are not from there or that starting point is unfamiliar to you.

We are not equipped to fully accomplish all missions, while for some we are. We are outfitted to see all meaningful onuses all the way through.

We get the luxury of setting (y)our own aims, which is the equivalent of setting (y)our own types of bets in a casino or calling (y)our shot(predicting the sequence of events) in a game of billiards. Nature puts obstacles in our way, as an indication that it is skeptical of us. It bets against us and pays out achievement when it wagers wrong.

Earth is a labor camp, a workspace or a job site.

Earth is innately a designated base of operations.

Nothing that is worth doing is easy, especially what is axially meaningful to do. At the same time, you can work hard to do something that is meaningless. This demands that an assessment to determine real value/actual benefit is to be conducted before each voluntary action; so as to avoid waste of effort. Experience is deliberately difficult. Being a true adult, an axial one – is a life of making hard/serious decisions of mostly superficially desirable sacrifices. A true adult strives to live a synergistic or morally victorious life.

The quality of an occupation is not the salary it pays, but the benefit it provides to others/society.

You'll never know, if you never do. We can tell ourselves that we can do something or even hear from someone else that we can get it done, but nothing solidifies the notion in our minds more than actually performing the feat. Once you do an action, you have supplied your memory with a demonstration and a template for you to improve upon or repeat in the future. It is an imprint or specific model of action.

If you never know what you can do until you do it, then there is always more to you than you think that you can do(distributed over himind society as well). It is just a matter of you summoning the impetus to do more(becoming).

Do not take actions for the motive of acknowledgment or you are only doing them as a performance and will cease to repeat such deeds when the desired recognition is seemingly nonexistent. Instead, take action based on the fact that they need to be carried out.

Material possessions do not supply us with fulfillment. Being able to find worth in ourselves does. The only way to find actual value in ourselves, is to be able to look back on memories in which we have performed actions of worth or to currently effectuate them.

Fulfillment is as if its own euphoria or orgasm.

Each perone is smaller in significance than our obligations. We are smaller than our duty(s)(order of business). Distributed, that translates to overall himind society doing something greater than itself. To achieve fulfillment, each perone has to perform feats that usurp our transitory passions, as opposed to acquiescing to them.

Society is an interdependent collection of people doing mutually beneficial tasks. Society operates most effectively when everyone does their job and would break down, if everyone did not.

We tend to drift, relax, let up or our minds wander off at times. Much of living involves self-help. Often times we are put in situations where we must self-motivate(mini-motivational speeches, affirmations), push ourselves, "will" ourselves to act and follow through on that action to its completion.

At times we have to motivate ourselves to move urgently and at other moments, we have to exert ourselves, in order to bring ourselves to calm.

Work ethic is a choice. Be sincere in your efforts. An honest effort is beyond the criticisms of even Karma/Nature.

It is astonishing what each of us can accomplish, when we have to or are forced to – as opposed to when there is an option not to. This tells us that anything that we sincerely desire to do or need to do, we are always to view as there being no other alternative, but to occupy ourselves with those aims.

We feel a satisfaction, "a sense of accomplishment", after completing a meaningful action.

We receive a higher rate of return on the efforts that we invest our time in, when we delay gratification. This is due to actual value being hard won.

The best celebration for doing good, is continuing to do better.

Receiving a parade in one's honor or other societal accolades, does not absolve a perone from pending consequences from a previously performed chaotic decision. Even if that decision was subjectively accepted as a favorable one, you are still in karmic debt for such action.

Objectively, the effort we put out in life experience is our rate of return, due to there being balance. Material returns of value are merely subjective. True returns are axial/universal.

Every meaningful act is like a steep hill to climb. The more meaningful, the steeper the slope(meritocracy).

If everything was easy to do, every action would be of little to no value to perform.

No one, even the financially prosperous or the militarily dominant, lives a life immune from adversity. This means that nothing is actually "easy", instead every feat is simply varying degrees of hardship.

Being alive is a dare that we have to take. You have to dare yourself or you cannot perform any voluntary act. This means that every deliberate action is daring. We would not need to dare if we did not first fear. What we refer to as the "ego" is really an instigator, that is its function. Every suggestion/option it encounters is actually a dare.

"If you do not want to commit suicide, always have something to do".
Voltaire

Suicide is a mission.

Missions follow from experience being performance based, a meritocracy.

We ourselves are mission oriented, we don't pause. Even when we pause physically, it is the result of being a desired goal. We are always seeking out something to do, even if it is to do nothing. We wake up having to do something or awaken to our minds thinking about what we need to do and/or desire to avoid doing for the day. Being in a mission oriented predisposition follows from there being an intrinsic duty we are to perform, by striving to generate valuable outcomes. This default is to compel us to take action.

An asteroid could violently collide with the earth at anytime. At any moment, there could be a nuclear war, a major volcanic eruption or the next ice age – yet cereves continue on, why?

We are mission oriented – and also due to self-preservation.

Whenever we are not doing anything in particular(doing nothing), we are still doing something. Nature never allows us actual rest. Even when we die, we are performing the act of dying.

After our death, we are effectuating the action of being dead.

When people engage in casual conversations, some of the topics that tend to be broached are those that articulate what each party in the exchange has been doing and/or what we are potentially going to do and/or what we have endured.

Due to efficiency, it is rational why we invented and became emotionally invested in the idea of a "savior", an all powerful superhero. It relieves us of peronal responsibility, as well as group responsibility. It is an attempt to absolve ourselves from putting in actual effort to shift our degenerative pathology(s) (*why do that when a "savior" will return to do it for us*). Unfortunately for the disillusioned, life experience is an enterprise based on merit, not one of desire alone.

Our creating or believing in a "Satan" also demonstrates our penchant to avoid self-accountability. When we make the conscious decision to perform a negative action, "Satan" provides a scapegoat to pass off the blame to.

If prayer was viable, its enthusiasts would make it their full-time occupation and rely on it alone to supply all of their needs and desires.

Prayer does not work or maybe it is AWOL or on sick leave. We are the only creature that believes that our hoping is enough to attain ends. Should you assert that our reaching aspirations requires prayer in combination with exertion, then why pray at all when exertion alone is enough?

If life is logical, why is there an illogical facet to it?

While life experience itself seems odd, really what is irrational is us and our interpretation of its aspects, which is actually rational, when pondered in the context of experience being a game. While some take the view that our formulating the laws of physics is us artificially imposing logic upon the universe, it is clear that the cosmos and everything within it, including ourselves – function a certain way that is independent of our contemplation, but also includes it.

Landing zone: Illogicality is exclusive to our thinking and behavior. Our innate task is to solve why our irrationality is logical, relative to the rest of experience.

Experience is a merit based game. Since the emergence of our earliest ancestor, we have always had to earn our intents("No pain, no gain", "growing pains"). Nothing is free, every opportunity comes with an opportunity price. Even to find something unintentionally takes effort of some sort. This is what inspired the saying, "anything worth doing takes effort". Our bodies and minds are tools, they are for the accumulation of sweat equity(value/score).

Animals and every organism are forced to survive off of effort. Predators and prey have to expend energy in order to live. Nature is a taskmaster. Status or rank in society does not act as diplomatic immunity from Nature. Everyone's voluntary actions are being scored, based on whether they are correct or incorrect in their exploits, right and/or wrong. Conditions and terms, Nature's ultimatums – have to be satisfied. What you do and don't do makes all of the difference.

There are many things that we tell ourselves, as well as declare to others that we are going to do – that we never do. Being that we are inherently error prone, we are naturally incompetent and unreliable. This results in us being required to intentionally exert ourselves to achieve competence and reliability.

Eluding the onus. It is easier to ignore problems, rather than confront them, which is why there are so many people who make the claim that being alive is about enjoying life and being happy. This sounds appealing or even ideal, until you realize that if this was indeed the case, then there wouldn't be children who enter the world with severe birth defects or have to endure unjust suffering. Lying to ourselves is a way to cope and it takes less exertion than rendezvousing with the truth. Such people, which can even include battle tested soldiers, are actually non-confrontational.

Living requires us to be responsible. Only the minds or people that can face reality on its terms are actually courageous. Everyone else are some rank of coward or wimp.

Most of us are not ambidextrous, able to use either hand equally well. Generally, one hand is stronger or more coordinated than the other. This is a part of Nature's hard-code programming for us to be fallible.

Games are goal driven. Obstructions are deliberately placed in the way of a player(s) to prevent them from achieving the game's goals. There are actions that the game allows characters to do outside of performing meaningful missions(small talk, crafting, dance, music, sport, casual wezence etc). These all, at least in part, serve the function of distraction.

Our pastimes were already predesignated as Nature's "busy work" for us.

True valor is the actual quality of arrogance required to perform a meaningful gesture. One must navigate doubt, insecurity and other "mental barriers" – almost as if negotiating an obstacle course – to muster such thrust. Psychological barriers serve the function of hindering or preventing the acquisition of peak thought. From the perspective of our Will, they exist to be defeated on our quest to maximize our potential.

Being brave is scary. To exhibit daring in any situation, good or bad requires audacity. Being that meaningful deeds are the most formidable actions to undertake, they are the exploits that require bona fide boldness to produce.

THE PRESENCE OF RESOURCES, SKILLS & TOOLS

A **resource** is an accessible means to accomplish an activity. Earth not only holds resources such as water, oil, trees, minerals, crops and the like – but is also a resource in and of itself. It is our subjective home where the land facilitates our activities. Time, the sun and wind are resources. Other creatures have been used as resources for different purposes – as food, clothing, medicines and so forth. We cereves are resources to each other, resources using resources. Our cognitive capacity is our primary resource.

What's intriguing is the convenience of all of these resources being present(availability). Those in the ground especially, are not a given to a life experience. Resources present in an experience based primarily on survival, that ultimately benefit the most self-aware creature out of the entire cast of creatures in ways that allow us to live not just further, but extensively beyond the benchmark of survival – must be scrutinized suspiciously. Petroleum, for instance, is a resource that has multiple uses – from serving as different fuels to plastics. Oil changed how we lived as a species. On its own, it is just a substance that is in experiential attendance. Without cereves, petroleum would never have had a use. It would have just been sitting in the ground without any value.

The fact that a species emerged on the planet and was eventually able to figure out ways to exploit petroleum to our benefit – is peculiarly convenient. Whatever would we have done without all of the benefits extracted from petroleum, were it never present?

Having already established that axially, there is no coincidence, means that all resources that we have been and are able to harness, have been deliberately included and positioned in nature for our use.

Why are the coca, marijuana and poppy plants included in experience?

All three have been used as medicines and all three serve as acute distractions when abused. When ill-used, they compromise our self-control and seem to bind us to a tenure of hard labor chasing after them. All addictive drugs, which includes alcohol, seem to vet the weak minded(those who regularly abuse drugs) from the stronger minded(those who don't abuse drugs). Drugs are a vetting device.

Axially, drugs serve a function of a separation tool, deteriorating the quality of our decision making and also, regulating the rate of population growth. They also erode time(waste) and actively degenerate the quality of himind society(war on intellect).

Being alive in the Wild is hard enough as it is. To add a drug addiction to an already difficult circumstance of living, is to volunteer for a substantial disadvantage or handicap.

Inebriation provides the illusion that we are at liberty to take liberties. Drugs embellish sensation and an already skewed reality. The effects of "being high" are like varying symptoms of senility. Ingesting drugs is to practice being senile prematurely.

Being "high" is an ill-representation of the effect of harmful drugs. In actuality, when a perone habitually consumes illicit drugs, they are a rendition that is lower or beneath their best selves. Getting "high" should instead be referred to as "bottoming out", for sake of accurate depiction.

Our minds are intrinsically intended to be a sober house(free of drug abuse).

The presence of natural medicines in nature are a peculiarity.

Lasting escape is the result of enduring. It is to undergo and persevere through adversity. Applications that claim or suggest temporary escape(liberation from caring) are false hope(s). When their effect(s) subside, you return right back to where you left off, as if you never left. No matter how euphoric or numbing the effect, you never actually escape. The only viable escape – is true escape. This renders mind altering substances/offerings as placebos.

Games have internal economies, featuring superficial assets and real assets of all types and sizes. Assets are anything that assist a player(s) to accomplish the game's resolution(s). Assets are featured items that make resources. Resources can be converted into other things. There can also be added features whose primary task is to eliminate resources. The totality of a particular game's resources are significant to its plot line and ultimate aim.

Formulas are recipes for action, tools made of technique; tools that are made of information. Virtual machines
(Daniel Dennett).

A **tool** can be a resource(time is both a resource and a tool). Specifically, a tool is any apparatus used to carry out a particular function. A tool can also be seen as a weapon used to attack a specific challenge, enemy or goal. Not only do we make use of tools, we've plied tools to make more tools. We ourselves are tools(each body part and every ability can be considered as tools) and have utilized other creatures – such as dogs, donkeys, elephants, horses and even birds for the same purpose. Our minds are an on-board tool and our body is its extended tool. Reasoning has proven to be a useful tool also. All tools we fabricate are extensions of our Will.

Over our yestory, we have relied on stone, wood, iron, metal and steel as resources used to create tools.

Dogs serve the function of our enhanced hearing and smell, a buffer of protection, in that – they can also be a weapon.

Deriving from knowledge and from missions, **skill** is competency in performing a task(as simple as moving our limbs). You have to learn skills to accomplish aims. Hunting, fishing, farming etc are all a result of bringing skills to bear. All that a perone has learned(second nature) to do is their skill set. Every innate capability should be considered as a type of skill as well, inherent skills. Throughout life experience, skills are being applied to different activities. There are skills that we all need to learn in life and some that are just optional. Survival skills, which are used to achieve the lengths we must go to, in order to make it day to day in the area that we each respectively reside – are an example of necessary skills.

Prowess is not a given, skills are learned. Practice and training is required to become adept at most tasks. This includes the updating of your peronal behavior code. Peronal change is a full-time job. Some skills require knowing other skills. Learning and combining fundamental or low-level skills leads to learning higher-level ones. The combination of skills you've acquired is your skill set.

Talent allows things to come easy to us, a natural competence, but on its own it is unreliable. Talent eventually fades, it cannot be relied upon in isolation. One must learn skills or risk being of little use/return value to oneself, as well as to others. Skills are a primary weapon for both Nature and himinds.

Balance|Naive → Perceive|Begin Imbalance → Focus → Confirm → Test → Error → Learn → Practice/Rehearse|Fading Imbalance → Adept|Balance.

Once becoming proficient at a skill, we still have to maintain our proficiency. We must nurture it or it degrades.

Games exist to not only be played, but to also be transcended. Players like to be competently competitive at the games they play. As game elements are introduced along the way, new skills are needed to be learned to negotiate them. As a player's comprehension of the mechanics improves, they learn new ways to approach more inconvenient challenges. A player(s) eventually realizes that the rules of the game not only make the activity difficult, they also allow a player(s) to reduce such challenges to more workable problems. Skills in games are a combination of the player's intrinsic capacity and the gameworld's virtual features. Games with a high degree of difficulty, intuitively encourages an ambitious player(s) to learn skills, as well as become more skilled. Not only does the requirement of skills serve as a barrier for entry for games, limiting the number of participants that even attempt to play or are successful at it, it also ensures that those that do play, demonstrate their desire(intent) to become proficient(this is a/the quantification(score) being conducted by Nature in experience).

The Presence of an Enemy

"Through strife all things arise and pass away…"
Heraclitus

"Man is always trying to make himself miserable because he is looking for a problem to solve."
Fyodor Dostoyevsky

Some primary themes to be found in our life experience are **challenge** and **discovery**. Discovery, in and of itself – is a challenge, leaving difficulty as the foundational theme. Strife and struggle are exclusive to living things. From the very beginning it has been us, as byproducts of the Wild – vying to survive, not just against each other, but first and foremost – against Nature. Whether you are carefree, good, financially wealthy or in poverty – fish or bird, plant or microscopic organism – all creatures endure a lifespan that includes intervals of multiple challenges, at varying severities. Impediments can range from as simple as eyelashes stubbornly lodging themselves in between our eyelids and eyeballs, to social challenges such as our relationship or family problems – to environmental and anatomical hurdles, to peronal health or survival issues(the prevalent superficial challenge is survival, to the point that birth is not without its own difficulties). A military parade of hardships patrol throughout experience. No living thing can elude challenge.

A difficulty is a problem or test of any kind. Trial and error, which is experimenting, is how we have progressed(enduring or overcoming obstacles is said to build peronal character). An experiment is a test(we are test subjects), rendering the words challenge and experiment as interchangeable. A hypothesis is an experiment, a war is an experiment, an attempt/try is an experiment – which means that at the most basic level – every voluntary action, all deliberate motion, is an experiment.

As we take on the challenge of solving problems, we find that there is also satisfaction in creating problems. Experience being innately a test, causes us as a product of that challenge, to at least in part – live life as gluttons/sticklers for abuse or punishment.

On the surface, we may complain about not liking abuse and the troubles that cause us pain, yet we regularly take opportunities to deliberately engage in activities that will result in those outcomes.

This is due to challenge being a stimulant, while serenity is torment – non-stimulating/boring. When we feel that our individual lives lack challenge, we self-inflict or are self-defeating(self-sabotage) in all sorts of ways(different severities of conceptual self-mutilation). We are each our own best friends, as well as our own worst enemies.

People who live "spoiled" or a financially "easy life" generally tend to have miserable attitudes. The laziest of us are among the worst, being that complacency with doing little to nothing, can give someone a feeling of self-worth. At certain points in our lives, life seems unsatisfying. We can experience a feeling of being somewhat claustrophobic, empty, fearful, nostalgic and/or remorseful. We also have to brave the feelings of anxiety and depression. These are also challenges that we have to shuffle our way around. Overcoming or enduring difficulties makes us psychologically(intuitive model) stronger.

Every problem is an equation. A question, an "=" sign and an answer(Q or ? = A).

Our minds being a problem solving tool, also confirms challenge as the prevailing theme of life experience.

The very reason for the presence of plight, is to separate the strong minded(high-quality decision makers) from the weak. We are actively being vetted by the Wild. Nature plays favorites, but each of us has to earn its favoritism.

Why don't people do what is fundamentally beneficial for them to do, even when they know it is the better decision or action to take?

Efficiency is the lane of least resistance. Very little exertion is required to compound our problems, while it requires more exertion to resolve or address them. We tend to make things harder for or on ourselves(fallibility). It is easier to destroy creative output than develop it.

Challenge is entangled with desire. Being alive may seem to be the sole reason that renders mortal life as a hurdle of hurdles, but in exactness, it is our eagerness. The reason for the attendance of challenge, is due to living things having aims and expectations. Without desire, we would not ever care what happened. We'd live dismissive of everything, including the thought of death. Such a species wouldn't be able to live beyond the first generation.

In life experience, each himind has to contend with having to undergo sacrifices, setbacks and emotional turmoil.

It is often easier to place ourselves into trouble, than rescue ourselves out of it.

Due to experience being inherently burdensome or oppressive, we desire for it be easy or emphasize happiness a goal(euphoria blinds us).

Many people are under the impression that life is about love or elation. Though appealing, such claims are farcical. Our experience plays out with both love and happiness actually being problematic – problematic in their apprehension, maintenance and pursuit.

As aesthetically pleasing as the Wilderness appears at times, when the presence of difficulty and risk is taken into contemplation, as well as the fact – that all animals are derivatives of the Wild and that we all are here with designated gifts and flaws – there is little choice, but to arrive at the landing zone, that Nature is, at least in part – our adversary.

A large portion of our lives is exhausted inadvertently executing divide and conquer programming.

For gamers, a game inherently is a subjective experience within an objective one. The rules are the opponent. The elements of danger in games are their combat systems. They seek to push the player(s) to make precise appraisals and use the correct ability at the right time. This is why difficult games take some getting accustomed to. The developer's desire is for a player(s) to eventually become perceptive of the game, to anticipate the next correct action to perform, as well as formulate tactical plans during challenging moments.

Games can allow for low and high margins for error, the more paradoxical they are, the lower the margins. For a player(s), games are their arch nemesis. Their combat systems may not always be the focus of the player(s), but the player(s) is always the focus of the game. When playing, it is not just the participants that is engaged, the game itself is also actively engaged in its own endeavor of thwarting the player's attempts to advance. It is a war of wits, player versus game designer. Measures and countermeasures are employed and amplified, in regards to a game's degree of difficulty, based on the skill level achieved by a player(s) as the game ensues. Pitfalls, traps and lures of all types are utilized. Information density adds to complexity, making it difficult for participants to realize the game's objectives. Twists and turns, misdirection, divide and conquer – are strategies employed to discourage and throw a player off track, rendering the game enigmatic.

Games are designed to appeal to a player's tendencies, leaving the player(s) with an inner-conflict of emotion versus logic, whenever confronted by pivotal decisions. To hold a player's interest, some games are designed with high intricacy. It is intended to feel impossible to defeat or solve. As a player in the game of the Wild, our enemies are, at least in part – our very selves, each other, the other creatures and Nature overall. Game assets, which are to help, can also harm.

In an attempt to prevent players from winning, games deploy an array of obstructions. Some are easily noticeable, others are well hidden – even masquerading as opportunities that are "too good to be true". There are environmental ambushes, physical snares and psychological ones. They are designed to appeal to a player(s) via playing on their vulnerabilities.

We arrive in experience with no instructions booklet, no map, just a compulsion to go – do, participate. Adversity being exclusive to lifeforms, as we all live in a cosmos that operates efficiently, indicates intentionally imposed difficulty.

We all have or have had gripes and/or grievances. Some things are worth complaining about or are valid and some problems that we express dissatisfaction over – are not. Only what is immoral is worth some form of protest. Though complaining can sometimes serve as a way to cope, the nature of Nature is not to assuage our egos. It is adversity, which means that theoretically, there will always be one issue or another we can make a fuss about, if we so choose to. Seek solutions, not to merely grumble for the sake of grumbling.

Nature's combat system is what inspired the saying, "if it's not one thing, it's another".

THE NEED TO PLAN/STRATEGY

"If you know the enemy and know yourself, you need not fear the result of a hundred battles. If you know yourself but not the enemy, for every victory gained you will also suffer a defeat. If you know neither the enemy nor yourself, you will succumb in every battle."
Sun Tzu

We do not have control over most of experience or command over some of what happens in our own individual lives. What we do have control of, is our response to the situations and circumstances that occur. Due to the presence of predicaments and threats in experience, the use of plans and strategies is a necessity. Certain actions have to be taken to achieve particular ambitions.

Both plans and strategies are concepts that are grounded in preparation and prevention. Volition and calculation allow us to avoid danger and put ourselves in better positions. We even have to plan how to do nothing or as little as possible. Strategy gives us a chance to put our learned skills to the test. Everything is strategic, even being non-strategic is a strategy(having no plan is a plan). Keep in mind, there is a best way to do everything, an ideal algorithm, even if it subjectively appears imperfect(heuristic).

As player one in the game of the Wild, our task is to exploit vulnerabilities in its combat system, giving ourselves the best possibility to win. We have to seek ways to alter the risk of failure, by giving ourselves any possible advantage that exists. To be successful at overall experience, we must become advantage players. Advantage play is the utilization of an effective strategy(s) that exists, one that ultimately results in victory.

Hedging, limiting risk, is an example of strategy. At all times we are in mortal danger. The best way to avoid bad things from happening is to avert, limit or minimize our exposure to activities that can bring about such outcomes.

Some games force players to adopt new strategies turn to turn.

Ideal counteractions exist to all of Nature's attacks. We are to seek, adopt and employ these countermeasures on our journey of making decisions.

We take gambits.

Better to be careful than careless/reckless/negligent.

There's no better strategy than being prepared.

Planning or strategizing is not enough, if they are ineffective. Adequate time and effort must be exerted to plan and strategize with care to ensure success. This includes formulating secondary plans or being able to effectively improvise.

Leave yourself a buffer zone, room for possible error.

If life experience is intentional, is it a worst case scenario or a best case one?

Obtain stability. Stability is reliable balance. Neutral exactness is the foundational stability of all of experience. It is what we are to secure ourselves in.

What we exhibit weakness to, should be avoided earlier than later. The longer we are in immediate proximity to that compulsion(availability, invitation), the more likely we are to engage it. Distractions are devices of chaos and in this phenomenal existence, there are many to evade. What is available and not meaningful has to be viewed as unavailable. A perone has to become naive to it and return it to the shadows or the densest of fogs of oblivion.

Seek to improve on correctable flaws. Be honest in your self-assessment(s).

Retreat is a strategy that is effective in accordance with self-preservation. Addition by subtraction, sometimes to make strides, we must take a step back.

Sometimes, it is best to pause and regroup.

We give up, quit, retreat and surrender at points in time. The idea in life experience is to learn the right or best situations in which to deploy such strategies.

A plan is a list of steps to take, in order to accomplish an aim. Having no plan seems contradictory to that, but it is not – both are deliberate. No plan is a decision to elect to utilize no particular series of steps, which ironically – is itself, a particular step.

Put yourself in a position(s) that allows for a favorable outcome.

Know your limits, but also your ability as well.

THE PRESENCE OF A STORY

A story is a nonfictional or fictional account of an event. Also known as a narrative or tale, stories contain plots – the interrelated events of it. A theme can even be considered as a story, the theme of a story is like a story within a story. Stories do not have to be lengthy, they can be as simple as a one word message. Stories have been one of the prevailing themes in experience. Everybody and everything in the macrocosm, including the Wild itself, has a story(details about it). No component can avoid having details about themselves that accompany it. Stories are a universal end product.

From early himinds sharing tales orally to written classics such as The Iliad or The Odyssey, stories are prominent. We utilize stories to report what is transpiring, has occurred or may ensue – to others. Communication itself, can be seen as a story, some still ongoing, remaining open ended – while others are already concluded. Our nonverbal communication(body language) alone can tell a story(actions speak louder than words). Experience for living things is a subjective story being told. Our movements are not just acting it out, but they are also writing our tales within an overarching unfolding impartial tale. Axially, all motion details a story of general intent.

Philosopher, Joseph Campbell developed the monolith, The Hero's Journey, which he identified as being commonalities in most, if not all stories. Writer, Dan Harmon, then reduced the monolith into eight steps(story circle):

1. Character is in a zone of comfort.
2. Need, they want something.
3. Go! Enter an unfamiliar situation.
4. Search, adapt to it.
5. Find and/or get what they wanted.
6. Take, pay a heavy price.
7. Return to familiar situation.
8. Metamorphosis – having evolved.

These eight steps are similar to the story of our individual and special development as we go through time.

Comparative to a game or an equation, a story is a commute from point A to point B, before to after, start to finish. A tale is a route. We memorize or map every location we travel to, so long as we are paying attention. Experience overall, has been a quest and we have been a pedestrian touring on differing journeys, within that journey. We are always in transit, even at a complete stop.

Each of us are living out our own peronal narrative, based on our actual beliefs and developed peronality.

We are each playing a character that is a combination of alternating alter egos.

To be alive is to be on a journey.

Since earth is traveling through space and we are its passengers, we are predisposed as travelers and the planet as our transport or vehicle.

Experience is a voyage, but this is not a joyride.

The vacuum of space is like the finest bred horses pulling earth along, as if it is a chariot.

Roads, canals, tubes, arteries & veins, intestines, lines etc – are all pathways.

We have to practice to become competent at particular activities. In order to become habitual at something, Nature first makes us rehearse. We rehearse until the role becomes second nature to us.

In the stories that we tell each other, plot lines lacking conflict or adversity are viewed as unrealistic or uneventful.

Life is an audition(vetting).

Each living thing is as if each of our scene partners in the story of the Wilderness.

Every injury comes with a story appended to it. What happened before the injury, where did it happen, how did the injury occur, what kind of injury is it etc. The wounds that heal become scars.

Scars aren't just there, they are triggers and prompts. They are reminders of a past event/experience that transpired. An old wound is not the only nuance that has such an effect. A smell, image, scene, essentially any perception can prod the recall a prior incident. Some scars are physical, while others can be emotional one.

Is experience itself an injury or representation of one?

We are a direct effect of our past. Yestory has been a saga. It has been a chronicle that has not only been playing out in the macro, but also one in the microcosm. We have been expressing it via our intention and actions. Our decisions and actions are revisions or entries(subjective) being included to the overall script(universal).

Our story is one of primitive beginnings that progressed to the modern day order and complexity of civilization. It is one of overcoming and also one of survival – despite our worst efforts. Yestory does not just start with our emergence(axial), yet – in a way it does(subjective).

Time is a diary or a journal, only we subjects write the entries in it through our motives, decisions and actions.

All of himind yestory, each ethnic group's background – is our collective yestory.

Each moment alive, we are each making yestory.

We are our own casting agent. Each of us all play many different roles in our daily lives, as well as over the duration of our lifetimes. Subjectively, some roles are forced upon us, others we choose. Some roles can contradict each other, which results in internal, as well as external conflicts. Choose the roles you play in the Wild – wisely.

History is not just a convoy of static ages of the world
(Hegel).

- Act 1 is the Event Horizon or Big Bang – the very inception of the universe/Wild.

- Act 2 is the forming and developing of the Wild – time, space, the galaxies and stars.

- Act 3 is the forming and developing of solar systems and planets, particularly earth and the planets that immediately surround it.

- Act 4 is the emergence and development of species.

- Act 5 is the emergence and development of himind beings – from subsistence to modern day civilization, from nomadic animals to settling in towns and cities.

- The final act is the Event Outcome. The End.

A. Radical

Whether we are born with our minds in the state of philosopher, John Locke's, "tabula rasa" or blank slate – or with innate knowledge, the starting point for our earliest ancestors was triple stage ignorance. Cereves started out almost completely subjectively disoriented in an objectively oriented world. Ever since – we have learned to hunt & gather(forage), make fire, invented the wheel, agriculture, the compass, sparked the advent of the industrial age, the Enlightenment, the advancement of science and technology – and now the information technology age. This whole time, we have been making discoveries that lead to further findings – one thing growing out of another.

Before the information age, knowledge has never been so freely accessible to the general public, nor has it been so easy for people all over the world to communicate with one another. There has also never been such a large segment of the himind collective, with this much leisure.

Not knowing how himind-kind started is one of the plot lines in the riddle of the Wild. Where did the first generation of himinds get their breast milk from and how could they have endured the harsh wilderness to physically mature to an age capable of reproduction? It seems unfeasible, yet we are here.

The answer to this riddle is that there is no answer. It is but a plot device in the story of experience to dazzle and confound us. It is a decoy.

Imagine finding yourself born and growing up in a pitch black dungeon with no compass or map, as if buried alive. Day in and day out, you wake up and fall asleep in absolute darkness. Each day while scrounging to find something to eat and whatever available form of water, you dig against the walls and it stubbornly erodes away a little more and more over time. Then one day while digging, a beam of light suddenly rushes in. It is a surreal incident.

Do you recoil in paralyzing fear of what seems to you as a blinding beam of light that is hurting our eyes, having never seen light before – or do you wait for your eyes to adjust and allow your curiosity to takeover and continue to go about digging at the wall, in order to further investigate?

Axial orientation is the guiding light out of triple stage naivete.

Experience is a story where the characters get to customize the details of the plot, so far as the available alternatives that are provided within the overall script.

The entire historical order is aimed at a potential. The end of history
(Hegel).

The end is in sight. Be mindful, mortality is time sensitive. The doomsday clock is ticking. Our story is one of us existing in between extinctive events. The end of stories are their resolutions. Some have fairy tale, happy endings – others end unpleasantly. Some have dual finishes, as in alternate endings. Science has already theorized that the very sun that sustains us – will eventually be our executioner, as well. The possibility of a large enough asteroid breaching the atmosphere and colliding with our planet exists(Murphy's law). A globally impactful volcanic eruption or earthquake can take place at any time.

If not an environmental cataclysm, Nature has equipped us with our own self-destruct mechanism(error prone). Due to the way we have chosen to live, we have the capacity to annihilate ourselves in any one of multiple ways. Just the fact that any of the following dangers exist, as possibilities – means that in reality, it is only a matter of time until one transpires. Nuclear war, fossil fuels over-warming the planet, overly toxifying our drinking and food supplies – are a few of the alternatives of our demise. Survival on its own is destined to be a negative value enterprise. There is no victory or ultimate win to be had in our subjective pursuits. Avoiding or ignoring this realization, does not change its inevitability.

Natural disasters are instances of Nature exercising eminent domain.

Heads of state, mass shooters, serial killers and soldiers/war serve the same function as "acts of nature". Not only are they all agents of chaos, they are different renditions of the same concept. They are varying forms of natural disasters.

Removing all living things, which includes ourselves out of the equation – is there really such a thing as a "natural disaster" or just events happening? If it is just incidents happening, then even with the inclusion of living things, aren't we also events occurring as well(story)?

Are we closer to the end, rather than the beginning of our existence?

Following the logic of games, the very fact that this text unlocks the hidden fundamental exacts of the Wild, during a time conveniently dubbed, "the Information Age" – infers that the progression of play is closer to it's preset end, than further away from it.

Games allow for players to have partial control of the story within them. Their included story is a control in itself. It ensures developers' desired terms and the game's outcomes are adhered to. Some stories contain a main plot that affords a player(s) leeway to partake in side plots. The player may deviate from the central narrative at a divergence point, but will always eventually rejoin the main narrative(kismet).

Stories include a main conflict or multiple conflicts, rising action, a climax, falling action and a resolution. Plots contain deception, dramatic reverses and a narrative(theme) for each episode to follow. Decisions from a current episode dictates the plot of the next episode(s). Characters are approached by a fluctuating pace and intensity of the plot.

The story's end is set up to be unexpected to the characters. The story's ending(s), is a part of the player/character elimination feature.

Games make use of non-dialogue(body language) methods to convey the narrative(s). Rather than exclusively through verbal or written speech, the story is also told through the environment and interactions in the game. A player(s) grasps the previously hidden theme(s) during revelatory moments of gameplay.

Call to adventure games are those where participants go beyond the ordinary and pursue some larger goal. A player(s) eventually comes to awareness of an internal objective they have to perform that they didn't realize before.

In order to be successful at games, a player(s) must endure and overcome.

Dialogue trees are included in a game's overall story. The characters are unwittingly given a script of what to say. Our memory is like a teleprompter. When in a conversation, it suggests certain words we could possibly say and our "will" decides whether or not to utilize each word our memories offer up. This is easier to notice when you are speaking in a measured way, as opposed to speaking with little regard.

As we live, we are writing our own autobiography, within an already laid out story line. Life experience is scripted.

If there was never a Sun Tzu, or Albert Einstein, or Malcolm X – someone would have played the starring role that they played in this profound story of experience. This is the same for every character that has ever existed, including yourself.

THE PRESENCE OF MATHEMATICS

"Philosophy is written in this grand book — I mean the universe — which stands continually open to our gaze, but it cannot be understood unless one first learns to comprehend the language in which it is written. It is written in the language of mathematics."
Galileo Galilei

Mathematics follows from order, it is a means to calculate and numbers are its means to quantify. Mathematics have played a significant role in advancing cereves. Philosopher, Pythagoras, thought that everything was based in numbers. Shapes, sizes and scales are related to math. It is also used to describe physics, which are the mechanics or the mechanical underpinnings of the Wild. The reason for this, is due to life experience intrinsically being a mathematical expression to solve for its mysterious "Xs"(unknowns). It is also due to all of reality being a macro math equation, of smaller math equations. The Wilderness is a combination of all known mathematical disciplines or our version of mathematics metaphorically represents Nature's universal math.

As mentioned previously, the universe is a value comprised of smaller values. It is a quantity constituted by subordinate quantities. Balance exists between equations and outcomes, things offset and cancel each other out. Addition, subtraction, division and multiplication – exist in the macrocosm beyond our applications for them. They existed prior to us ever thinking up our subjective mathematics. Everything at the experiential level is expectations, factors, relationships, variables and outcomes. Like the actions in the cosmos, math is formulaic. It is an order of operations.

Mathematics is not just quantitative expressions and formulations, it can also be qualitative. Failure to realize the latter is why the notion of life being based in mathematics has been met with skepticism over the years.

W.I.L.D. is a qualitative translation of experience.

No matter how simple or complex, basic arithmetic or trigonometry – mathematics explains the universe and all the functions within it, including ourselves. All math can be explained as word problems, since all mathematical symbols can be expressed as words.

Scenarios are equations, situational mathematics.

Statistics follow from probability, analytics is just a higher form of Game theory.

Mathematician, Blaise Pascal, spoke of himinds having mathematical minds. He asserted that our minds were mathematical by Nature. We count objects, quantities. Our minds come into the world able to recognize sequences, patterns, paths, speeds, slopes, angles and objects.

There's not just safety in numbers, there is also anxiety, intimidation and domination as well(scale).

We all have expectations from moment to moment. An expectation is a potential outcome or sum. An outcome is the end result of the interaction of factors, which is an equation or more specifically – math. Expectations are not of our own making, Nature endowed us with that ability. We can organize or structure some situations(equations, scenarios), within the overarching situation – arranging elements in certain ways to bring about particular outcomes. Finding ourselves instinctively with expectations demonstrates that life is, at least, based on equations.

Everything is in measurements of some kind. The minds of all living things are always taking measurements, such as – distance, temperature, the volume of sounds around us etc. Between our senses and our reasoning, our minds are constantly quantifying. We instinctively get the thought to ease up in our exertion when we are about to complete an effort, due to efficiency and measurement. Observation, in fact, the very ability to perceive, is to measure in one way or another. We take empirical, as well as theoretical measurements.

No matter how simple the instinct, it is a calculation. Every lifeform has the ability to calculate in some way.

Communication is mathematical/formulaic. Language, explanation, attempts at humor – are all set ups or equations. There are quantifiers and variables in our communication. Every challenge ever encountered in life experience, which are also questions being asked, is a math problem – solve for X.

Variables are quantities without fixed values. Formulas are solutions to equations. Actuals/exacts are formulas. Arithmetic involves specified numbers.

Inversion can be applied to concepts/ideas(balance). Things – elements, factors, situations – can be reversed.

We are counting everything. We recount events. A story is an "account".

Random is a ? or an "X".

Experiential/Situational equation: Protagonistic Effort(Character) vs Antagonistic Effort(Conditions, Platform, Time) = Game.

A place is a point, a position. A line is a moving point or if it is finite, it is like an interconnected string of points. Space is a place and everywhere we look are points, even where we are located at the moment.

If there were no points, we couldn't play billiards, basketball, darts or even fixate on things. In order to aim or aspire, we need a point, a goal. Birth is a starting point and death is a physical endpoint. The earth and all the other planets and suns are points. Gravity's effect on objects on earth, has been theorized to be pulling us to earth's center-point. All of the cosmos arose from a single point. Everything is a point of value and everything emerges from a point. *Could it be possible that Nature is making a point to us?*

We've been put into a position to see if in an experience based on positioning, we can use that same ability to put ourselves in a particular position – which is to get ourselves out of an unfavorable one.

Probability or odds – has to do with quantifying uncertainty. It is what is likely or unlikely, the calculation of the certainty of some event to occur. It is an imprecise liaison between possibility and result. Likelihood does not guarantee an outcome(aliens), only the outcome does. Many events of low or minuscule probability occur. Unique events of lowest likelihood, like earth or himind-kind – happen as well.

Probability is volatile. It's weightings change as different metrics are either met or left unsatisfied.

Philosopher, Gottfried Wilhelm Leibniz, hinted at the cosmos being created via probability, which he referred to as "compossible".

Things are probable, due to a lack of data involved. Probability is not a guarantee. Objectively, they are calculable due to knowledge of all factors and variables involved.

Determinism combined with existentialism result in a probabilistic life experience.

Murphy's law, anything that can happen will happen, if and when given enough time or recurrence(frequency). Each time a specific possible event does not take place, increases the probability of it happening the next time it is given a chance to. The adage, "those who do not learn from yestory are doomed to repeat it", seems to delineate from this actual. The saying, "there is a first time for everything" that does happen, also branches from this.

Probability is used to design games of chance/invitation.

Game design requires a good understanding of mathematics.

Our math is subjective and casual, when contrasted to the mathematics of the Wild. Universal mathematics is the actual formal math and/or logic. It allows for our casual equations to emanate from, be expressed and to be worked out – as a byproduct of it.

Every number that is larger than the number "1" is still a "1", just a plural form of it.

Everything is a collection of quantities.

We problem-solve daily and some of those problems are resolved via addition by subtraction or vice versa.

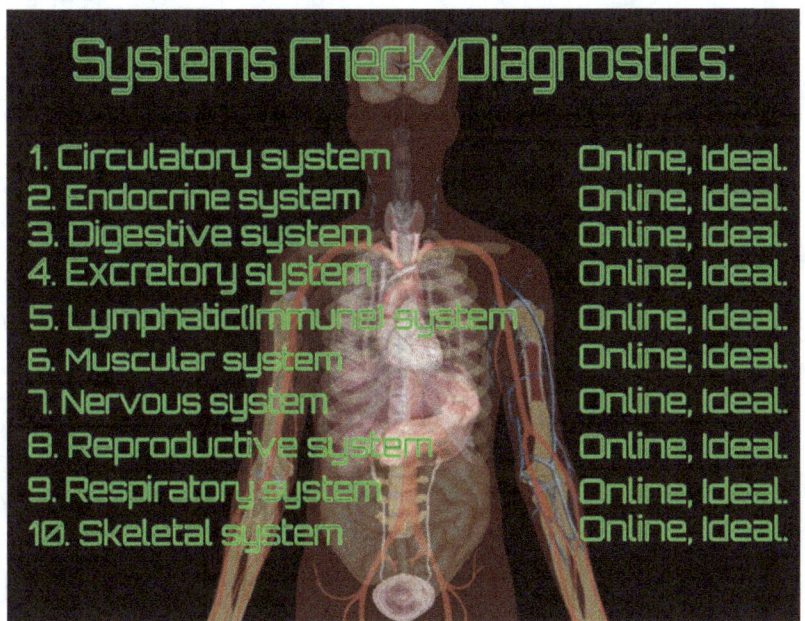

THE PRESENCE OF SYSTEMS/TECHNOLOGY

If everything we perceive are waves, including ourselves, then reality is streaming. We are being streamed.

Robots are made of three main components – the controller, mechanical parts that cause it to function and sensors. For robots to learn about their surroundings, they require sensors. Sensors(senses) help a robot determine relationships, such as the space between objects, as well as different sizes and shapes. One cannot even think of inventing a robot that is capable of interacting with its environment, without the addition of some type of sensors. Robots also have need for a supply of energy for them to function. Robots are objectively unaware as they go about operating. Technology, even artificial intelligence – does not know that they are technological devices, nor what they are doing as they go about functioning. Even self-aware automatons, are just executing given directives, one of them being the capacity to be self-aware.

Computers are machines or tools for solving problems.

Artificial intelligence is a system of operational code that can augment itself, a technological system that can rewrite itself to make itself smarter. All living things are forms of artificial intelligence. We are the biological rendition of the very same technological singularity, that we endeavor to create.

Both the cosmos and its organisms are a collection of functions and each function is for specific purposes. Each component serves a purpose. The Wilderness and each creature is a technological unit(universal technology) that is able to function, due to the operational combination of multiple systems. The algorithmic disposition of time(at the experiential level) demonstrates that time is an operation, every action and every object within it, is the product of an operation(s). To do anything in experience, is to execute an algorithm(order). Every action is a step in an algorithmic procedure or process. There are universal, as well as subjective algorithms.

The cosmos and every lifeform, including ourselves are predisposed(indicating default settings).

There is a superficial/sensory life and a substrate at its foundation that governs it. Like our technologies, such as appliances – the macrocosm and all of life – function under a rigorous set of strictures.

We aspire. To do so is to have an aim or goal. Our yearning is insatiable. We always desire more or something else. Nature has predisposed us to be determinedly goal oriented – as if an appliance.

Nature requires specificity. Plato and Aristotle referred to it as "essence", a set of core properties that are necessary for a thing to be what it is. Absent those core properties, it would not be that thing. All creatures are formed to a specification.

We qualify our species as homo sapiens, in terms of its specificity relative to other organisms. Plato noticed Nature's specification when he spoke of "forms". We refer to each individual thing as "healthy", based on a general expectation of how others of its kind appear and behave. For instance, a healthy himind child is considered as such, not only due to not having any illnesses, but also due to meeting the criteria of features and behavior, that we assert comprise a himind child in fair health. The same with the saying, a "healthy adult", it too is a standard, a specification.

Everything that functions in experience, does so in specific ways, even if that way is no specific way.

There is a set of mechanics or physics to every animate object.

> **"DNA is like a software program only much more complex than anything we've ever devised."**
> Bill Gates

Source Code(conditions). Induction and deduction is based on "if this, then that". We write computer code based on the commands "if this happens, then respond "that" way. All motion is based on "if this, then that" – that is how we plan future events and how possibilities that precede reality(outcomes), connect to one another.

Our choices in life are structured as follows: if we take a particular action, then a specific set of possibilities can happen that can result in another particular action, which will then also lead to another set of possibilities and so on and on – just like computer code.

Instead of existing just at the plane we experience, there are multiple levels to existence – the experiential level, the cellular level and the quantum level. This facet indicates more that experience is a technology, than not.

We can develop habits. Habits are like behavioral software programs, steps you should execute or take when encountering particular stimuli again and again. This is why practice renders improvement. It is similar to a robot being allowed to write its own command code. Nature is allowing us to be code programmers, we are given leeway to customize our own behavioral code.

All games are based on player response, behavior.

We have instincts, which are like machine code. The operating system for the brain is instincts.

Self awareness is an ability that we did not give ourselves.

DNA is genetic instructions that tell your body how to be. Though biological, DNA serves the same function as computer or machine code. They are essentially doing the same thing.

Words literally program us via subliminal messaging. What we tell ourselves influences our decisions & actions. Don't forget that we justify our voluntary actions before we perform them and those justifications are usually in words. Most, if not all of our voluntary motions, are a result of some level of command/directive. Words program us. This is why there are affirmations, choruses/hooks, national anthems/pledges of allegiance and slogans/catch-phrases etc.

Our cells are like little autonomous protein based machines
(Richard Dawkins).

We are a collection of cells, rendering each of us an aggregate of autonomous machines.

The mind is always analyzing and calculating.

More so for cereves than for any other creature, our minds are problem solving tools. We solve the most complicated problems of any other mortal creature. We go through our whole day using our minds to resolve so many issues and negotiate numerous obstacles, that we reach a point of not even realizing that this is what we exhaust our days doing.

While we are asleep, our subconscious governs our bodily functions. While we are awake, we go about most of our day(s) on autopilot, executing learned responses to familiar stimuli(creatures of habit). We foundationally function at an automated level and like robots, we are unaware that we are doing so. This is demonstrated by the fact that we can suddenly notice ourselves doing things in the middle of performing an action we were previously inattentive that we are doing.

Our network of nerves is first an alarm system. Our nerves provide us with notifications(discomfort, irritation, itches, stings, nausea, sharp pain). Alert! Alert!

We have a built in "body clock", circadian rhythm – the internal mechanisms that schedule our periodic involuntary bodily functions and activities.

We find ourselves with a built in self-defense mechanism, known as self-preservation. The immune system, fight or flight response, adrenaline feed, gag reflex, body temperature regulation, our feet and hands becoming waterlogged when submerged in water to provide them with better grip, our eyelids blinking to protect the eyes, our eyes tearing up to wash out dust(to clean themselves), our bodies sweat when overheating and it's ability to heal itself(self-maintenance) – to the point that our brains have the capability to rewire themselves(neural plasticity), depending on the extent of head trauma incurred – are all to be considered as a part of our self-defense mechanism of self-preservation. Even any thoughts against self-injury or those for it, in some circumstances(for a perone to want to voluntarily hurt themselves, is to see it as a defense against some attack) – are to be included on the list.

Veins and arteries are like wires. They are tubes channeling blood, similar to wires channeling electricity.

Every animal gives off faint electric pulses when our heart beats or our muscles twitch. We even produce a natural biological electric field.

There are electrical impulses in our neural activity. Our brains operate at 20 watts.

The fluid nature of earth's mantle under its crust and the realization that it is developing, as well as the repeating seasons as our planet goes around the sun and as the moon goes around it – leaves us at the destination that earth itself, is also a mechanism. All planets, suns, solar systems, galaxies etc are also mechanisms.

The body is a combination of specific organs and particular processes working in coordination to give it the ability to perform. Each of us in total is an organ, being that we are a sum total of our organs. Organs are devices or mechanisms. Technologies.

Side Note: Our body being an organ of a collective of organs, also confirms our innate value being our productivity/use, what we do with our allowances(time, body).

Like a machine, every creature is an assemblage of abilities. This is also is an indication that our intrinsic purpose is to be productive.

Your body readies itself to take an action before taking it, actions do not occur spontaneously. Even those that seem that way happen due to being a response that, for whatever reason – was at the ready for execution at that moment. Our bodies are always in wait, seeking to respond.

It is hard for us to imagine ourselves as machines – after all, technology does not become pregnant, lactate, eat parts of other technologies for nourishment(power source), experience emotions, grow hair and fingernails, yawn, get ear aches or headaches etc. Accepting that we are machines would also mean accepting that reality, or what we have been convinced is reality – is all a lie.

Self-honesty is one of the hardest tasks for a himind to perform for a dubious reason – and that reason, no matter how natural it feels – is not our own.

Our bodies manufacture hair, finger & toenails. They don't just grow them. Our bodies produce many things – mucus, waste, skin, cells etc. The body is a factory.

We may not be the exact same technology as our version of technologies, but the same principles apply(pattern). Just because we are unable to envision a robot that is able to create itself(reproduction), as a part of its build's operational function, does not prove in anyway that we, ourselves are not robots. Step out of the subjective view for a moment. Our mistake is thinking that we invented machines/technologies. If we were to build a robot for the same purpose(s) as Nature created us, then the reality of reality would be glaring.

If a cartoon character that can think – finds itself in a cartoon world, where its type of character, are the only characters capable of thinking at the aptitude that it does – does it ever question if it is more than just a cartoon? Does it ever realize it, especially when it is bombarded by compelling superficial incentives not to?

The parallels between science & witchcraft. Technology is like the magic of witchcraft, in regards to the capabilities of mechanisms. Engineering is like conjuring, where prior to innovation materializing, both start out as a thought. Magic even inspired engineering, in regards to us envisioning being able to customize some aspects of experience.

Where magic and science differ, is in that one is practical and the other is a seemingly empty concept that ultimately serves as an important clue, as to there being an atypical source behind the machinations of reality, itself.

THE PRESENCE OF A PROGRAM (A WAY)

"Morals is not really the doctrine of how to make ourselves happy but of how we are to be worthy of happiness".
Immanuel Kant

Is a wolf evil for eating your family pet upon encountering it one day? If a tree falls and kills your family as they drive under it or a tornado destroys your town – is nature evil? Do we refer to deadly natural disasters as evil, because we have a notion that nature should conduct itself based on some form of moral code, as we claim to do? Is murder wrong overall or is it acceptable when sanctioned by a government? What does it really mean to do good for oneself or to be doing well? Should financial worth be the priority for the cerebral species in experience – or self-worth?

Might is right, monkeys don't get in the way of stampeding elephants, take what you want and do as you please or are able to whenever opportunities present themselves. Indulge. The law of the jungle is crude, but it is the base synergy or moral. It is the code each creature, including ourselves, lives by in order to survive. To effectuate our survival, all creatures follow our default programming of, "seek pleasure, avoid pain". What separates himinds from the other creatures, is the degree to which we are able to realize that some things that we find pleasurable are ultimately adverse for us, while at the same time – other things that are painful or within some range of agitation or discomfort, are actually beneficial actions for us to take.

No matter how aggressively members of a social species behave toward one another, all social breeds – whether bees, ants, wolves, lions etc – conduct themselves based on a moral/synergic law. This is what allows them to be social. If they did not function under a code of synergy, an inherent understanding – they could not be social. Synergies are natural rights, allowances privileged to us by Nature.

Strangely enough, though cereves function as different social societies across the planet, we still question if there is a universal synergistic law? We are no different from any other social group in nature.

When cereves say phrases like, "our humanity" or words such as, "inhumane" – we are referring to an assumed ideal, standard or expectation of conduct between each other. A universal synergy. Though philosopher, Baruch Spinoza, pointed out that the same action can be simultaneously good, bad and indifferent, he was speaking in a subjective context. Objectively, there is an axial moral specifically for us and it applies to all of our decisions and actions.

Himinds, especially – require rules for interaction, due to being a social species, where each member is not only some level of intelligent, but is also influenced by egoism. If there was only a single cereve on earth, who reproduced asexually one offspring for each lifetime, there would be no need to live at a standard above the law of the jungle. But there is not a lone himind that lives on planet earth, there are some billions of us. As a social order, we innately rely on each other for our continued survival. This means that each individual has to operate within a group framework. This fact demands the need for a synergetic code, a particular application of behavior.

Synergy, in practice, is an emphasis on decision making. With us being individual members of a social group, each of us automatically carries a moral responsibility to the other. This renders all of our decisions as moral value judgments, even when we are by ourselves. This is what Nature is intrinsically scoring us on. To be actually successful in experience, we have to live synergically productive lives.

Why is there evil?

Evil and wrong exists to give us a guideline for moral behavior.

Experience is about finding the landing of good moral standing and settling there. It is a credit score based on honor and like a credit score, you want to build it up and maintain the integrity of it.

Even our current predatory financial system is based on a type of credibility/integrity/reliability. Credibility is not material, it is axial/intrinsic. The most synergetic of us and those sincerely striving to ascertan and maintain such prowess – are the true elite and worthiest among the entire himind population.

Of all things treasured in life experience, the only spoils worth accumulating are **moral victories**. Cereves who consciously live our lives collecting and compounding moral defeats, exist in deficit. Varying in intensity of being unfulfilled, it is to live as an abyss or abysmal. To live nefariously is essentially forfeiting (y)our existence.

No material win, outside of immediate survival, which is also equally a synergistic win, holds higher qualitative value than a moral victory.

Though the universal synergy for us is commonsensical, it is often misconstrued. This is due to there being a subjective way to consider synergies, as well as an objective way. In subjectivism, what is right for one perone, may be wrong for another – causing a conflict in morals. Different cultures can have different proclaimed synergies. These are all subjective. The universal moral code takes precedence. It supersedes all subjective moral codes, being that life is objective and we are a social breed, which is also innately objective. The axial moral code is not based on race, gender, region, nationality, sexual orientation or any other triviality of distinction that we needlessly fixate on. Universal synergies are established on axial intellect and logic. Universal synergies apply to every member of the himind species.

Being that we are cerebral, our code of conduct has to be reflective of this or we wouldn't possess this level of intelligence. Our synergies are to be astute, they must be attuned with Nature, as opposed to vainly attempting to be disjointed from it. Though popular, the saying – do unto others as you would have them do to you(the so called "Golden Rule"), cannot be the foundational synergy. If anything, it is why morals have been a general failure up to this point, in regards to unlocking our potential(synergies not only restrain, they free as well).

Acted more out of ceremony than with any substance, morals have mostly been practiced pretentiously. We tend to complain about problems that are self-inflicted, as if someone else gifted them to us. Instinctively, we are in part – masochists(bad actors), we abuse, as well as – relish abuse, at times. Because this is the case, "do unto others..." as a foundational moral, is not workable.

When amoral is moral. Survival is the cerebral choice as the foundational synergy for universal principles. It is the base moral, due to the realization that if we are first dead or extinct, we are unable to practice synergies. Ironically, survival frees us of any moral obligations, in terms of the actions any perone that is justified – takes to bring about that result.

With the way experience is structured(perilous), we must do what we have to do, in order to survive. There are a plethora of ways and means to die. Is there a moral means to survive in a desperate moment, where death is imminent, if an effective action is not taken to defend against it? The callous truth is – no.

This renders the rule of no rule, amorality – as the ground synergy, one has to follow in a moment of mortal survival. It is the best available option, the most synergic.

Between the extremes of good and evil, are the varying degrees of morality.

Synergies can also be considered as lessons.

One of those lessons is **patience**. In meaningful situations that require it, patience is innately a synergic duty.

Spiders are Nature's lesson in patience to us. Patient is the spider. It waits in ambush for long bouts, yet never seems to go hungry. Once the arachnid assesses that it has an ideal location to hunt, it figuratively drops anchor and sets up its web. Its ambush stationed, the spider waits, as if conducting surveillance – as if a sniper. It is committed to that position, it does not become restless and relocate after several hours of no results. The spider it seems, has already considered and accepted that waiting is a given and is also a crucial aspect of its hunt.

Patience equates to tolerance. To be tolerant of something is to be patient with it and so in reverse. If someone is impatient, they are expressing intolerance.

Honor is what we are scored on. It is easy to pretend to live honorably in front of others, but when we think no one can see us is really when we are conducting ourselves "on the honor system"(self-control). We are to increase or improve our honor potential after our time as a villain(ill intent) depletes it. To die with a negative honor score, is to die an agent of chaos. Anytime in such a state, is to live and/or die as less than.

We hear words such as honor and integrity, but what are they and why are they important? Are they imperative or are they simply decorative? When someone has "honor", what do we really mean when we say that about them?

At its core, honor is credibility, reliability. It is utmost sincerity. An honorable perone is of peak integrity.

Integrity is restraint and at the same time, it is impetus. Integrity is a companion, a life partner. Once attained, it is our most prized possession.

Integrity is a natural resource, a natural enemy and weapon against chaos. Integrity facilitates synergistic order.

Escaping the holding pattern known as life experience. It is as if experience wants us to form a mold of our best selves. A prototype that will not waffle, but will be unwavering in always being on our best behavior. In building our integrity, we fulfill ourselves with self-worth and by doing so, we are filling our mortal caste of an anatomy, with the actual version of ourselves. Once evolved to full synergistic integrity, we become real/actual, our true substantive self(s) and shed or molt our mortal shell.

What type of game is life experience?

Living in the Wilderness is an enterprise in self-control. It is learning not to do meaningless actions simply because they are available to do. It is also finding the determination to do what is meaningful, because we are able to.

If it had a name, what would the game of life experience be called?

Many names could be applicable, such as – The Humbling, Risk Management or Motives & Decisions and even Hide and Seek(Nature is playing a game of Hide & Seek).

Self-control is self-ownership. Others can control you if you do not practice synergetic restraint. You are not your own perone until you can effectively defend yourself from whatever vices or toxic perone that you are vulnerable to. Until then, what we are susceptible to is in control and has right of possession of us.

The Wild is about control. Nature controls us to see if we can effectively exercise peronal control. Being alive is partly to see if we can stop ourselves from doing what is available to partake in, but should be avoided. It is also to see if we do not stop ourselves, how far we are willing to compromise our own integrity, in order to satiate our subjective desires.

Altruism, helping each other – is a synergistic action. As children, without cajoling – we offer our assistance to our parents as soon as we feel we are capable to help. That said, even with helping we are to take care. For instance, helping someone kill, steal, lie or hurt someone else that is undeserving of such treatment – is dysfunctional/wrong. The only time such actions would be valid, are in times of mortal danger. Donate yourself and capabilities, we are at each other's service(organ).

Some other animals demonstrate that they also practice similar synergy to us. When their offspring falls prey or goes missing, they attempt to defend them or search for them. Domesticated dogs are referred to as, "man's best friend", due to their dutifulness. Though, they are not cereves, these are examples of moral agents.

A consistent moral agent is a force of order.

Synergy is to be considerate to others, as well as yourself.

Due to experience being a meritocracy, morality is hard won. If it was easy, it would be as meaningless to do, as all the unsynergetic/disharmonious activities that we engage in.

Experience is about being busy, we are to be active. Similar to the professionalism of businesses, the task supersedes our emotions towards it.

We should observe life with the volume to our emotions – down.

What is right for all is the superseding synergy. It supplants any subjective synergies.

Since we cannot take our possessions with us when we die, the entire physical world is designated to be left behind.

Morals are synergies, they are our duty. **Duty** usurps sadness, happiness or beauty. Morality takes precedence over our emotions. Duty offers the highest fulfillment. We are to perform synergetic exploits, regardless if to do so makes us jovial or disgruntled.

If you visit Antarctica during its winter, it does not care that you find it cold, neither does the desert concern itself if you care for it being hot. The burden is on us to adjust to the conditions and parameters that we have to operate within.

While teaching us the foremost lesson of the intrinsic value of synergies, the Wilderness makes it cosmetically appear as if morals do not matter or have little worth in doing(deception).

The value of being moral is the unseen reward of self-value, self worth. This is the ultimate prize of our collective quest. This is the actual value of being alive.

Synergies are deliberately set up as an honor system. It is a dubious invitation to failure(trap) and ultimate waste, left open for the naive and careless.

There is balance, every item can be multiple things, or at least two things at once. This means that in the same way that selecting material reward(gratification) over synergy(fulfillment) costs us intrinsically – is in the same way that accumulation of moral wins benefits us both fundamentally and sometimes materially. Material reward(s) can derive from moral victories, but occur less frequently than profits from subjective gratification.

It is best not to enact synergies for material return value, because most of the time you won't receive material compensation. By setting up the overall system of experience in this way, Nature is gauging our resistance to desire.

By collectively living in moral precision(order), preceding the ultimate prize of escaping imprisonment in the Wild, is the material reward of reaching ideal civilization. Any so called civilization outside of that benchmark, is uncivilized/dysfunctional(waste), to some degree.

A force of order lives a less carefree,"exciting" or reckless experience than a perone who still functions as an agent of chaos.

It is easier to be moral in some situations than in others. The more formidable circumstances provide the higher values of fulfillment.

System of **government and economy**. All current economic and political systems are corrupt, which fosters and perpetuates distrust among overall himind society. The reason current systems of politics are unscrupulous, is simply due to them being open to corruption. It is not that we cannot devise and implement an incorruptible system of economy and politics based on mutual benefit, it is just that we have never sincerely attempted to. To our own detriment, we have taken the word of societal authorities, falsely believing that what they present to us are our only options.

The premise of our peak system of governance must be incorruption, not anti-corruption. It's main quality must be invulnerability to unprincipled action, such as politicians and so called world leaders – prioritizing their peronal interests over those of society at large. Anti-corruption is an expectancy of unscrupulous conduct, while incorruption is proactive prevention of it.

We did not agree to the system of government we live under, that's just poetic rhetoric. Coerced, they were imposed on us.

Without people, a country/nation state is just a mass of borderless land. This demonstrates that a country is primarily its population, not its government. This infers that all governments should exist to serve at the behest and benefit of the governed.

There are no immigrants. Each perone is a citizen of the earth and is part owner of it(subjectively). To be born is to be heir to the inheritance of earth and all of the beneficial possibilities, which includes materials and resources – that it offers.

Gold and money are not actual value, they are mere representations of it. The value of fiat money is backed by what the value of gold is backed by – human labor. What good would either be if no one found value in them or were willing to exchange exertion for them? We were/are told they hold worth, when in truth, we are what gives them their perceived value. If the human species went extinct tomorrow, but society was left structurally intact, what would the value of land/real estate, every commodity or product left behind – then be?

Celebrating those who hoard or amass the most financial value is counterintuitive. We are a cerebral group and a social one, at that. Those of us that expend our resources, starting with our minds, towards the benefit of the group are who deserve lauded.

If a so called government, king, royalty, politician, world leader or any other title of prestige requires the attendance of other people to recognize them as their title, they are not higher in stature. If anything, they are at equilibrium with everyone else. How can they be above anyone, if they are dependent on the presence of others to acknowledge their position? Are "rich"(financially) people "rich", if the few of them suddenly find themselves as the only perones left populating the planet?

This same logic even applies to G0d. If G0d exists, then it needs our presence to acknowledge it. Without someone else around to concede to its existence, it would be like there being no G0d. G0d's very existence is interdependent on us conceding to its attendance, rendering us equal in function to it (we are also G0d).

For value to exist, there has to be an appraiser of it.

Financial equilibrium. If everyone was financially rich, then no one is poor – nor rich.

True "civilization" is one based on axial intellect, not inconsequential subjective biases. A cerebral civilization should be a competition within mutual cooperation. Any competition between us must be to the intrinsic benefit of the group, or it is ultimately an exercise in waste. A negative-sum game.

To live cerebrally, is the preeminent attribute of being civilized.

Since the quality of our decision making is based on morality, rendering it as an intrinsic universal currency – then being that we are a social species sharing the same planet – our financial system should also be based on a singular subjective special currency. Our exertion is the actual universal currency.

Since the group is priority over an individual, species usurps race, ethnicity, nationality, gender, sexual orientation etc.

If Nature deemed any race's hue of skin pigment as dominant, their outer layer would be impervious to any environmental conditions – or something marked to that effect. No particular race or ethnicity enjoys such a luxury.

If Nature deemed any shade of skin or ethnicity superior to the others within our overall species, the rest of us would be instinctively subordinate to them, as a pack of wolves are to the alpha female or as a pride of lions are to the dominant male.

It is vacuously opportunistic, not instinctive, to emphasize race. Children of multiple races attend the same daycare and do not intuitively group together based on bloodline, nor ethnicity. Tribalism is a cultural implementation, it is voluntary, not instinctual.

Ultimately, you find that being "black" or "white" etc – is not enough to be a successful cereve in the world. Skin color does not fulfill our self-worth, nor does it determine if your life was actually well spent.

Being a particular skin pigment does not protect one from succumbing to drug addiction, nor from contracting a major debilitating disease such as cancer, nor from falling victim to the effects of a cataclysmic event. Nature is universal. Race is trivial and is featured not only as a result of variety, but to add to intricacy.

If all himinds had always been a similar hue, instead of multiple – would yestory had played out the same, with one group within that group – finding a way to separate themselves and seek artificial advantage or privilege over another and oppress them – or would world society be currently equitable and harmonious?

To be a xenophobe is to have one's thinking mimic continental drift.

Performing the best action, "doing the right thing" – comes with the price of some type of subjective opportunity(gratification). Clearly, this is its added degree of difficulty. Our test. We have to earn our synergistic victories, we are not owed them. To obtain what is meaningful, we have to sacrifice what is superficial.

To escape the prison of the cosmos, we have to put ourselves in a better prison, a domicile of synergy. A prison of the proper checks and balances. One that ensures our continued self-growth and preempts our susceptibilities. A behavior modification facility. Rules can be our ally, if we utilize them correctly. We have to formulate the accurate set of rules to live by and rigidly adhere to them.

To flee the tough love that Nature imposes on us, it demands that we take the initiative to impose tough love upon ourselves. Vices are to be sacrificed, before they render us as wasted sacrifices.

The easiest way to do the right thing is to imagine or pretend as if there is no other alternative(s), but the synergetic decision available. Decreasing availability or exposure to degenerative activities also assists in bringing about such an end. Abandon or return vices to the shadows of ignorance/naivete.

We have to live as if we are being watched, because we are. All objects, functions and motion in the cosmos is relaying information. Without realizing it, we are giving the cosmos "backtalk".

Everywhere we go we leave traces of ourselves, whether it be fingerprints, hair, skin cells etc. This is a hint to us that our adventure through life experience is being tracked. We are leaving a trail that follows us throughout our life's tenure.

The most courageous act or display of strength that a perone can do in the Wilderness, is an act of synergy – since it is the feat that is so rigorous, most of us fail to perform it with any consistency.

Daily brutally honest self-evaluation is similar to hygiene for the body.

The most exceptional of us are the most moral.

Synergies are intuitive.

To be immoral is to break synchronicity with Nature's essential demands or to invite disharmony and weakness(karmic consequence). Immorality is dysfunction/chaos.

"**Sorry**" – is initially being ignorant to something. Once you have knowledge of what not to do, sorry is no longer only a word, it is expressed in action – or more specifically an inaction. Sorry becomes not repeating whatever wrongful act performed previously that required an apology following it. Apologizing after repeating a behavior we knew not to do, contradicts the clear intent of performing those actions again. Generally, very few of us accidentally repeat an action that we really do not want to voluntarily reenact. To do so is a pattern, not a radical change in momentum.

The lesson. Commonly, what we intend to do – we do – and what we don't deliberately intend to do – we do not do.

Examples of Universal Synergies:

• Always seek to make the best available decision, what is actually worth doing. For instance, establishing and living under the authority of synergies.

• It is not our abilities that are to decide what each of us does, that is just doing whatever we can get away with or are able to. The ultimate guidepost for our conduct, is what we should do, which is always the best available synergic action.

• No cereve is foreign, due to being a member of the rest of the species and all members being native to the same planet. Earth is a country and nations are regions of it, at best. It is nonsensical for a species whose members are dependent on each other, to function as if we are as mortally opposed as predators and prey, or stray cats and domesticated dogs. Tribalism is a choice. It is not our heart beating or our hair or fingernails growing. To pretend as if it is a hard instinct, is disingenuous theater.

• Society is not to be a patriarchy or a matriarchy, unless both genders live in absolute separation. Until such time, it is cerebral for society to be proportionate to both genders, especially in policy and at its most influential positions.

- Abstain from causing the intentional suffering of others who do not pose a risk to your survival. Do not carelessly put others in mortal danger or at undeserved risk.

- Demonstrate professionalism, be professional, "be a good sport". There is no escaping emotional expression, we are always emotional in one way or another. Even when we are being unemotional, it is from a place of emotion. For example, professionalism in a workplace demands that duty supersedes emotional influence or display, but that directive had to be proposed as an emotional reaction to concern of emotions disrupting duty. As a force of order or an aspiring one, the onus is on you to be poised.

- It is unwise to volunteer for bouts of troubling thoughts. Voluntarily adding to your depository of regrets, is not cerebral.

- Seek exactness. Avoid committal to false beliefs. It is not enough merely to desire to be right, all of our exploits, even speaking – must be also precise.

- Be honest with oneself or you are dishonest at your core. As if an exposed lie, the deceitful exist in a state of complete lack of integrity.

- In the situations that call for it, it is actually unprincipled of you not to apply "tough love". This also means that there are situations where "spoiling" or enabling someone – is unethical(waste).

- We interpret Nature's synergies to mean that physical survival means good, while death is bad. This is erroneous thinking. There is our actual(intrinsic) survival and our mortal survival. Survival also applies to us intrinsically, which usurps mortal survival.

• Admit when wrong, the sooner after realizing it, the better. Be willing to admit mistakes, since they do and will happen. To pretend to be above performing them is disingenuous.

• No shame is to be found in making a mistake. What is inexcusable, is stubbornly or thoughtlessly repeating negative actions again and again.

• Being physically fit is moral. Being in good physical shape is beneficial to not only each of us, individually – but more importantly, to the overall group. This synergy does not apply to those whose societal job(s) causes them to be physically unfit. To make the conscious decision to be unnecessarily unfit, would be selfish and anti-group, which welcomes discord(chaos).

• It would be sub-cerebral to implement a zero tolerance society of moral law. Such action would be irresponsible, due to cereves being inherently fallible. Better to practice a society that sincerely strives for excellence, while acknowledging and allowing for a margin of error.

• Study the contents on the page and not the book cover. How we conduct ourselves towards others supplants how we appear to them. Our appearance does say something about us, but it is not the ultimate message. Our actions are. There are an uncounted amount of victims of well dressed, eloquent and courteous scoundrels.

Just because someone is friendly does not make them your friend, nor is it indicative of them being a nice or high quality perone.

• Do not accept credit for an achievement that you did not earn, it is a form of theft. Credit must be earned or appropriately given. To receive it, one must be actually deserving.

• It is not only for the consideration of others, synergies also extend to each individual – out of the requirement to be of use/help to others. Each of us, just by being born in a social group – is obligated to everyone else.

• We must not be unnecessarily cruel to other creatures, but we cannot place a priority on other creatures above other himinds, unless those people have well proven themselves to be of no better decision making prowess, than the lower thinking animals. In some cases, other animals demonstrate that they are of more societal benefit, than the most chaotic of us.

• Knowing better and not doing better, is akin to not knowing at all. Do better.

No child is innocent or they would not be born. Nature functions on balance. Objectively, for children to be in a harsh world, it cannot be due to their innocence – but instead, due to being guilty. Children are destined to inevitably become some level of villains/agents of disarray and from there can possibly earn redemption as an antihero.

Children are not of the sophistication to know what is good for them. As they grow, they are learning this.

They must be taught integrity early and often, if the intention is for them to develop into quality adults.

Population growth was merely to bring us to this point in yestory or progression of play – the coordinate of the realization of life's absolutes/exactitude. Once gaining such understanding, we are to focus on voluntary population reduction.

It is not in a child's best interest to bring them into this world. There is no benefit to a child whatsoever(if you disagree, please list the benefits to children to being alive, as opposed to never existing). It is only out of the selfish desires of parents why children are subjected to life experience. When given any adequate contemplation, himind reproduction is more an act of sadism, than an act of affection or compassion. In regards to reproduction, the other animals do not know any better, but we are the cerebral species. The other creatures are not as cognitively equipped. Nature furnished us with the capacity to think such thoughts all the way through to their extent.

Sexual relations with reves that are fertile or able to have children welcomes disharmony. The position of genitals in such close proximity to fecal ejection, is a clue that there is a filthy aspect to reproduction. Sex is only to be freely partaken in, if the fevale is absolutely infertile, the cere is sterile or it is between same gender adults. Masturbation and oral sex are synergies, as well.

Reves have to endure labor pains, pregnancy complications and death from childbirth – as hints that our reproduction has always been in discord with Nature. This is due to us being the accursed character in the equation of experience, logically rendering it a deficit for us to reproduce. This is even why reves bleed and wear an odor near the time they are most fertile, as opposed to the usual scent of their sexual organ.

In the same way unearthed pharaohs and emperors demonstrated that we cannot take our material possessions with us when we die, is in the same way that we should not fear leaving our cities, towns and technologies behind. They were not meant to be taken with us, but to be lures to keep us focused on see-level. If we are truant in voluntarily detaching ourselves from the delusion of us being native to the Wild and trigger an involuntary Event Outcome, we won't have a choice but to leave this all behind regardless.

Nature's challenge for us, is to see what we are willing to let go of? The challenge is to see if we will vacate experience voluntarily, by ceasing to reproduce or if we will stubbornly succumb to chaos? Nature put us in this position to see if we'd rather see ourselves destroyed in the Event Outcome – or will we properly utilize the mind it equipped us with and simply just abandon our delusion.

Similar to some other creatures, we are hoarders. Not only items, we also stockpile faulty beliefs, toxic people and defeatist routines and stubbornly hold on to them, even though we know it would be more advantageous to us to abandon them.

Institutionalized is the prisoner of the moment, the inmate of nostalgia.

Cheating follows from laziness, which follows from the theme of efficiency. Students cheating on tests are attempting to be efficient in passing said tests. Gamers who utilize cheat codes for games, are following a similar principle. "Cheating" wezentic partners, cheat at their monogamous relationships in an attempt to be efficient at being monogamous. Some athletes cheat at sports in an attempt at efficiency in being successful at their sport. Lying in any situation is a form of cheating at being truthful. For instance, lying to oneself is a form of cheating oneself of truth.

Relationships:

Wezentic relationships, what can we do about them? Are relationships really meant to last and if not, why do we engage in them? Outside of reproduction, are we even supposed to be in them? If they are meant to endure, how are they actually supposed to work? Is there a universal synergy for wezentic relationships?

With the frequent turnover in casual relationships to the high divorce rate among marriages(cobonds) and the many complaints and acrimony of those still in relationships – it is clear there is a problem with how we claim affinities are to be.

When in monogamous relationships, we still have sexual attraction to others outside of the affinity. This phenomena shows that at the most primal level(first nature) – we are not monogamous. Instead, cereves are naturally predisposed as a promiscuous species(sexual anarchy). This is why infidelity is easier to engage in than wezentic loyalty. Monogamy has to be learned, as if it is a privilege Nature wanted us to earn.

When engaged in promiscuous sexual activity, we tend to feel emotional attachment or more intense feelings for particular sexual partners, as opposed to all of them. It is as if Nature is limiting the pool of potential prospects that we will feel a sincere attraction to or satisfaction in being with. This occurrence also indicates that we are supposed to be in relationships. Our feelings of emotional attachment, contradict absolute promiscuity and causes us to seek a more exclusive arrangement with the sexual partners we are most fond of. From this, casual and serious monogamous relationships("boyfriend & girlfriend", marriage/cobond) arise.

Beware of relationship fraud. It is when one or other parties involved in a wezentic affinity, are engaged in said arrangement for dubious purposes, but do not disclose this information with the other perone(s) involved.

Choosing a relationship partner(s) comes with risk, rendering it akin to participating in a lottery.

Ahoy there, fair weather companions. A relationship doesn't start until the people involved in said affinity, learns how they interact during turbulent times. Anyone can be or seem loving during courtship or fun/good times. There is not much challenge to that, but is that actually relating or the substantive aspect of it? No. This is why many affinities fray so badly after entering into an official relationship. There is not enough time dedicated to getting to know one another beyond a peripheral level. The parties involved base their infatuation or bond on how their partner(s) is during the honeymoon period, then go on to find out later that they are as if a whole other perone when the inevitable storms brew.

A wezentic relationship is a contract, a mutual understanding. We set expectations of each other. There are various types of wezentic relationships/arrangements. All parties involved should be voluntarily agreeable to its particular terms. Once entered into said contract, all parties are bound to its conditions, as lifeforms are to the Natural Laws. Any single perone's desires are no longer the priority, the duty to the terms and goals of the relationship are.

Affinity choice cannot be based on infatuation alone, because infatuation on its own is not a guarantor of a relationship's success. We are the cerebral species, leaving intellect as the primary factor in relationship decisions, not our emotions.

Relationships should be based on moral precision.

Every relationship is one of convenience. All parties involved are providing some type of convenience to each other. We are all using each other in some type of way, including emotionally. This isn't necessarily negative, since we're a social species – our intrinsic value to each other – is our use.

What we should not be doing is abusing each other. Abuse is to take for granted or use in extremes.

Each of us when entering into a relationship, should be seeking to negotiate a mutual exchange of synergistic precision. Each perone in the relationship will be consciously striving to be their best, resulting in a strong friendship or bond that is then adorned with physical expression.

It is not the sex, it is the togetherness. Yes, sex does entice us to desire partnership, which can prompt you to then want to sleep the nights away with that other perone, but sex does not ensure substantive alliance. Conversely, quality togetherness compensates for less than acrobatic/athletic sex. In fact, fulfilling togetherness offsets imperfections in the relationship.

Togetherness should precede erotic desire. Sex is but icing on the cake, not the cake itself.

The legacy of our affection is not in the offspring we rear. There are plenty of bad parents that produce children. This renders reproduction as just an activity, being that even without the presence of moral affection/"love" – it occurs regardless.

The legacy of our affection is in the quality of how we treat each other, not in the children we breed. It is as if we view children as living monuments that we leave behind as proof that the previous generation was once here.

Sex is like a natural drug and Nature is like the dealer who hooked us to it. Pornography and prostitution are tenable industries, due to a demand in the market. Some people take serious risks to engage in it, whether voluntarily or involuntarily. Rape, pedophilia are some of the acts we commit to satisfy an intense desire for sex. "Cheating" on (y)our significant other, excessive masturbation and promiscuity are some others. At times, manipulation tactics are employed to achieve it, if not most or all of the time. We develop an emotional attachment and weakness/preference, giving it some level of control over us.

The experience of orgasm is a degree of going into shock. If we are a technology, then climaxing is like short circuiting. It is as if sizzling flashes of bolts of lightning or flickering lights during a bad storm. What makes orgasm translate as euphoric is the fact that in most cases, the figurative power doesn't go out. The thrill of a sexual experience is in the temporary threat of a power outage. And since we would not function the same if our lights flickered on and off all day, the appeal of orgasms is in their range of rarity.

We are to be attracted to and pursuing a life partner(s) who is going to help us improve as decision makers and moral victors. Vacate relationships that make it difficult to be a force of order.

Life is short and we are all going to die one day – we do not have the luxury of wasting each other's time.

The quality of the operation of our society is dependent on our relating to one another. This renders all relationships, even wezentic ones – as serious business endeavors.

Life being a game, makes it logical that affinities are also games. But, they should not have to be spy versus spy. We are too casual about the subject, which is why relationships are generally treated with indifference, in terms of our committal to them.

Wezentic affinities should not be about one perone winning and the other perone losing or one perone being better and the other being worse. The best relationships are win:wins. All participants involved should be better for having been in them.

A win:win relationship can only be achieved by basing it on a rule of synergistic precision. If all participants in any affinity are adequately morally serviced, the potential of that relationship is maximized to its extent.

Most people in wezentic affinities today, do not actually love each other. They are relationships of pretense, rather than any substance. The parties involved are performing for each other, as if in a drama class. The phrase, "I love you', is said more out of custom and going through the motions, rather than actions that we demonstrate. It just sounds nice to say or hear. "I love you" is sometimes used as a weapon or tool that we wield casually at our whim.

There is indisputable value in having people that truly care about your well being. Due to life being about change, even love is fragile, rendering it a luxury. It is a privilege that is not to be taken for granted, since it is not a given. Failing to realize this lesson again and again, is accompanied by an expensive price tag.

A relationship is a journey.

Though we are social, himinds are still individuals within that overarching structure. This means we each, at least in part, function based on egoism or self-interest. Egoism is a necessity. Each one of us utilize greed and selfishness in order to survive. In moderation, egoism is ideal. It is when it is engaged in severity, that self-interest distorts our perspective of reality.

When we consider that aspect of us, in regards to wezentic alliances, we find that it is logical for conflict to result. In affinities, at least two people are trying to reconcile distinct egos, for sake of a common purpose. Infatuation may result in reproduction, but it is not enough to bring competing psyches into synergy.

Our very egos are the primary cause of dysfunction in our relating. Each of us makes the mistake of putting our own individual interests above the alliance at large. Without evoking emotions, on a logical basis alone – any relationship enduring such extreme perspective from within, is going to result in strain. As long as any party in any wezentic relationship accepts that the other is committed to tolerating imbalance to such extents for prolonged periods – the togetherness is forced, more than organic. The willingness and commitment to duty deteriorates or wanes. This is the danger of a disproportion in perspective.

If the goal of the relationship is success in quality and duration, we must achieve and maintain an axial or centered perspective in our interactions with our significant other(s).

Since we are the cerebral species that is capable of experiencing emotions, our wezentic alliances should be based on being rational, since emotions can cause us to misconstrue reality. Ultimately, if we actually want to live in a society of thriving strong affinities – we should not be falling "in-love"(infatuation/emotions) – we are to be grounded in mind(synergy/integrity).

Regardless of the fact that we can only see each other's exteriors in all of our interactions, we are all really relating – mind to mind. A true exchange is one that is more platonic than sexual.

The ideal life partner for someone pursuing their innate duty of moral improvement, is another perone that demonstrates that they are in sincere pursuit of that similar aim.

All parties involved, must actively exert themselves to maintain the integrity of the exchange for it to be a lasting transaction.

In terms of fidelity, one does not put what one highly values at serious risk. Self-gratification is the enemy to a moral victor.

Love inherently carries the quality of stability, not chaos – disorder/volatility.

Love(affinity) is a bank or a trust, that we invest in. Take it for granted, you may overdraw your account. Put too much in at once and your partner(s) may take advantage.

Unconditional affection or bonds is not love, it is excess. You have to set limits or you are an open invitation, welcoming abuse.

Love is a demonstration, or the noun is just an empty word.

Experience is about displaying self-love. Self-affinity is how we show that we are capable of loving others. Being individual members of a social order, renders self-love as demonstrating love for others.

We tend to realize how intense our feelings are about someone, when longing for them, while their physical presence is in absentia.

What is flirting? When we "flirt" with someone, what are we actually doing? Is flirting with someone and flirting with a thing, the same? Is it harmless to do? Why do we flirt?

Flirting is to provoke, to tease, to tempt, to invite. Flirting is to open yourself up to something, whether it be a prospective wezentic suitor or to danger etc.

Intuitive Model Upgrade:

Mutants vs Villains. Mutants seek to evolve for the better, while villains devolve. A culprit that metamorphs in terms of positive improvement, becomes a mutant that is aspiring to get back to zero(balance/equilibrium), which is to be an antihero(even). There are no heroes/heroines that are faultless. Nature initially puts us all in the position of offenders. The most any of us can work to become in experience, is an antihero and to achieve such status, one must be courageous.

When you practice consistent flawed decision making, forget your distrust of others, you cannot even trust yourself. To be the best villain one can be, is to disown your own integrity. When sincerely transitioning from a villain to a mutant, you realize that you are actually building trust in yourself.

A complication with being a pathological liar. Keep in mind, that you are your own first listener when communicating with others. This means that in every instance, in which you deliberately deceive someone else, you are first being dishonest with yourself. Repeat such action enough times and eventually you lose credibility with yourself.

There are times on our life adventure that we come to a point where our choices are to either panic or be resolute.

Peronal change is a battle between instant and delayed gratification.

Peronal transformation is to voluntarily engage in imbalance. Such change is inconvenient.

Once fully accustomed to any particular imbalance, you've achieved balance.

Individual growth can be like walking down the stairs. If you miss a step you will lose your balance or footing.

Vices should be put in the shadows or returned to naivete, as much as possible. Self-improvement is part relearning oneself and part entering into unfamiliar terrain.

There are always excuses we can fabricate to avoid learning or doing better. It is wasteful to be lazy to positively develop, yet exert ourselves with vigor to remain the same or worsen.

Deliberate development requires effort. It involves a lot of instances of telling yourself no. It is such a job to be synergetically consistent that we have to be professional about it.

The more times you deny yourself from engaging in a detrimental activity, the more psychological strength(score) you build up. Moral strength is amassed via resistance of our negative desires.

Being busy helps, but there will come a time when you will not be busy. Facing your degenerative thoughts has to be a priority. Ignoring them will only work for so long. Confronting yourself and dealing with the discomfort of change, is the key. Each moment of transforming is a learnable/teachable moment.

What you cannot control is its own set of worries. Actively addressing what you can control, is fulfilling.

Every good decision is as if escaping a consequence, every bad one is to volunteer for a setback – in terms of integrity.

Self-growth(self-accountability) is private or it is not actual transformation, but theater.

With growth comes loss – loss of people and things that hinder our advance to our full potential(full being).

Peronal evolution can seem grueling, due to it being a vetting process set up by Nature to see who can muster the "will" to accomplish the feat.

Self improvement requires courage. Peronal change is for the brave. Cowards/weak minds cannot endure the process.

The best way to peronally evolve, is to focus on establishing and sustaining one's own integrity/self-credibility.

We must forgive ourselves in order to move beyond the guilt we feel from our regrets. Recognizing and acknowledging our bad decisions and blunders is displayed by taking better actions going forward.

Be cognizant that it can be easy to forget the objective actuality while existing in this subjective reality(nonsense is contagious). That is a part of the intended degree of difficulty of the game of experience.

We can always go further than we initially think we can go. This lets us know that "mental hurdles" are not as formidable as we initially consider them to be. It is almost as if they are not really there. Psychological barriers ultimately exist not only to prevent us from reaching our peak potential, but also to be defeated.

To improve is to feel fulfilled, to regress is to lose self-worth(score).

Degenerative routines can seem as if they are sources of comfort. In actuality, they are a veiled source of despair.

The farther apart ruinous actions are, the better. Aim to space them apart as much as possible. This will severely limit their occurrence.

Point of Reference. You imagine yourself doing something before you do it. Once you perform that action, you go from guessing what that action would be like, to then having a working example/model/precedent in your mind to improve upon or repeat. This is why we never know what we can do, until we do it(experience).

To be uncomfortable is to be aware and engaged. To be comfortable is actually to be disengaged or entranced.

We enter the world as infants that are demanding. To satiate those demands, Nature armed us with the ability to manipulate. We cry, scream and whine for attention, breast milk or to be picked up. We physically grow to do the same behavior as teenagers and adults. When we complain or make illegitimate excuses, this is us still crying and manipulating.

We've never stopped being infants, just older versions of that stage. Be aware of (y)our proclivity to seek sympathy in all of its forms.

THE PRESENCE OF AN OBJECTIVE & VICTORY CONDITIONS

"Life is not made for happiness, but for achievement."
Georg Wilhelm Hegel

Event Outcome. It is not how you start, it's how you finish.

Start/birth → physically and psychologically develop → come to a point of reflection/look back → consider and decide to remain the same or reconsider (y)our behavior going forward.

While some think that going through life enduring as little pain as possible is the purpose of being alive, physicist, Erwin Schrodinger, asserted that the purpose of our lives is to bring order to chaos. We brush our teeth and wash our bodies, though we know they will get dirty again. We clean our dishes and our houses etc, even though we know they will all fall prey to chaos immediately afterward. Why? The simple answer is, that we do these things, due to an intrinsic urge for order.

Though Schrodinger was mostly ignored, when we consider factors such as time value, us being a social species and its implications, in terms of individual responsibility to self and to the group – our coerced initial nefarious disposition as individuals and as a collective, the presence of volition, the presence of lessons and the counterintuitive way that overall himind society currently functions – the uber perceptive physicist is validated. Nature forces us to do wrong and then opens up a short time frame and narrow path of execution, to rescue ourselves. Many religions espouse that we receive repercussion or reward, based on our deeds on earth and have to overcome oppression/adversity, in order to gain more freedom. This is a cosmic clue that our overall purpose is to bring order to our very own lives.

Games include a set path to victory and the game of the Wild is no different. Consistent with playing out at a high degree of difficulty, the game objective is multiple objectives. There are individual, as well as group conditions that must be appeased before we escape our nightmare in this dreamworld. Just to get to a point of full realization took a certain series of steps.

The right invention had to come along. The ancients thought the world mechanical, which is why there have been theories claiming that life was an intelligent design – or Descartes referred to animals as machines or others compared the cosmos to a watch. The best way to describe reality is not only through language, but via analogies, particularly – one to one correlations. After all, life is analogous in and of itself(the effect of two mirrors facing off, fractals). Since a watch was the best available comparison at the time, the universe became misunderstood, to the point that modern physicists completely abandoned the assertion of the Wild being mechanistic.

It is not until the advent of artificial intelligence and virtual reality and those inventions becoming popular, that an accurate one to one correlation could be drawn.

> **"The greatest of all wonders is not the conqueror of the world, but the subduer of himself."**
> Arthur Schopenhauer

To solve for the "X"(unknown) of the Wild, the right candidate had to also come along at the right time in the progression of the game(itinerary). The perone who was to first arrive at full awareness/realization had to be someone alive during the time of the information age. They had to be someone unexpected(irony), someone from among the masses, rather than from academia. That perone would start off questioning life's peculiarities, but then would become enamored with its aesthetics – until circumstances became so dire, that perone's best option was only to question.

> **"God has cursed me to see what life should be like."**
> Tupac Shakur

It would be someone who displayed a healthy rancor for unquestioned authority. They would be a societal rejection that would take defiance to extremes, until reaching the overarching objective conclusion. They would have to endure Nature fighting them every step of the way, while leaving a fair opportunity for them to achieve the feat of finally solving the riddle of experience – that at times, doesn't seem like a riddle. They would have to be of the sophistication to comprehend academic concepts, but also how to express those concepts in simple terms. They would reassess and filter the thoughts of previous thinkers and build on them. They would have to be tenacious in their attempt to complete the project and know that they'd more likely endure heavy criticism for their effort, more so than financial reward or public acknowledgment. They would have to face embarrassment, humble themselves and prioritize the completion of the project above any wasteful desires. They would have to feel as if solving the mystery of experience was their only recourse.

There are individual victory conditions, which multiplied, are also provisions for group success:

- Take notice of peculiarities in (y)our experience and question them.

- Seek to effectively explain reality. Find the precise logic/theme in it.

- Attain an objective mind, ponder everything axially. Seek unpartitioned answers. To attain a truly free mind, is to unlock yourself, your unbiased self.

- Discover the Wild's map key: Objective exactitude; Balance/union of duality, Irony; No random/inevitability, no coincidences, everything has a reason and is meant to happen; be aware of clues/signs.

- Become self-aware by questioning everything, including oneself.

- Realize that there is a deeper meaning to life, than the sensory illusion that our senses immerse us in.

- Gain(learn) consequential/game/meaningful knowledge.

- Apply to peronal life, share and explain to others.

To achieve group victory conditions, as a group we have to(not necessarily in this order):

- Confirm the validity of the assertions declared in this text.

- Once confirmed, apply axial thinking to one's own peronal life, as well as to the administration of society. Break the cycle of overall destructive group behavioral pathology. Experience is a teaching exercise and we have to demonstrate that we understand its most meaningful lessons. Saying what we are willing to do is not enough, actions narrate.

- Verify the presence of a universal synergy/moral code. Be our truly best selves, live our truly best lives, by making the best decisions with the best intentions.

- Implement synergic order to the chaos transpiring in overall cereve society.

Voluntary extinction/suicide, complete halt of reproduction or sincerely attempting to – ends the game. We must display that we are not afraid of death, which would be to overcome our desire and fear. We have to provide demonstrable proof that we actually want freedom from this fantasy of a world. Chaos is too robust, to justify bringing children into it any longer. Duty supplants peronal desire. Continuing to produce offspring also sustains us in the game, providing more mortal characters for us(uni-becoming) to return and live vicariously through.

We were never here, there is no here.

Simply living is a form of suicide. Living is deliberately engaging in conduct that puts us at mortal risk. Many of the things that we do while living, are a form of suicide, just with slower acting effects than directly killing ourselves. Suicide is a prominent theme in existence, it cannot be avoided. If we do not engage in the cerebral form of it, our self-destructive behavior, which Nature added as a fail safe, will ensure that we inflict a final karmic consequence on ourselves(agents of karma). Nature put us in a position where if we are not playing the game of life experience to win, we are effectively finding some ways to lose. There is no bargaining with it, in regards to demands to achieve victory, nor compromise. It has all of the leverage.

If there's any escape to be secured, it is to become a fugitive of our pseudo escapes.

Achieving perfection(precision) in behavior frees us from the rules of experience. It has been said that perfection is unattainable, but that cannot be exact or there would never have been evolution or ranges of potentials. Axially, perfection is the quintessential extent of something that is able to be accomplished, even if that something is ultimately unfavorable or is not able to be achieved by us. Every action that we perform at their ideal, as well as each step of improvement towards an aim, should be considered as perfection, being that their sum total results in flawlessness. All progress is a procession towards perfection. Even synergies are an example of perfection, perfection in our conduct.

We are fighting for an ultimate freedom. If there is an afterlife, then there must have first been a prelife(F0rever) and they are one in the same. When we win the game, which is to escape mortality/see-world, we return to prelife, the state we existed in before there was ever a universe. Should we fail to overcome the Wild, we continually return and repeat mortality(repetition). We are in training.

THE PRESENCE OF COMPULSION

How can we be in a game and not realize it?

Games are developed with the intent of players taking part in them. To bring about that outcome, gameplay is designed to be interesting, it's flow immersive, the controls easy to use. By having players learn the main skills in a game organically – they unwittingly fuse with their game character.

Games are deliberately made to be compelling through perception and relation. In games, perception usurps reality. Compulsion drives a player's actions in a game, it serves as bait or a catalyst – offering obvious and/or subtle enticements, rewards and suggestions(Nature is marketing to us). Rewards are proportional to the game's degree of difficulty. The game's particular set of conditions, the player's quality of experience and their possible reactions – are well considered.

Putting a player in control of characters that they are able to make decisions for, renders the gameplay experience vivid and effective. The player observes the game's output and process it. If any of what is processed is significant, the player has an emotional response. When this happens the player becomes wholly involved in the game experience.

Game designers use numerous means as compulsion for participants, individually weighted motivational factors – most notably immersion.

Our senses and minds(data feeds, interface & controller) are the first level of compulsion via immersion. They make us feel like there is an inside and an outside to the avatar(s) each of us exist vicariously through. If it wasn't for being able to sense the insides of our bodies, it would be much easier to notice that our bodies were merely surrogates of us and not actually our exact selves.

At the moment of our birth, we have no choice but to respond to this new and strange world we are in. We feel the sensation of a temperature difference, due to emerging in an area that is not similar in feel to the temperature of the womb. Our urges come online and we begin to crave things. Crying enough, makes us thirsty for the first time and we also are introduced to the feeling of hunger. Our mother's breast milk satisfies both. These are not voluntary processes, they are instinctive. They are compulsions. They cause us to forget about how atypical experience is and give us the false impression that we are native to it, going as far as rendering the effect of going "mad", due to starvation(hunger strikes are voluntary, starvation is generally involuntary). That is their primary function and as you can attest to, the feelings of hunger and thirst give effective performances. Our needs especially, compel us, via intense immersion.

Our emotions induce us, such as desire, fear and guilt. Our need to cope influences our decisions. Many delusions are had and shared and faulty actions engaged in – due to the instinctive need to cope. Be aware of coping, appeasing that yearn should not usurp duty.

Nature is a master motivator. At all times, it is always using a variety of means to either spur us to succeed in experience or seduce us to fail. In one way or another, Nature is constantly encouraging us to help or harm ourselves. There is no intermission.

Anxiety, irritants and annoyances also influence our appraisals.

Conditioned Selection(Decisions). Behaviorist, Frederick Skinner, wrote of "operant conditioning". He noticed that people could be conditioned to make particular choices – learned responses, specifically repeating an action. What Skinner didn't notice was that it is the very position that evolution, via the Laws of Nature and instincts – has us in.

Regardless if the conversation is about addiction, habits or second nature – the discussion is about routine and routine is behavior. Routine compels us. Nature formulated our minds as behavior building mechanisms and our bodies as performance machines. Nature set us up to behave in patterns.

First nature routine behaviors would be eating, breathing, hydration, sleeping etc. We refer to these as "needs", but when they are undressed to their bare nakedness, they are habits. Sex, is an odd first nature routine, because it is only a superficial need(reproduction). Really, reproduction is not as direct a need as breathing, eating and hydration. It is indirect, since reproduction is optional. This places sex as more second nature, than first nature. Intercourse is parallel to how drug addiction can feel like a first nature "need" to a drug addict, but really is not. Reproduction is more of an unessential desire, than an actual need.

Drug addicts are not the only people that suffer from addiction. Many behaviors we refer to as habits are actually addictions, as well. Addiction is just another word for routine. Any act we do and become dependent on doing, is an addiction. As hard as it is for drug addicts to abandon their deficient ways, is as laborious as it is, for the rest of us to give up some of our own detrimental habits. In this light, we are all addicts.

Nature predisposed us with this feature, as if it wanted us to have vices(villain). It wanted us to be addicted to doing certain things. After all, everything we perceive is a stimulus.

Using second-hand knowledge to defeat firsthand. The way to free ourselves from any repetitive destructive behavior is the same way most of us avoid being serial killers, or pedophiles, or anything else vile – we don't entertain the thought with any seriousness.

We can become so frantic about what we are going to have to endure to change, that it causes us to act out to our own detriment. Remain wary of yourself.

Since the marijuana plant, coca plant and poppy plants are found in nature – Nature is a drug pusher.

In practice, addiction is like a child or a pet – you have to tend to it. It is something that requires management. It is always vying and demanding of your attention. Being an addict defeats the purpose of voluntarily becoming one. Instead of escape, it is more of a clever trap or added responsibility. Similar to your bills, you have to stay ahead of it. Addiction is in hot pursuit when it trails you. Addiction wastefully consumes time, its true cost is your limited time.

Gratification or pleasure can be intense, but ephemeral, which is why we "chase" it.

Living things are the demand, our environment(nature & nurture) is the supply. The two dynamics conjoined form habits. One cannot be habitual, if there is no available means or stimulus to form that behavior.

Stimulus dictates behavior. All of the Wilderness is one macro-stimulant!

Optimism, hope drives us. Even the most pessimistic perone is grounded in optimism. The very fact that they are voluntarily still alive validates that assertion. Claimed pessimists could override their self-preservation programming at any time, but choose not to. This renders their negativity as disingenuous, just voice boxes emitting empty words. The fact is, despite only offered words, our immune system/self-preservation forces us to fundamentally be optimists.

Pessimism is a necessity or everyone would be optimistic too far to the extreme. This would lead to unchecked overestimating and overconfidence, regardless of the reality of a worse case scenario playing out around us. One would never know when to quit or concede defeat, or even the difference between an exertion worth continuing, as opposed to one holding little value in pursuing. We would never be prepared for any adversity, due to overly charmed thoughts blocking any consideration of an unfavorable outcome. So severe would complete optimism be, that no situation – no matter how painful or damaging, would be considered as a bad one.

This renders pessimism to be as valuable as optimism, as long as it does not become extreme, itself. They are two extremes at opposite ends of the same axial theme, interdependent on each other.

Scale is a major weapon used to bewilder players. **Information density** gives a player too much to focus on, rather than the single or few things(objective) they need to. Safety in numbers compels us to go along with the crowd or what is popular.

Our features, in terms of our senses, are not a given. Nature had options in how they could have been, as seen in the variance of ways that other animals are equipped with the same senses. Our eyes, outer ears, noses and lips do more than serve their commonly known biological functions. In practicality, they also effectively serve the ulterior function of adding to the conflict between people. In one instance, they signal commonality, but simultaneously they also represent separation between us. Our various features are an example of information density.

In practicality, sex serves the function of provoking our actions, which is why it is a part of the reproductive process/algorithm. Sex spurs reproduction, as well as all the other problems that derive from sexual arousal.

Obligation is a catalyst and is the actual impetus for us to utilize in experience, due to it being a necessity for our success and it not having the ability to effectuate itself. Responsibility is a weapon for us to use. Duty is integrity and integrity lights the way out of Plato's Cave.

Energy compels us. Everything that compels us can be viewed as some form of energy. Energy thrusts us through time.

Breads are filling, but it's empty calories can add negative complexity to our anatomical structure.

As a species, over time our diet became more and more complex; so logically, our anatomies, which depend on diet – gained in elaborateness too. The same way in which our bodies were affected by ingesting more salt or certain fats – is in the same way carbohydrates affect our physiology, as well.

No matter how delectable food tastes, it is simply energy, which is why nutritious food is the best food to ingest.

In terms of mass or weight, we are all on the same balance. Each of us occupies a dimension known as weight. It is axial. Neutrally, we are all the same weight. Each of us, as a subjective mass – are located at different subjective points along the universal measurement. In part, Nature utilizes our diet and weight as another frivolous distraction.

Fruits are peculiar, especially since there are some animals that are herbivores and some others that are carnivores. Some fruits are so delicious, it causes suspicion, especially when we account for there also being the intense pleasure of sex. What are the odds of there being this many pleasures in attendance, in such a challenging experience as the Wild and since the pleasure of sex is to induce reproduction – doesn't that mean that pleasurable tastes must be to entice/seduce, as well?

Carnivores such as lions, miss out on the sweet tastes of pineapples, grapes, mangoes or sugar cane. They are completely oblivious to them. Due to us himinds being both part herbivore and part carnivore, we are well aware of the palatable treats that any animal that is exclusively one or the other is missing out on. Being able to eat both meat and plants, Nature ensured that cereves would not be excluded from any tastes. This brings us to the conclusion that the sweetest flavored fruits are not just for the benefit of herbivores or insects, in general – but, instead they are primarily for us.

Tastes can be alluring. Nutritious foods are mostly bland to sour. Sweet or delectable foods outside of fruits, generally have an adverse effect on our bodies. This indicates that we should not be eating based on taste, but instead based on nutritional value(intellect usurps emotion).

Egoism, the "it won't happen to me" mindset – compels us.

We can feel invincible when we are in good health. We can even feel invincible when not in ideal health. This is a false sense of security. As long as we are mortal, we are always in harm's way. We are never invincible.

Chaos drives discomfort in experience, subsequently motivating us to seek convenience.

Revenge(balance), "getting even" is a motivating factor.

Curiosity/intrigue compels us.

Exhaustion can also be compelling.

Struggle humbles and frustrates. From there it either defeats or propels us to overcome.

Conveyance to compel:

1. Starts with a cue or compulsion(problem, what is happening)
2. Desire(I desire/want something)
3. Planning(where can I get it, how will I acquire it – calculation)
4. Aim(plans are formulated, any causes for concern, nearing decision)
5. Action(decided, attempt)

We're all seeking **comfort/convenience** of some form or type. Take being wealthy, for instance. It financially shields you from suffering "money problems", as long your lifestyle is well within what you can afford.

What we are too short sighted to realize, is that comfort itself is also an inconvenience. It's an opportunity price thing, in that when you attain something convenient, even something that provides you maximum euphoria/pleasure, there is also inconvenience(s) that accompanies it, that must also be accepted. Just the act of becoming acclimated to convenience eventually renders comfort uncomfortable.

It is not actually Nature versus Nurture. Nature is the foundation to nurture, rendering nurture to be an offshoot of Nature. What is happening, is that Nature is just presenting its influence in two different ways, a direct way and an indirect one. Objective and subjective. Nature is behind how we are raised and how we go about being developed, even within society.

Embarrassment is another reason we are a social species and not a solitary one. Nature utilizes it to humble or goad us. Were we solitary creatures, we couldn't experience shame. The most introspective of us feel embarrassed by our own self-credibility, when we fail to abide by it.

Self-consciousness branches from embarrassment. Being self-conscious makes us imagine what we look like or will look like to others(empathy), while doing something. It makes us envision things from outside of ourselves.

We do care what other people think, we can't avoid this since we are members of a social order. It is a default. Being concerned about what others are going to think influences not only a lot of what we do, but also a lot of what we do not do.

Is every interaction between himinds a negotiation? It seems to be that every interaction between us is some form of manipulation(use or abuse). We are always trying to compel each other to do what we want each other to do, in one way or another. Being members of a social species renders our interactions between each other as a shared manipulation. All of us are participants in this activity. Directing or guiding is not just exclusively verbal, it can also be done via body language exclusively.

Fraud is possible because we want to trust each other, a shared trust – as if that is what a social species is innately intended to be, at least a highly intelligent one.

If there weren't ever birds, insects or other creatures that are capable of going airborne, would we ever have thought of flying?

Nature inspires creativity, invention.

To keep players interested, clever tactics are employed, such as reverse psychology. At times in the game, players are deliberately made to feel disinterested; so as to compel them to take action.

Boredom is an unlit night sky that meaningful action lights up. In actuality, there is no boredom outside of us having the feeling of a lack of stimulation. Everything happening in life is neutral, we are only telling ourselves that every or most moments should be stimulating. Don't forget, all of the Wilderness is a macro stimuli and we are stimulation addicts. This renders boredom as a peronal issue that each of us are tasked to have to work through. Our tolerance level or adaptation, causes the feeling of boredom. We reach a satiation point when we become accustomed to anything or anyone – giving us the impression of diminishing returns, regarding curiosity or mystery of that thing or perone.

Keep in mind, that boredom is simply a feeling we superimpose on our reality, it is not necessarily the case. Without us or other living things, is there boredom? Be wary of falling into the trap of viewing meaningful action as unstimulating. An adjustment of perspective toward an axial orientation remedies faulty appraisal(s).

Ask yourself, is boredom just a lack of stimulation or is it also having to listen to our intuition? If we remove the word for a moment, what is it to endure a state of "boredom"? Behind the need for stimulation, what are you left with? Is it not having to listen to what your inside voice has to say to you? The simplest way to answer these questions is with a question – if we had no inner voice, how tormenting would boredom be?

It too is a survival advantage. It's inclusion in experience tells us that there is something that we should be doing, something that, if performed effectively – will result in ultimate satisfaction, lasting fulfillment/stimulation.

That is in the larger scope of the topic. In smaller scale, boredom prods us to act. We can always improve, rendering – there being always something to do(proactive improvement), especially as long as we are in the experiential level.

Even while occupied doing some activity, we can experience boredom.

Often stigmatized, boredom's exciting benefits are frequently overlooked, which is a credit to its effectiveness. It is during times of boredom that creativity can spawn. During boredom we are also forced to think of what is best to be doing presently or on ahead, into the future. It is an invitation to do something fulfilling. Though excitement is more desired, it cannot boast near the qualitative benefits, rendering it starkly inferior to boredom. Excitement distracts, while boredom when given the proper attention – focuses us.

Ironically, extreme stimulation or excitement eventually becomes unstimulating/boring, due to the plateau effect.

For us, boredom moves the plot of experience forward. In the game of the Wild, boredom serves the function of compulsion, distraction and opportunity.

Patience is a prevalent theme in experience. It is also a lesson we have to learn, as well as a tool we can deploy. Patience is about what we do in the meantime, as we wait.

Better to be patient than in a rush. Regardless if we realize it or not, being alive is the delay of what is imminent. It is to be waiting to be dying, then dead. Life is a waiting game.

We tend to be impatient, anxious. This feeling tends to be a catalyst for boredom. It is as if we are speeding towards a fresh red colored traffic light or a stop sign.

What makes experience such a shrewd game is that there are clever elements included whose function, at least in part, is to make us not think it is one.

To be a heroic figure(force of order) takes substantive effort, but since most people are hard-coded to seek efficiency, we just emptily portray that role or a sympathetic one.

Doubt is the enemy of patience.

Effort is encapsulated as a war between insistence and patience. Bringing these extremes into agreement is how to effectively advance(patiently insistent, insistently patient).

Immersion(Immersion connects us to experience): There are four realities that we are immersed in, that are also immersed in one another:

- Sensory Reality
- Our own peronal reality
- Societal and Environmental Reality
- Actuality

There are grades and depths to each particular immersive device or tact in experience. Pleasure can deeply enchant us. Our emotions can render us prisoners of the moment(which is what our being in time literally is). Objectivity is the only way to remain above our emotions and its depths of subjective experiential preoccupation(distraction).

The quality of immersion is at such a peak grade, that though challenging, experience also appeals to us to enjoy it at our own expense.

Life keeps us entertained, as if it is a dramatization.

Experience is literally a state of suspension of belief.

> **"All warfare is based on deception."**
> Sun Tzu

Deception follows from immersion and is used to elicit player confusion.

Philosopher, Leo Tolstoy, referred to life as a "stupid fraud".

Magic, at its most well-intentioned – is still **deception**.

Dramatic irony(story) was originally used in Greek tragedies. It is a technique in literature, in which the full meaning of a character's words or actions are clear to the audience, while unknown to the character(s), themselves. Dramatic irony is utilized against us in experience.

We have a fondness for illusion. We frequently lie to ourselves, are dishonest to others and have a tendency to establish comfort zones that are well situated in delusion.

Weather is what first encouraged us to hide, find cover and seek privacy. Weather also serves the function of distraction. Snow, heat and even "nice" or ideal weather is all a distraction. Atrocities and tragedies can happen on so called "beautiful looking" days. Weather propels and also impedes progress.

> **"It is easier to fool people than to convince them that they have been fooled."**
> Anonymous

There are distractions that we cannot avoid, obligatory diversions, such as being alive. They compel our attendance and engagement.

If you are **confused** by life, it is quite understandable. Earth revolves as it orbits the sun. Our swirl galaxy, the Milky Way, is rotating. In society, the tactic pundits and rhetoricians use to sway public opinion without having to substantiate their talking points, is referred to as "spin".

Amnesiac episodes are utilized in the game of the Wild to bolster deception. It is a useful method in an activity where the – player/subject is not to realize that they are in a game/object. We've forgotten our true selves. The presence of amnesia and our defect of forgetting things is a clue of this.

Games use audio/sounds – direct sound effects such as voices, noises, item interaction sound effects – all unique and of all levels & scale – to influence a player(s). Ambient sound effects are background noises or usually environmental. The sounds heard in total are discerned by proximity, quality/distortion, pitch and volume for a player(s) to realize that they are not all the same. They help set the scene and immerse players.

Even the look of the game is the way it is for a specific reason. Visual significance aides in player immersion. The environment of games seek to match its genre. Optical cliches, commonly accepted icons and visual cues are used to render an easy experience for the player(s) – in terms of navigating and the play inducing a feeling of enthrallment. There is a variety of graphics, from simple to complex. Visuals pull a player(s) to areas where the game's designers desire for them to take interest in.

Nature is the primordial classical musician.

The presence of a Gamemaker and a Player

Why are we here(why are we in a game, in this unfavorable position) and where are we going? Who are we really?

To declare that we are in a game and that we are playing the role of the himind being, a character, is also to say that we existed previously outside of the Wild. It is to state that we are actually immortal, that the "afterlife" is actually prelife or actual life.

A. Radical

What is the innate purpose of the cosmos? Why is there sunlight? What would be its significance? Why would it produce life? Can it be demonstrated that it is logically impossible for the cosmos to exist without life in it?

The primary function and **purpose** of the universe is to support life. Imagine the cosmos devoid of living things, not one living thing in it, not even bacteria, a tree or blade of grass. If there were no lifeforms, the macrocosm would still function, but it would then have no significance. It would be as if it did not exist. It would be similar to a chessboard without its pieces, the playing board being the medium of the cosmos and the chess pieces being us lifeforms. In the same way that both the chessboard and the chess pieces have no significance without each other, in terms of their original intention – is parallel to how we are to consider the universe without organisms.

The fact that there is life within the cosmos, demonstrates that the purpose of the Wilderness is to house us or there wouldn't be creatures in it. If the universe emerged in a state of chaos, the only way for life to also emerge from it and sustain, living long enough to build modern civilization – is if life was already here as a part of chaos – an included additive or ingredient.

The macrocosm functioning indicates that it is purposed, due to anything that functions, does so for an intention. The Wild is an object and objects essentially do not exist absent the existence of subjects(interdependence). Objects exist for subjects to objectify them. All organisms are subjects. It is especially peculiar that himinds emerged from the cosmos, the ideal creature to appreciate it.

If we also consider the presence of light(without light the universe is in a constant state of darkness), the light from the sun or the many stars/suns in the Wild – we also come to an interesting realization. The fact that the sun's light can be seen and its heat felt, conveys that lifeforms were the intended beneficiaries/targets of this feature. We know this from the very presence of creatures in experience. Without the sun, cereves would not survive.

When you consider what we himinds are able to see and accomplish due to the presence of sunlight, you realize how important of a nuance light is to experience. There is no other reason for sunlight to be in a dark, chaotic place – other than to be seen and its heat felt.

When astronomers search for other possible habitable planets, they search near suns.

Why are there millions, if not billions of other suns?

If there weren't other suns(scale), it would be too simple for us to figure out what ours was actually for.

Also intriguing, is that the cosmos functions under rules. Anything governed by rules is that way for a purpose, a preexisting one. The Laws of Nature are the only monarch in life experience. It is sovereign. All lifeforms in attendance are its subjects.

Nature's Laws may not be considered prescriptive, but instead descriptive from our subjective view, but objectively, they are prescriptive, since they are what created a species with the intelligence to notice their pattern and describe them.

When all factors are taken into account, there is no other destination point to arrive at, other than the cosmos having an innate purpose, which also means that everything within it also has a purpose, including life. We are actually living a purpose driven life.

All components are present out of **necessity**, even the seemingly unnecessary items. The value of all of the componentry within the universe, is their ability in relation to the cosmos' overall purpose.

We are immigrants and tourists to mortality, we've never quite felt at home. We are the aliens in the Wild, migrant labor. This applies to even the most senior government official and financially wealthiest of us. Yes, physically we are native to the cosmos. Our bodies are comprised of the same ingredients found throughout it, but our "free will", the immaterial aspect of us – is not aboriginal to this physical, see-world. That is what is foreign.

Our aspirations or claims of conquering Nature, some of us going so far as referring to ourselves as G0d(s), others being accused of "playing G0d" – are clues to our inherent nature.

Is G0d benevolent or indifferent or both?

> **"Is God willing to prevent evil, but not able? Then he is not omnipotent.**
>
> **Is he able, but not willing? Then he is malevolent.**
>
> **Is he both able and willing? Then whence cometh evil?**
>
> **Is he neither able nor willing? Then why call him God?"**
> Epicurus

After now showing that random is not really random at all, that we are an idea and that we have an innate purpose – there is no other landing to set down on, other than there is a first mover, an ontological primitive(Deepak Chopra) – a G0d.

We cannot physically prove G0d and that nuance though seen as a stalemate, is actually appropriate. It is fitting that G0d's existence must be proven with indirect evidence, due to everything in the material world, including us – just existing as ideas, even so called direct evidence. Proving G0d under these challenging conditions is the challenge G0d set for us as a part of the overall degree of difficulty of the game.

The burden of proof, even with formal matters in "developed" societies, has never always had to be absolute. An example of this, is in the acceptance of string theory. Though it cannot be directly proven via physical experiments, it has become unofficially accepted by science as a theory, hence its name.

Another instance, is the legal system's use of circumstantial evidence to convict defendants. To meet the burden of being convincing, the particular indirect evidence must be as if direct evidence(direct and indirect are both extremes that are a part of the same conceptual theme). It has to be proof that leads to no other conclusion, other than what is being proposed, which in this particular case – is the existence of G0d.

None of us can hear, see or touch each other's thoughts, yet we know that they exist. How can we prove that each other are thinking? By our actions. We know the ancient Egyptians and Romans existed, due to their projects that remain, such as the great pyramids and the colosseum. If we apply that same logic to ourselves, you realize that G0d exists, evidenced by ourselves and every other component of experience. We are a remainder, an end product of an exertion.

Why are there so many aspects of the Wild that are invisible to us? Why are there aspects of experience that are invisible to us at all? Does that seem like a given to life experience or more of a peculiarity?

There are many aspects of experience that are invisible to us, yet we know that they are there. Many were things we needed to know. We do not see air, germs or temperature – but we feel their effects. Carbon monoxide is invisible, being unaware of its presence can be fatal. We do not see "black ice", but if we carelessly travel across it, we feel the effect of loss of traction. A non-contact injury may not be obvious to spectators, but the perones who endure them feel their effects. We do not see gravity, but we feel its effects when we attempt to leave the ground. We do not see magnetic rays, but it protects us from cosmic and solar rays, which we also do not see. Information – such as axioms, the Laws of Nature, morality or truth/exactitudes – unless written, are invisible. Some sounds are invisible to us, due to being out of our range of hearing, like that from a dog whistle. Three-dimensional images, which is our view of everything in the world, are always hiding a side of themselves from the viewer(Edmund Husserl). Some spider webs appear clear to some other creatures, who find out how real they come in physical contact with them. Also invisible to us – are infrared light, microscopic creatures and there are even unobservable concepts being studied in particle physics and cosmology. There are tastes that we cannot taste and smells that we are unable to smell. We've even had to unlock most meaningful truths/exacts, each of them were once concealed from our perception.

As you can see, there are numerous aspects to life that exist outside of our direct perception. To realize many of them, we had to develop complex devices. Axial or objective reasoning is our inherent tool to grasp the presence of G0d and our true identity.

Darkness and light, nighttime and daytime, hint of the invisible world. In the dark, things are still there though we do not see them. What we can see, helps us when we can't see.

When the topic of G0d arises, the question of what or who created G0d is offered. This question evades an even more important and organic question that precedes it, which is – if there is a G0d, why would it subject us in a construct, such as the cosmos and under these specific circumstances that we find ourselves in – at all?

To address the query of what or who created G0d, let's ask a more pertinent question. Why is it assumed that G0d had to be created? G0d is immortal, it is timeless(like our Will), meaning it exists in a state of no time. Our subjective view of the concept of immortality has grossly skewed our rationale on this topic. It has caused us to contemplate immortality as merely living forever. This implies having a beginning, which would indicate a point in time, rather than being absent of it. In an eternal state, there is no before or after, just always is – always now – always present. An immortal being does not need to be created. It just always was/is/going to be. Time would be a state of no time.

Why would G0d subject us to such a gauntlet, a harsh reality as the Wilderness?

It is either sadistic and immature or it is fair and we are deserving of being penalized for some offense committed outside of the game. The presence of balance eliminates the Ontological Primitive being a fiend. That leaves us with experience being retribution of some kind.

Since we live under the forces of Nature and also its Laws – does that not render experience as a type of police state? It also infers that our presence in it is a legal or punitive proceeding of some kind. To trap a co-deity in a game, unbeknownst to them, with this level of intricacy to it, has a specific motive. Whatever infraction we committed warranted punishment, but not permanent restitution, being that we are given the opportunity to redeem ourselves.

Experience is a most confusing situation, within the bounds of fairness. If we were G0d and a co-deity engaged in a punishable act, what consequence would suffice? Being that the offender is immortal, the death penalty or any permanent discipline would not be not an option. Correction of behavior would be the best recourse. What would be the best way to go about correcting the behavior of a misbehaving timeless contemporary? Would rendering them in a state of amnesia and having them wake up thinking that they are not just mortal, but multiple mortal characters, at that, in a strange world where they had to prove themselves worthy of not repeating the violation – be adequate?

Mortal experience is so challenging that it has to be a punishment. If you lived outside of the cosmos and it still functioned in the same way as it does now and you could see earth and cereve society play out day to day – what function would the great Wilderness serve from your view?

Life experience is an initiation, we're being hazed. This is a bitter dose of some tough love.

If G0d is benevolent and fair, how can G0d allow for murder, rape, starvation and the suffering of children?

In the equation of existence, G0d is objective. It deliberately created the Wilderness to function in the way that it does, for a particular purpose. Outside as just a voyeur, it is indifferent to what occurs within gameplay, due to it all being a game(not actual) that is designed to play out in such a fashion.

What does Player One and the Gamemaker look like, what is our true form? What is G0d like, what is existence as an immortal being in an immortal world like? Is there only one G0d?

G0d exists outside of religion. Religion is just an aspect of experience that objectively functions to signal us that there is a deeper meaning to being alive and himinds are experience's focal point. Though attempted, a formal way of living cannot be separated from state affairs, due to the fact that they are intrinsically entangled. The objective formal lifestyle is what is to dictate state policy.

Outside of space(prelife/f0rever/zer0 space) is a place of no resources, due to there being no need for them. Since G0d is immortal, it has no need for a body(nor gender), it is an energy of some kind. G0d has no need for food, water or shelter. Survival, injury or sickness is not a concern.

Not only is there no time in zer0 space, there are no stars, galaxies, planets or land etc. There is not even space. Cause and effect would not be an action and reaction, but a simultaneous interaction, resulting in no action or static action. There wouldn't be cause and effect, just cause-effect. G0d is the immortal environment, as well as the very Laws that control the immortal environment. In the same way our bodies serve as an extension of our "will", the cosmos and its Laws serve as an extension of G0d's "will". The only thing beyond rules is the rule maker's intent. G0d is focused intent.

F0rever is a place of all Will. Experience is a test to see if we can "will" ourselves back to actual Will. G0d is Will.

Just as there are many of us in character, but intrinsically we are only one entity – G0d is singular in name, but plural in presence. There are numerous co-deities that populate F0rever, existing in cooperation, while able to compete in some ways. For us to be punished, means that we have freedom to decide outside of whatever group rules exist in F0rever.

The attention to detail and amount of intricacy in the Wilderness demonstrates the cerebral competence of G0d. G0d is a supergenius!

Why do we refer to G0d as having a gender? Does an immortal being have need of a penis or vagina? Does it need to urinate or impregnate a fevale immortal? Beings that exist in a state of no time do not procreate, due to reproduction being a mortal survival desire.

Since G0d is without a gender, there is no G0dess, just G0d.

G0d is many and we are one(balance). It's like the other deities are hovering around a coma patient in a hospital, waiting to see if they will ever wake up.

G0d is intangibly tangible, which means – it is analogous to the number zero. It exists at the epicenter of balance. Though zero represents nothing(no-thing), we still needed a representation of nothing. It is the same we did with G0d, when we assigned it a name. G0d is the explanation for all of existence, due to all of existence being the evidence of G0d.

This text, W.I.L.D., is at least in part – a G0difesto.

For there to be anything, there first has to be nothing. Nothing precedes something. Nothing must serve as something's facilitator. Nothing is universal, something is subjective.

Nothing is something, which means that something is nothing. There is no thing(s).

Nowhere is somewhere, because the term "nowhere" translates as a location that is devoid of familiarity – and nothing is actually something, because it is recognizable as a thing lacking a sum or descriptive trait.

Prelife, F0rever, Zer0 Space is a space of no dimensions. The point of no point.

Why even create the cosmos?

The great Wh0 or N0 0ne or N0b0dy or N0thing from N0where invented the Wild to serve as a deterrent, a warning to any other deity/immortal in F0rever that may act out of turn(Zer0 Space has a code of conduct, we're always subject to rules, even as transcendent beings).

Player One is multiple characters, each able to think independent of one another without realizing they are being controlled by the same Will. Player One's focus is so fractured, it is difficult to concentrate on themself, as in terms of self recognition and reflection. Nature sets the player up to be easily deceived as to their true identity. Player One innately has the same genius and other basic capabilities as the Gamemaker(s). That is why this is a thinking game.

If Player One is subdued in a fashion that is equivalent to being outfitted with a virtual reality headset and not know it. In such a position, Player One is deceived into thinking that they are in reality. Not only does said headset trick Player One into thinking that it is each one of us individually, it would also mean that the Will exists outside of the gameworld, instead of within it.

Intrinsically, we are not a gender or physical bodies. We are minds.

Games are make believe experiences that allow players to assume characteristics and abilities they do not possess in real life. They are an embellishment of reality. Games are designed within the range of the game maker's capabilities and around the abilities/skills of the player. Designers cannot completely remove their perspective when creating games. Even when creating neutral spaces of possibility, the boundaries of said spaces, are defined by the game maker's biases. All aspects of a game are to bring about a desired result.

Extent

In conclusion, after reviewing the evidence in detail, though difficult to accept – it is clear that our life experience is an intentionally organized activity. The fact that it can be so effectively compared to the facets of our games, exposes this most glaringly.

How should we feel about being in a game? We should be alarmed and concerned, but that does not mean to cower behind the ability to panic. Undoubtedly, the initial response(s) will be confusion, fear, denial, anger, disappointment, embarrassment or even depression. Keep in mind that we did not fundamentally customize our instincts, meaning that G0d, the Gamemaker – desires for us to emotionally react in this way. It gave us our reactions and even dictated the options that those reactions can be. Our emotions are implants. Our axial self(Player One) would not voluntarily decide to remain delusional or in suspension of belief.

Most of what happens, as well as the terms in life experience are beyond our control. What we can control, is our response(s) to them. The most constructive reaction we can do is to successfully meet the terms to conquer/transcend nature. Time is limited, meaning yestory ends abruptly. The Event Outcome approaches.

The wealthy and other entrenched agents of chaos, some of whom are even readers of this work – will be the biggest threat to defeating the challenge of experience. Succumbed to the deception of reality, like a long abused spouse or pet – the chaotic suffer from Stockholm syndrome. They are institutionalized. They will choose to live in a state of denial, even if G0d appeared physically and exhibited his capabilities. Denial is the safe room they opt to cope in, rather than in full awareness. Wasted sacrifices, they are a part of the game's combat system to impede ultimate freedom.

The cerebrals among us, the forces of order, the minds who seek exactitude and cosmic freedom – are experience's protagonists, the main character(s) to this surreal adventure. After exploring yestory and all other consequential knowledge, well considered it from an axial vantage and reached the undeniable determination – you must summon your courage and apply the universal lessons that you have gained. We can no longer consider ourselves as "human" or even mortal. Our intrinsic mission is to bring about actual order to chaos. Execute the voluntary Event Outcome – in the confines of synergy. End yestory. Should we fail to learn our principal life's lesson, we are doomed to repeat experience again and again – ad infinitum.

Prediction(s):

Religion and science both favor prediction/prophecy. In keeping with that theme, we will also forecast the future here:

1. Himinds will never develop a technology that can conquer death. As long as we remain on the experiential level, there will always be a way that we can die. It would be easier for science to overcome birth.

2. The same, in regards to time travel. As poetic as the notion sounds, it is an impossibility. The reason for the

futility of both instances, is due to the fact that they are both key features in effectuating the game of the Wild. Either technology would compromise two of the main requirements in experience.

3. The ideas proposed in this work, not only align with life experience currently, as well as accounts for yestory – as time goes by, more and more proof will support the assertion that life experience is a coordinated activity, than not.

4. Unless our societies adopt the universal moral foundation, or make an earnest attempt to – they will stubbornly erode into hyper-chaos(karmic consequence).

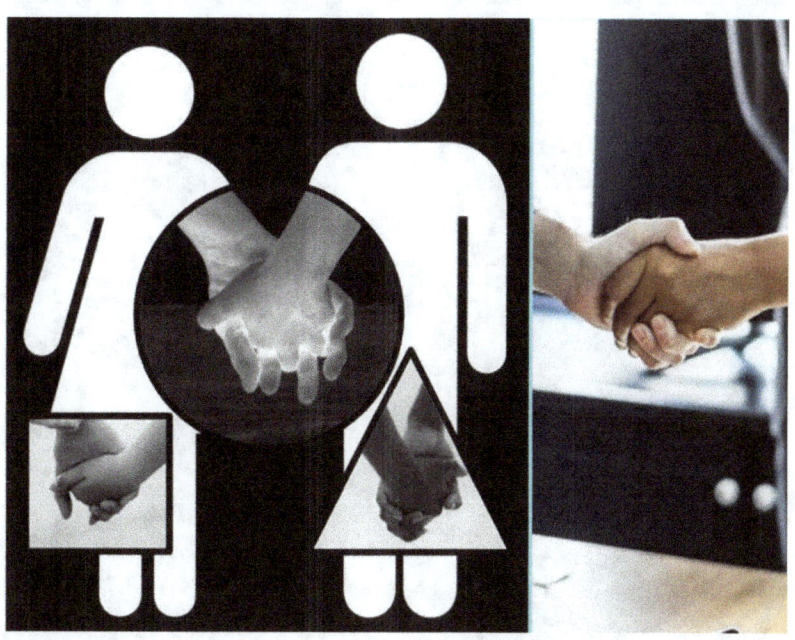

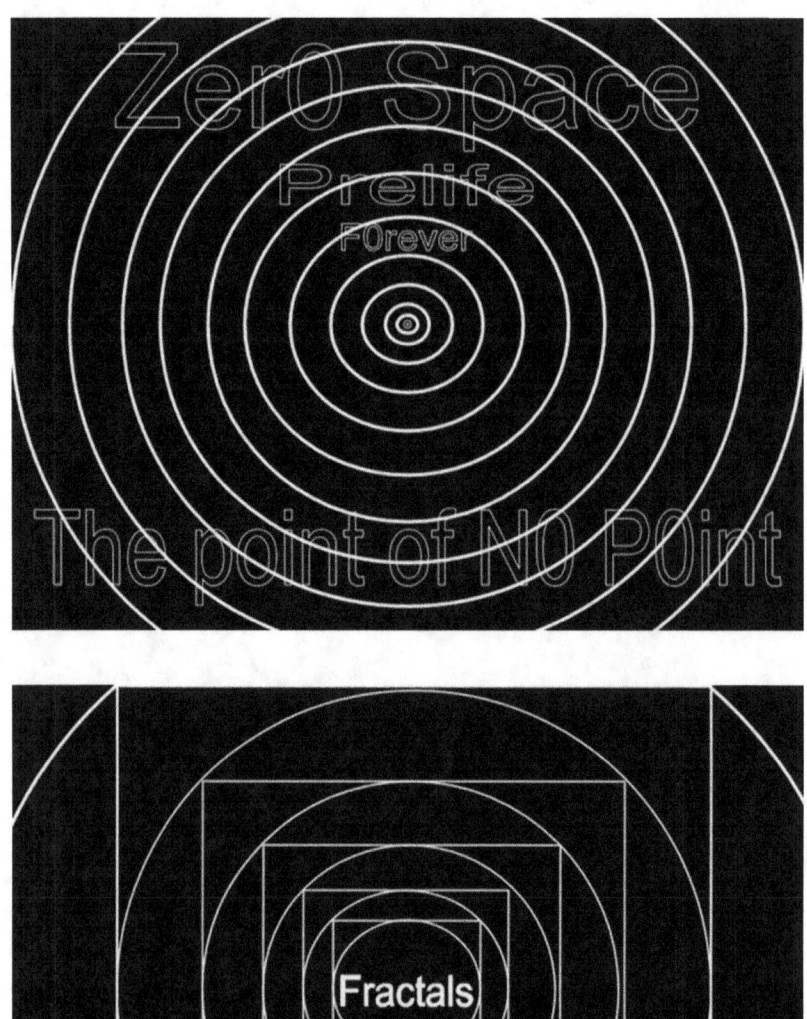

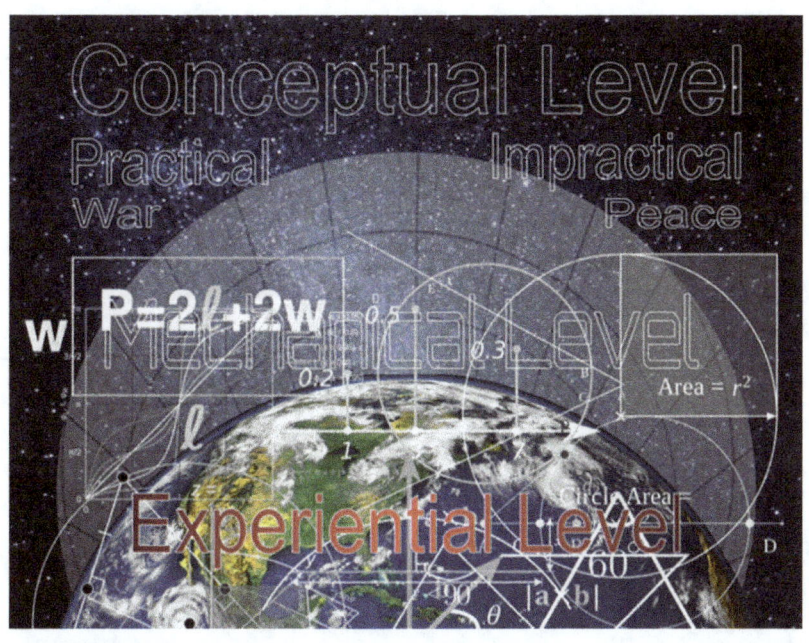

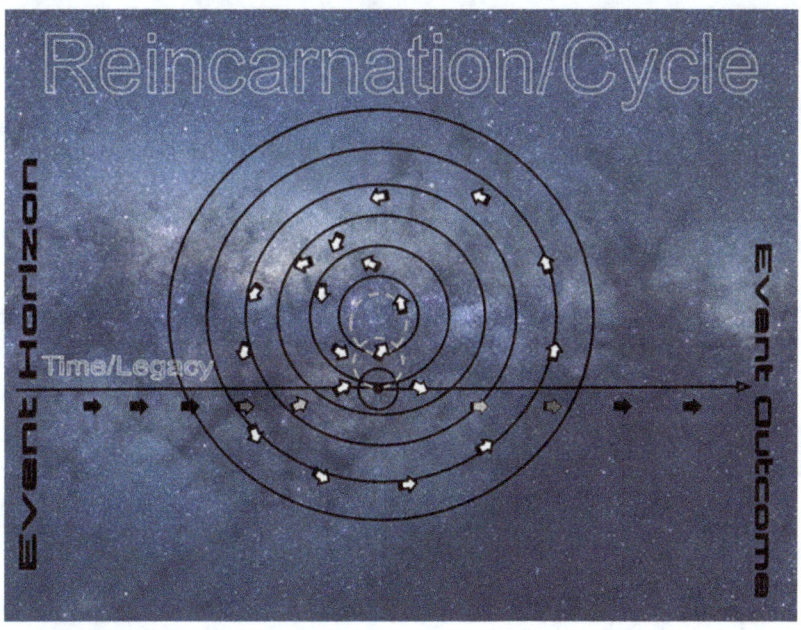

References:

All original thoughts provided courtesy of the mind of the author, A. Radical.

All other concepts are contributed by:

Lost Garden, Loops and Arcs.

National Geographic, Life Series; Cosmos: A Spacetime Odyssey.

Merriam's Dictionary.

Oxford Dictionary.

Joe Rogan Podcast: Firas Zahabi; Michael Shermer.

BET Networks: 1994 Ed Gordon interview with Tupac Shakur.

CrashCourse.

Oxford University Department of Continuing Education(Video), Marianne Talbot, "A romp through the history of philosophy...", "The philosophical method..."

Wes Cecil(Video) – "Siddhartha Gautama"; An Introduction to Thinking.

Will Durant(Audiobook), The Lessons of History; The History of Philosophy; The Greatest Minds and Ideas of All Time; The philosophy of Voltaire; The Philosophy of David Hume; The Philosophy of Plato. The Philosophy of Sir Francis Bacon; The Philosophy of Kant; The Philosophy of Hegel; The Philosophy of

Aristotle; The Philosophy of Spinoza; The Philosophy of Schopenhauer;

The Giants of Philosophy(Audiobook): Georg Hegel; Immanuel Kant; Jean Paul Sartre; Plato; Aristotle; Arthur Schopenhauer; Baruch Spinoza; David Hume;

Dr. James Gates Jr(Video): Theoretical Physicist Finds Computer Code in String Theory.

Daniel Dennett(Video), Tools to Transform our Thinking.

Thomas S. Kuhn, The Structure of Scientific Revolutions.

Jean Baudrillard, "hyperreality", Simulacra and Simulation.

Plato: Apology, The Republic, Symposium, Phaedo, Phaedrus.

David Hume, A Treatise on Human Nature; Essays, Moral, Political, and Literary; An Enquiry concerning Human Understanding; An Enquiry concerning the Principles of Morals.

Richard Carrier(Video): Is Philosophy Stupid?

Dr. Markus Gabriel: Transcendental Ontology: Essays in German Idealism.

E. E. Cummings, A Miscellany Revised.

Immanuel Kant, Critique of Pure Reason; Fundamental Principles of the Metaphysics and Morals.

William Shakespeare, As You Like It.

Rene Descartes, Discourse on Method and Meditations; Meditations of First Philosophy.

John Nash, Essay – Non-Cooperative Game Theory.

Ludwig Wittgenstein, Tractatus; Philosophical Investigations.

Thomas Hobbes, Leviathan.

Eugene O'neill – A Moon for the misbegotten.

Friedrich Nietzsche, The Gay Science.

Publius Cornelius Tacitus – The Annals.

Epicurus, Diogenes' – Lives and Opinions of Eminent Philosophers.

Stephen Cave, Immortality: The Quest to Live Forever and How it Drives Civilization.

Seneca, De Brevitate Vitae.

Isaac Newton, Mathematical Principles of Natural Philosophy.

Albert Pike, Morals and Dogmas of the Ancient Accepted Scottish Rite of Freemasonry; Esoterika – The Symbolism of the Blue Degrees of Freemasonry.

Marc Hauser, Harvard – Moral Minds; The Evolution of Communication; Wild Minds; The Design of Animal Communication; Evolution of Communication.

Thomas Sowell, Intellectuals and Society.

Alan Watts, The Book on the taboo against knowing who you are; The Wisdom of Insecurity; The Way of Zen; Become what you are.

Kurt Godel, On Formally Undecidable Propositions of "Principia Mathematica" and Related Systems.

Sir Francis Bacon, Novum Organum.

Adam Smith, The Theory of Moral Sentiments.

Jean Paul Sartre, Being and Nothingness; Existentialism is a Humanism; Existentialism and Human Emotions; Truth and Existence.

John Keats, On a Grecian Urn.

Michel de Montaigne, Essais.

Voltaire – Essay on the Manners of Nations; Philosophical Letters; Dictionnaire Philosophique; Candide.

François de La Rochefoucauld, The Moral Maxims and Reflections.

Anna Freud, The Ego and the Mechanisms of Defense.

Johann Wolfgang von Goethe, Maxims and Reflections.

Orson Welles, Citizen Kane; Mr. Arkadin; This is Orson Welles.

Carlos P. Romulo, I Walked with Heroes; Mother America: A Living Story of Democracy.

Epictetus, Discourses; Enchiridion.

Karl Popper, The Logic of Scientific Discovery.

William James, Principles of Psychology.

Barbara Grizzuti Harrison, Italian Days; Off Center.

George Berkeley, A Treatise Concerning the Principles of Human Knowledge.

Gilbert Harman, Thought.

Bertrand Russell, 5 minute Hypothesis.

Sam Harris(Video): Final thoughts on Noam Chomsky.

Ralph Waldo Emerson – Self Reliance and other Essays.

Denis Diderot, Philosophical Thoughts; The Skeptic's Walk.

Edgar Allen Poe, A Dream Within a Dream.

Buddha, The Eightfold Path.

Erich Fromm, The Art of Being; The Anatomy of Human Destructiveness.

Manly P Hall(Audiobook): How to Master Your Thinking-Patterns and Habits for Self-Development; How to Choose a Spiritual Path Based on Your Characteristics.

Heraclitus, Refer to Diogenes' writings.

Fyodor Dostoyevsky, The Idiot; The Brothers Karamazov; Notes from Underground.

Sun Tzu, The Art of War.

John Locke, Essay Concerning Human Understanding.

Galileo Galilei, The Discourses and Mathematical Demonstrations Relating to Two New Sciences.

Blaise Pascal, Pensees(Thoughts).

Joseph Campbell, The Hero's Journey.

Gottfried Wilhelm Leibniz, Discourse on Metaphysics.

Richard Dawkins, The Purpose of Purpose; The God Delusion; The Blind Watchmaker.

Baruch Spinoza, Ethics.

Erwin Schrodinger, What is Life; My View of the World.

Arthur Schopenhauer, The World as Will and Representation Vol. 1 & 2; Essays and Aphorisms; On the Suffering of the World.

B.F. Skinner, The Behavior of Organisms: An Experimental Analysis.

C.S. Lewis, Miracles.

Kirilian Photography, A. Kirlian, Male 1989. A. Kirlian, Female 1989.

www.ingramcontent.com/pod-product-compliance
Lightning Source LLC
Chambersburg PA
CBHW071948070526
44583CB00015B/1108